BLENDER RECIPES

through the magic of *Osterizer* blender spin cookery

BY JOAN OSTER

TESTED RECIPE PUBLISHERS, INC., CHICAGO, ILLINOIS 60648

CONTENTS

INTRODUCTION, 3

BLENDER BASICS, 4

APPETIZERS, 10

BEVERAGES, 18

BREADS, 28

BUTTERS, 38

CAKES, 40

CAKE FROSTINGS, 51

CANDIES & CONFECTIONS, 56

COOKIES, 60

DESSERTS, 68

ENTRÉES, 80

FRITTERS & DOUGHNUTS, 102

CHILDREN'S DELIGHTS, 105

OUTDOOR COOKING, 110

PIES & PASTRIES, 118

PRESERVES & RELISHES, 130

SALADS, 138

SALAD DRESSINGS, 149

SANDWICHES & SPREADS, 156

SAUCES & TOPPINGS, 165

SOUPS, 173

SPECIAL DIETS, 182

VEGETABLES, 187

INDEX, 194

SECOND REVISION JOAN OSTER EDITION
PRINTING: 6 7 8

ISBN 0-88351-003-0
Library of Congress Catalog Card Number 77-98169

INTRODUCTION

The modern multispeed Osterizer blender is a wizard at performing kitchen tasks. Exciting things can be done with the blender; it can transform mundane ingredients into culinary creations, speed up the preparation of the family food and handle scores of difficult everyday tasks with the greatest of ease and efficiency.

Don't let the fantastic blender stand unused! Discover the ease and convenience of blender cooking. With the high-speed motor and whirling blades, tedious jobs are mastered jiffy-quick. It will blend, chop, grate, crumb, shred, purée, grind, or beat, make fancy drinks, turn left-overs into exotic dishes, crumb cookies for pie crust, chop an endless variety of foods, finish preparation of convenience foods or fix tasty foods for baby, junior or convalescent.

This book covers Controlled Cycle blending. Cyclomatic and Pulse Matic operation and the use of the Mini-Blend containers.

Get acquainted with your blender. Read the instructions supplied by the manufacturer, then try a few of the simple recipes that follow. Recipes which can use special equipment have these symbols:

CHAFING DISH   FONDUE

ICER ATTACHMENT   MINI-BLEND CONTAINERS

Soon you will enjoy preparing many of the gourmet recipes included, they're marked with this symbol

In all the recipes in this book the blender speed to be used is given in **CAPITAL** letters. Thus a recipe tells you to **STIR**, or **BLEND**, or **PURÉE**. This tells you where to set your blender control, dial, or pushbutton after you have placed the recipe ingredients in the blender container.

The recipes in this book were developed using multi-speed blenders. The chart shows the 16 speed settings used in developing and testing the recipes in this book. Select the speed column which fits your blender and project your setting to the left column (16 speed) and this will give you the setting used in the recipe in this book. With this chart and a little experimentation you can make adjustments if you find it necessary.

Blender Control Settings

MY SPEED SETTING	16 SPEED (SETTINGS USED IN THIS BOOK)	14 SPEED	10 SPEED	8 SPEED	4 SPEED	2 SPEED
	STIR	STIR				
	BEAT	BEAT	STIR	STIR		
	PURÉE	PURÉE				
	CREAM	CREAM	PURÉE	PURÉE	STIR	
	CHOP	CHOP	CHOP			
	WHIP	WHIP	WHIP	CHOP		LO
	CRUMB	MIX	MIX	MIX	LO	
	MIX					
	MINCE	MINCE	GRATE	GRATE		
	GRATE	GRATE			MED	
	CRUSH	BLEND	BLEND	BLEND		HI
	BLEND					
	SHRED	SHRED	GRIND	GRIND	HI	
	GRIND	GRIND				
	FRAPPÉ	FRAPPÉ	FRAPPÉ	LIQUEFY		
	LIQUEFY	LIQUEFY	LIQUEFY			

BLENDER BASICS

OSTERIZER BLENDER COOKING IS QUICK AND EASY

The electric multispeed Osterizer blender makes food preparation easy, interesting and trouble free and saves time galore since mixing time is measured in seconds! Follow these rules and success is assured.

1. **Before using blender read the manufacturer's instructions carefully!**

2. In case you are interrupted during a blender preparation, turn blender off. Never leave it unattended while motor is running.

3. Since the blender is so fast, approximate timing is included in the recipes in this book as well as description of finished product; i.e., until smooth; until well blended. Due to variations in size, consistency and age of food items to be processed, these times serve only as a guide.

4. CAUTION: Follow these important steps to assemble, tighten, and mount blender container quickly and correctly. Injury may result if moving blades are accidently exposed.

a. ASSEMBLY OF CONTAINER

1. Turn container upside down so the small opening is at the top.

2. Place sealing ring on container opening.

3. Turn agitator blades upside down and place in mouth of container.

4. Thread container bottom to container. Engage threads properly. Screw on firmly.

b. TIGHTENING THE CONTAINER

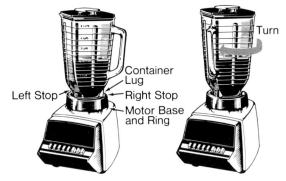

1. To tighten container bottom, put assembled container securely into motor base ring with handle and lug in front of the right stop.
2. Using container handle, turn container to the left as far as possible. This insures that the container bottom is tightened properly. Remove Container from Motor Base and follow mounting instructions below. Do not attempt to place the container on, or remove it from the motor base while the motor is running.

c. MOUNTING

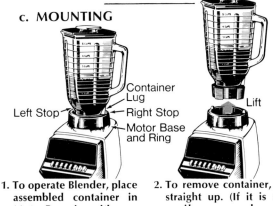

1. To operate Blender, place assembled container in Motor Base ring with container lug against flat side of right Motor Base stop. If container lug does not rest against flat side of right stop, remove container assembly and place against flat side of left stop. Seat container firmly and operate.
2. To remove container, lift straight up. (If it is not easily removed, rock gently and lift up. Do not twist.) If container bottom cannot be loosened by hand, place assembled container into the motor base ring with handle in front of left side stop. Using container handle, turn container to the right until container bottom loosens.

ALWAYS HOLD JAR WITH ONE HAND WHILE PROCESSING

"MINI-BLEND" Containers (8-oz. or 30-oz. sizes available as an accessory . . . Not normally included with your Osterizer blender.) For proper assembly and tightening instructions, see above directions. The **"MINI-BLEND"** Containers allow for processing and the storing of foods in the same container. They are heat- and cold-resistant and are specially constructed to Osterizer blender specifications. **DO NOT USE OTHER TYPES OF JARS FOR PROCESSING FOODS.** Ordinary jars may break or unscrew during processing. Do not wash any parts, including container, in an automatic dishwasher. **DO NOT** fill "MINI-BLEND" container above **MAXIMUM FILL LINE** to allow for expansion of foods while processing. **ALWAYS HOLD JAR WITH ONE HAND WHILE PROCESSING.**

5. Slice, dice or cube ingredients as directed in the recipe or in crumbing or chopping directions on the following pages before adding to container.

6. Pour fluids (liquids and semi-liquids) into container before adding dry ingredients unless specific recipe suggests otherwise. It makes blending easy.

7. Cool very hot foods slightly before adding to container unless recipe suggests otherwise.

8. Process, chop or crumb food in 1 cup amounts. Food will be more uniformly chopped.

9. Most foods chop more uniformly when using controlled cycle blending. Due to variations in size, consistency and age of food items, check the food often to avoid overblending.

10. If the motor labors at the speed suggested, use a higher speed to complete processing.

11. HOW TO USE A RUBBER SPATULA WITH YOUR BLENDER (Fig. 1).
When blending ingredients of a heavy consistency, such as cheese dips and sandwich spreads, it is necessary to use a rubber spatula to help the mixture get down to the blades. To use spatula, TURN MOTOR OFF, remove cover, move spatula up and down rapidly along sides of container. Push ingredients from sides of container to the center. Do not use metal knives or spoons (Fig. 1).

Figure 1   Spatula Use

12. Remove heavy dips and spreads, nut butters, mayonnaise and products of similar consistency, by removing the processing assembly and pushing the mixture out through the bottom opening into serving dish or storage container (Fig. 2).

13. Pour mixtures of liquid or semi-liquid consistency, such as muffin and cake batters, from the container.

Figure 2   Removing Heavy Mixtures

14. Always disassemble container and wash and dry all parts thoroughly. Wash in warm, soapy water. DO NOT WASH ANY PARTS IN AUTOMATIC DISHWASHER. Reassemble container for future use—never place processing assembly on motor base without the container!

CONTROLLED CYCLE BLENDING: The most modern blenders have Controlled Cycle blending, an important feature which enables you to obtain perfect results when pieces of food are desired, such as chopped vegetables, nuts or cheeses. There are several different kinds of Controlled Cycle blending, but all involve turning the motor "On" and "Off" intermittently. During the "On" cycle the food is tossed up away from the blades, and during the "Off" period the food is redistributed around the blades to make processing more uniform. On the following pages one cycle means that the motor is "On" for about two seconds and "Off" for about two seconds.

"CYCLOMATIC" BLENDER OPERATION: Cyclomatic blenders are completely automatic. They provide the homemaker with a cycle counter which turns the motor on for about two seconds and off for about two seconds automatically, once for each complete cycle.

"PULSE-MATIC" BLENDER OPERATION: "Pulse-Matic" blenders are not as automatic as a Cyclomatic blender, but the homemaker is still able to achieve perfect results with a very little bit of practice. Simply push the desired speed button and momentarily activate the pulse button as often as desired. Hold the button in for about two seconds, then release and let the blades coast to a stop. This is one cycle as used in the charts on the following pages.

BLENDER TECHNIQUES

CHOPPING

CANDY: Hard candy (candy canes, stick candy, toffe bars, brittles) is easily chopped in the blender. Just add a few pieces to the container at a time. **BLEND,** switching motor on and off, 4 to 6 times, until candy pieces are desired size. Watch closely; the blender is fast! Empty container. Repeat as necessary.

SOFT CHEESE: (American; Cheddar or Swiss). Cut cheese into ½-inch cubes. Chill well in refrigerator. **GRIND** 1 cup of cheese cubes at a time, switching motor on and off until cheese is desired fineness. Empty container; repeat as necessary. About 4 ounces of cheese makes 1 cup of grated cheese. Mild, or young, cheese may require the addition of a half slice of bread to absorb the natural oils and keep the cheese from sticking together. USE LARGE CONTAINER ONLY.

PARMESAN AND OTHER HARD CHEESES: Prepare as directed for natural cheese above. **GRIND** ½ cup of cheese cubes at a time until fineness desired, 10 to 15 seconds. About 4 ounces of cheese makes 1 cup of grated cheese. USE LARGE CONTAINER ONLY.

CHOCOLATE: Cut squares (1 ounce) of unsweetened, German sweet or semi-sweet dipping chocolate into small pieces. Chill well. Process 2 or 3 squares at a time. **BLEND,** switching motor on and off until chocolate is finely chopped.

COCONUT—FRESH: To grate fresh coconut set speed at **LIQUEFY,** remove feeder cap from empty container, start motor and drop coconut pieces into revolving blades. After grating 1 cup of coconut, empty container and repeat process until all coconut is grated.

COOKED MEAT AND POULTRY: Cut well-chilled meat or poultry into ½ to ¾-inch chunks. Set speed at **LIQUEFY,** remove feeder cap from empty container, start motor and drop meat pieces into revolving blades. After chopping 1 cup of meat empty container and repeat process until all meat is chopped.

EGGS—HARD COOKED: Quarter or slice eggs. **CHOP** 2 eggs at a time, switching motor on and off until fineness desired, 4 to 6 times. Empty container. Repeat as necessary.

FRUITS—DRY CHOP METHOD: Slice or dice raw, well-drained cooked or canned fruits into 1 inch chunks. **BLEND** 1 cup at a time, switching motor on and off until desired fineness (Fig. 3, Page 7).

NUTS: Pecan and walnut halves, blanched or toasted almonds, hazelnuts, cashews or peanuts can all be chopped jiffy-quick in the blender. **BLEND** or **CHOP** ½ cup of nuts at a time, switching motor on and off until desired fineness. Use the lower speed for the soft nuts, such as pecans, walnuts and cashews, and the higher speed for the harder nuts, such as almonds, peanuts and hazelnuts. Watch closely; the blender is fast! Empty container; repeat as necessary. About 1 cup nuts makes ¾ to 1 cup chopped nuts depending upon the fineness. Large container can also be used; processing 1 cup at a time.

RIND—LEMON, ORANGE OR LIME: A mite of citrus rind adds a distinctive flavor to sauces, desserts, salad dressings, etc. all rinds chop beautifully with foods and liquids. When adding rind to a favorite blender-made dish, chop it in one of these ways.

a. Carefully trim the rind from fruit with vegetable peeler. Cut the rind into thin strips and blend it with other foods as specific recipe directs.

b. Freeze thin strips of rind and then process ½ cup at a time in "Mini-Blend" container at **SHRED.** Store in freezer in "Mini-Blend" container and use as needed for pies, cookies, breads, etc.

RECONSTITUTE

FROZEN CONCENTRATED JUICES: Put water and juice into the blender container, cover and process at **STIR** only until well mixed.

DRY MILK. Put water and dry milk solids into the blender container, cover and process at **STIR** only until well mixed.

GRINDING

Coffee beans are quickly and evenly ground, ½ cup at a time, in the "Mini-Blend" container, or 1 cup in blender container.
GRIND—10 cycles for percolator
GRIND—15 cycles for drip

For finely ground Nuts, Rice, Oats, Wheat, and Peppercorns—Put ½ cup in "Mini-Blend" container or 1 cup in blender container, cover and process at **GRIND** until desired grind is obtained. Longer processing will give a finer grind. Whole spices, such as Ginger Root, Nutmeg, Cloves, are extremely hard and should be processed only in the glass blender container. Process only two or three 1" pieces at a time. Break nutmegs with a nutcrackers before processing. Process only in large glass container and grind at **LIQUEFY.** Don't operate blender continuously with dry ingredients for more than two minutes.

BLENDER-CHOP (dry method)

Cut foods into pieces about ¾" in size and place recommended quantity in Osterizer blender container or in "Mini-Blend" container (1½ cup only). Process at Cycle: (Fig. 3).

Figure 3   Dry Method

FOOD	SPEED	CYCLE	YIELD
Apple— 1 cup	**STIR**	2 cycles	1 cup
Carrot— 1 cup	**GRATE**	2 cycles	1 cup
Celery— 1 cup	**STIR**	2 cycles	1 cup
Green pepper— 1 cup	**STIR**	2 cycles	1 cup
Onion— 1 cup	**STIR**	2 cycles	1 cup

Cheese, Cheddar			
½ cup	**GRIND**	3 cycles	½ cup
Cheese, Swiss— 1 cup	**GRIND**	4 cycles	1 cup
Eggs, Hard cooked, 2 quartered	**STIR**	2 cycles	½ cup

BLENDER-CHOP (water method)

VEGETABLES FOR SALADS AND RELISHES: Water Chop Method (Fig. 4): Cut vegetables into pieces about one inch in size and place recommended quantity in the blender container. **COVER** vegetables with cold water, cover container and process:

FOOD	SPEED	CYCLE	YIELD
Apples— 3 cups	**MIX**	2 cycles	2 cups grated
Cabbage, red— 3 cups	**SHRED**	1 cycle	1½ cups
Cabbage, white— 3 cups	**GRIND**	1 cycle	1½ cups
Carrots— 2 cups	**LIQUEFY**	1 cycle	2 cups
Green Pepper— 3 cups	**CHOP**	1 cycle	2 cups
Onions— 3 cups	**CHOP**	1 cycle	2 cups
Potatoes 3 cups	**GRIND**	1 cycle	3 cups

When processing is finished, immediately pour through a strainer or colander and drain well. The speeds and number of cycles listed above produce a medium-size chop. If a finer size is desired, process one additional cycle.

*For detailed information on cycles see Special Blender Features on page 6.

Figure 4   Water Method

LUMP-FREE GRAVY AND SAUCES

To smooth gravy or white sauce which may be lumpy, put about half a cup into the blender container, cover and start processing at **STIR.** Remove cover and with motor running gradually add remaining gravy or sauce. Continue to process until smooth.

GIBLETS FOR GRAVY

To chop giblets for gravy, cook the giblets in water or broth, then cool to room temperature. Cut giblets into 1-inch pieces, put into blender container and cover with cooled cooking liquid. Cover container and **CHOP** until pieces are desired size.

CRUMBING

BREAD: Tear one slice of fresh or dry bread into six to eight pieces, put into blender container, cover and process:
BEAT—1 cycle—½ cup coarse crumbs
GRATE—2 cycles—½ cup medium crumbs
LIQUEFY—Continuous—½ cup fine crumbs
Empty container and repeat as necessary.

BREAD CRUMBS—BUTTERED: Spread bread with softened butter or margarine before cutting or breaking and dropping into container as above.

BREAD CRUMBS—CHEESE: For casserole toppings, au gratin, vegetables, etc. Break one slice of fresh bread into six pieces and drop into blender container, add 4 to 6 ½-inch cubes of American or Cheddar cheese. Cover container and **GRIND,** switching motor on and off until finely crumbed (Fig. 5).

CEREAL CRUMBS—COARSE OR FINE: For crusts, cakes, desserts, casserole toppings, meat loaves, etc. Prepare ½ cup of cereal flakes at a time. **BLEND,** switching motor on and off until crumbs are desired texture. Watch crumbing closely! About 1 cup cereal flakes (corn or whole wheat) makes ½ cup coarse crumbs or ¼ cup fine crumbs.

COOKIE CRUMBS: For crumb crusts, desserts, etc. Break cookies into blender container, cover and process:
10 chocolate wafers—**GRIND**—3 cycles—½ cup crumbs
16 small coconut cookies—**GRIND**—3 cycles—½ cup crumbs
16 vanilla wafers—**GRIND**—3 cycles—½ cup crumbs
6 zwieback slices—**CRUSH**—4 cycles—½ cup crumbs

CRACKER CRUMBS: Graham, Soda—For crumb crusts, desserts, etc. Break crackers into blender container, cover and process:

8 graham crackers—**CRUSH**—3 cycles—½ cup crumbs
16 soda crackers—**GRATE**—2 cycles—½ cup crumbs

ICE IN THE BLENDER

The Osterizer container should contain at least 1 cup of liquid in order for whole ice cubes to process properly. Some of the recipes in this section do not call for this much liquid. In these recipes only, follow this simple step: Add all ingredients, cover container, process 3 cycles at **FRAPPÉ** to break cubes. Then process for a few seconds.

PURÉE

Fruits, vegetables (cooked and raw), cooked meats, poultry and fish or sea food may be puréed. Cut food into ½ to 1 inch pieces and **PURÉE** ½ cup of food and 2 to 4 tablespoons liquid (milk, juice, water, etc.) at a time. Stop motor and push ingredients into blades with rubber spatula as needed.

Figure 5   Blender Crumbing

WHIP

Heavy Cream: Put cream (add sugar and flavoring if desired) into blender container, cover and process at **WHIP.** Remove cover and use a rubber spatula to brush thickening cream from sides of container to the vortex. Do not overblend!

DO:

1. Use only the line voltage and frequency as specified on the bottom on the Osterizer blender.

2. Always operate your Osterizer blender on a clean, dry surface to prevent air from carrying foreign material or water into the motor.

3. Put liquid portions of recipes into the container first unless the instructions in recipes specify otherwise.

4. Cut all firm fruits and vegetables, and cooked meats, fish and seafoods into pieces no larger than ¾ to 1 inch. Cut all kinds of cheeses into pieces no larger than ½ inch.

5. Use rubber spatula to push ingredients to be chopped into liquid portion of recipe **ONLY** when motor is **OFF.**

6. Place cover firmly on the container before starting, and rest hand on the container cover when starting and running motor.

7. Remove heavy dips and spreads, nut butters, mayonnaise and products of similar consistency by removing the processing assembly and pushing the mixture out through the bottom opening into serving dishes or storage container.

8. Pour mixtures of liquid or semi-liquid consistency, such as muffin and cake batters, from the container.

9. Allow cooked vegetables and broth to cool before pouring into Osterizer blender container for processing.

10. Switch to the next higher speed if the motor seems to labor when processing at one of the lower speeds to prevent overloading of the motor.

11. Use a "Mini-Blend" jar to process citrus rind, coffee beans or cereal grains. Use only glass blender container to process whole spices and hard cheeses.

DON'T:

1. **DON'T** expect your Osterizer blender to replace all of your kitchen appliances. It will not mash potatoes, whip egg whites, or substitutes for dairy toppings, grind raw meat, knead or mix stiff doughs, crush ice or extract juices from fruits and vegetables.

2. **DON'T** process mixtures too long. Remember, the Osterizer blender performs its tasks in seconds, not minutes. It is better to stop and check the consistency after a few seconds than to overblend and have a mushy or too finely ground product.

3. **DON'T** overload the motor with extra-heavy or extra-large loads. If the motor stalls turn off immediately, unplug cord from outlet, and remove a portion of the load before beginning again.

4. **DON'T** put ice cubes into the container without at least one cup of liquid. Ice cubes will not process properly without liquid.

5. **DON'T** attempt to remove the container from the motor base or replace it until the motor has coasted to a complete stop. Blender parts can be damaged.

6. **DON'T** remove the container cover while processing, as food spillage can occur. Use the Feeder Cap opening to add ingredients.

7. **DON'T** place or store agitator blades or assembly on the blender base without first correctly assembling to the container. Severe injury can result if the blender is accidently turned on.

8. **DON'T** use any utensils, including spatulas, in the container while the motor is running. They can catch in the moving blades, break the container and cause severe injury.

9. **DON'T** use **ANY** jar not recommended by Oster for processing foods. Jars other than Oster jars can break or loosen during processing and cause severe injury.

10. **DON'T** use "Mini-Blend" jars for processing whole spices or hard cheeses, as they can break the "Mini-Blend" jar and cause severe injury.

LIQUEFY

The blender will liquefy, but it is not a juice extractor! Cut fruits, vegetables, etc., into ½ to 1 inch pieces. Combine 1 cup liquid (juice, bouillon, water, milk, etc.) and ½ cup food in container; **LIQUEFY** until food particles disappear. Remove feeder cap and add three or four ice cubes (Fig. 6), one at a time, to thoroughly chill the liquid. Continue processing until the cubes are dissolved. (If desired, this juice may be strained through a fine sieve to remove the heavy fibrous particles.)

Figure 6   Liquifying

9

APPETIZERS

PARTY TIME NIBBLERS

Appetizers arranged handsomely in the living room get any party off to a good start, whether it's a casual get-together or an elegant party.

It's easier than you think to serve swanky little appetizers. Interesting dips, dunks, patés, spreads and hors d'oeuvres can be whizzed up jiffy-quick in the modern blender. Try just a few of the recipes that follow to get acquainted with the blender and you'll quickly discover ways to adapt your own favorite recipes so they can be made the easy blender way. These few suggestions assure success.

1. Don't overload the container. If the mixture is a thick one, do several small batches; it will speed up the blending. Make no more than 1 cup at a time.

2. Make the blending easy. If a mixture is stiff and clings to the side of the container, stop the motor and push ingredients into blades with rubber spatula. Repeat process as needed.

3. Chop a small amount at a time (¼ to ½ cup) when nuts, cheese, ham, eggs or vegetables are being blended and a pleasing texture is desired. Set the speed and switch motor on and off until the food is just the right fineness. Empty container and repeat as necessary.

4. Chill dips, dunks, patés, spreads and cold appetizers very well before serving. Serve hot appetizers from an electric chafing dish, electric frypan or heatproof container over candle, canned heat or alcohol burner.

5. Group appetizers and go-with foods attractively on table along with serving plates, forks, napkins and beverages, and let the guests help themselves. It makes party giving easier for the hostess, and more fun for guests.

CRABMEAT
SPREAD OR DIP

½ cup Blender Mayonnaise (page 154)
¼ cup lemon juice or cider vinegar
1 (4-inch) green onion, cut in 1 inch lengths
1 (⅛-inch) slice unpeeled lime or lemon, quartered
½ teaspoon salt
⅛ teaspoon pepper
2 dashes hot red pepper sauce
1 tablespoon drained capers
2 cans (6½ or 7½ ounce) crabmeat, boned and flaked
Chopped parsley, optional

CRUMB first 8 ingredients until onion and lime or lemon are finely chopped, 3 to 5 seconds. Stop motor; push ingredients into blades with rubber spatula, as needed. Turn into bowl; fold in crabmeat. Spoon into serving dish; garnish with chopped parsley, if desired. Serve with chips, crackers or toast. Makes about 1¾ cups.

CRABMEAT FILLED PUFFS: Prepare or purchase tiny cream puff shells, about 1¼ inches in diameter. Cut tops from shells and fill bottom halves with Crabmeat Spread or Dip (above); cover with top.

CHICKEN FILLED PUFFS: Fill puff shells, as directed for Crabmeat Filled Puffs, with Pronto Chicken Spread (page 15).

TANGY HAM DIP

1 cup diced (¼-inch) fully-cooked ham (about ¼ pound)
1 cup (½-pint) dairy sour cream
1 teaspoon horseradish
1 teaspoon prepared mustard
1 (⅛-inch) slice onion, quartered

Pour ½ cup ham into container. Set speed at **GRATE** and switch motor on and off until ham is chopped moderately fine. Turn into mixing bowl. Repeat with remaining ham. **GRATE** remaining ingredients until well mixed, 2 to 3 seconds. Add to ham; mix well. Chill. Serve with crackers or Melba toast. Makes about 1½ cups.

CHEESE
NUT BALL

2 jars (5-ounce) blue cheese spread
1 jar (5-ounce) sharp American or Cheddar cheese spread
1 package (3-ounce) room temperature cream cheese, cubed
1 (5-inch) green onion, cut in 1 inch lengths or 1 (⅛-inch) slice onion, quartered
1 teaspoon Worcestershire sauce
2 dashes hot red pepper sauce, optional
2 cups peanuts, cashews or pecan halves

Remove cheeses from refrigerator and allow to warm to room temperature. Add first 6 ingredients to container in the order listed. Set speed at **PURÉE;** process until smooth, 10 to 15 seconds. Stop motor and push ingredients into blades with rubber spatula as needed. Pack mixture into plastic film or aluminum foil lined 2 cup bowl. Cover; chill well. Add ½ cup nuts to container. Set speed at **BLEND** and switch motor on and off until nuts are coarsely chopped. Empty container and repeat 3 times. Before serving turn cheese out of bowl; remove film. Cover top and sides of ball with nuts. Serve with favorite crackers. Makes about 2 cups.

STUFFED
KUMQUATS

¼ cup pecan halves
2 to 2½ dozen large preserved kumquats
2 tablespoons half and half (half milk, half cream)
2 tablespoons rum or orange juice
1 (⅛-inch) slice unpeeled lime or lemon, quartered
¼ cup pitted dates, quartered, or 6 to 8 medium-size pieces preserved ginger
¼ teaspoon salt
1 package (3-ounce) room temperature cream cheese, cubed
⅓ cup flaked coconut
6 or 7 maraschino cherries, quartered

Set speed at **STIR;** add nuts to container. Switch motor on and off, as needed, to chop nuts moderately fine. Pour out of container; save. Start at stem end of kumquats and cut ¼ way down from top with sharp pointed knife or scissors to form tulip-like shells with 8 petals. Remove seeds and pulp and discard; turn upside down on paper towel to drain. **GRATE** remaining ingredients, except coconut and cherries, switching motor on and off until dates or ginger are chopped moderately fine. Turn into bowl; stir in coconut and nuts. Fill kumquats with mixture. Garnish each with a maraschino cherry wedge. Makes about 24 to 30 appetizers.

Bagna Cauda

BAGNA CAUDA

See photo at left

1 cup soft butter or margarine
⅓ cup olive or peanut oil
3 small garlic cloves, slivered
1 or 2 cans (2 ounce) anchovy fillets, well drained
Bagna Cauda Vegetables (allow ½ to 1 cup vegetables per person)
French or Italian bread, cut in ¼-inch slices

Combine first 4 ingredients in blender; **CHOP** just until anchovies and garlic pieces are finely chopped. Pour into electric fondue pot; heat slowly at medium heat until mixture is bubbly. Turn heat to low; keep just hot enough to heat and lightly brown vegetables without burning. To serve spear a vegetable piece with a fondue fork or long heavy bamboo skewer and swirl vegetable in butter mixture until hot and lightly browned, do not cook. Hold a piece of bread under vegetable as it is removed from oil to catch flavorful drippings. Yield: About 1½ cups, enough for 5 to 6 cups vegetables, appetizer servings for 10 to 12.

Bagna Cauda Vegetables

Choose an assortment of any of the following:

CARROTS: peel and cut crosswise into ½-inch slices.

CAULIFLOWER: clean and break into flowerettes.

GREEN BEANS: clean, stem and dry.

CHERRY TOMATOES: wash and dry.

GREEN OR RED PEPPERS: clean and cut lengthwise into ½-inch strips.

MUSHROOMS: clean, dry, leave whole or cut in half.

ZUCCHINI: wash, dry and cut crosswise into ½-inch slices.

TASTY TUNA DIP

You can heat this dip to use as a sauce for hot, cooked noodles

1 (7-ounce) can tuna
½ cup mayonnaise
¼ cup coarsely chopped onion
¼ cup coarsely chopped green pepper
1 stalk celery, sliced
1 small carrot, sliced
1 teaspoon Worcestershire sauce
¼ teaspoon salt

CHOP all ingredients 30 or 40 seconds or until smooth. Garnish with lime slice and mint. Makes 1½ cups dip.

CHUTNEY-CHEESE SPREAD

1 (8-ounce) package cream cheese, cubed
¾ cup chutney
2 tablespoons lemon juice
1 teaspoon curry powder
¼ teaspoon dry mustard
¼ teaspoon salt
Flaked coconut

GRIND first six ingredients 45 seconds, stopping motor to push ingredients to blades, if necessary. Chill. Garnish with flaked coconut. Makes 2 cups.

WISCONSIN DUNK

Slice apples and pears to use for dippers here

1 cup cream-style cottage cheese
1 cup cubed Cheddar cheese
1 (3-ounce) package cream cheese, cubed
½ cup half and half (half milk, half cream)
½ teaspoon salt
⅛ teaspoon paprika

GRIND all ingredients 1 minute, stopping motor to push ingredients down to blades, if necessary. Makes 2½ cups.

HOT BLACK BEAN DIP

1 (1-pound) can black beans, drained, or 1 can black bean soup
1 (8-ounce) can tomato sauce
1 cup cubed sharp Cheddar cheese
1 small onion, sliced
½ teaspoon chili powder
Dash Worcestershire sauce

GRIND all ingredients about 15 seconds or until smooth. Heat through and serve in heatproof container or pour into chafing dish and heat. Serve with corn chips and crackers. Makes about 2 cups dip.

ROUSING ROQUEFORT DIP

1 cup cream-style cottage cheese
½ cup mayonnaise
4 ounces Roquefort cheese, cubed

GRIND ingredients 30 seconds. Chill. Makes 1¾ cups.

SHRIMP NEWBURGH DIP

1 (4½- or 5-ounce) can shrimp, drained
½ cup mayonnaise
⅓ cup American cheese, cubed
3 tablespoons milk
1 small onion, sliced
1 teaspoon Worcestershire sauce
Dash hot pepper sauce

Reserve a few shrimp for garnish. **GRIND** all ingredients 1 minute or until smooth, stopping motor to push ingredients to blades, if necessary. Chill. Garnish with reserved shrimp. Makes 1½ cups.

SHRIMP 'N DILL DIP

Frozen cream of shrimp soup makes this dip extra-fast

1 (10-ounce) can frozen cream of shrimp soup,
  thawed
1 (8-ounce) package cream cheese, cubed
¼ medium cucumber, peeled and cubed
1 slice onion
1 teaspoon dried dill weed

LIQUEFY all ingredients for 20 seconds or until smooth. Chill thoroughly. Makes 2 cups dip.

CAVIAR DIP

A most elegant dip for special occasions. Celery hearts and radishes make interesting dippers

1½ cups dairy sour cream
¼ cup tomato paste
1 small tin red caviar
2 tablespoons Worcestershire sauce
1 tablespoon lemon juice
Chopped parsley or green onions for garnish

GRIND all ingredients 10 to 15 seconds or until smooth. Serve with toast triangles and assorted crackers. Makes about 2 cups dip.

SAUCY SARDINE DIP

Use fresh vegetables — celery, radishes, cauliflowerets, carrots — for dippers

1 cup cream-style cottage cheese
2 (4-ounce) cans sardines, drained
1 tablespoon prepared horseradish
1 clove garlic, peeled
½ teaspoon Worcestershire sauce

GRIND all ingredients 30 seconds or until smooth. Makes about 2 cups dip.

DANISH HERRING DIP

Serve with radishes, raw cauliflowerets, carrot and celery sticks

1 cup cream-style cottage cheese
¼ cup marinated herring chunks
1 tablespoon onion from herring
1 teaspoon lemon juice
⅛ teaspoon paprika

GRIND all ingredients 30 seconds, stopping motor to push ingredients down to blades, if necessary. Makes about 1 cup dip.

DOWN EAST CLAM DIP

Try pretzels for dippers

1 (10½-ounce) can minced clams
1 (8-ounce) package cream cheese, cubed
½ onion, sliced
1 teaspoon celery salt
1 teaspoon Worcestershire sauce

Drain clams, reserving 2 tablespoons liquid. **GRIND** clams, reserved liquid and all remaining ingredients 45 seconds, stopping motor to push ingredients to blades, if necessary. Chill. Makes about 1½ cups.

HAM AND MUSHROOM DUNK

½ cup cubed cooked ham
1 (4-ounce) can sliced mushrooms, drained
¼ cup coarsely chopped sweet pickles
¼ cup mayonnaise
¼ teaspoon paprika

GRIND all ingredients 30 seconds or until smooth, stopping motor to push ingredients to blades, if necessary. Makes about 1 cup.

DEVILED HAM DUNK

1 (4½-ounce) can deviled ham
1 (3-ounce) package cream cheese, cubed
1 slice onion
¼ cup parsley sprigs
1 tablespoon catsup
1½ teaspoons Worcestershire sauce

GRIND all ingredients 30 seconds or until smooth. Makes about 1 cup dunk.

BACON DIP

Try this as a sauce for cooked vegetables or baked potatoes too. Great flavor!

6 slices bacon, diced
1 cup dairy sour cream
½ cup mayonnaise
1 slice onion
¼ lemon, peeled
1 tablespoon parsley sprigs

Cook bacon until crisp; drain. **GRIND** bacon with all remaining ingredients about 30 seconds or until smooth. Makes about 1¾ cups dip.

PRONTO CHICKEN SPREAD

For sandwiches or canapés

1 (5½-ounce) can boned cooked chicken, cubed
¼ cup mayonnaise
¼ cup coarsely chopped green pepper
1 whole pimiento, cubed
1 stalk celery, sliced
½ teaspoon salt

GRIND all ingredients 20 seconds, stopping motor to push ingredients to blades, if necessary. Makes 1¼ cups.

CREAMY ANCHOVY DIP

Remember this recipe for a great Beef Fondue sauce

¼ cup mayonnaise
¼ cup half and half (half milk, half cream)
1 slice onion
¼ cup parsley sprigs
2 tablespoons anchovy paste
2 (3-ounce) packages cream cheese, cubed

GRIND mayonnaise, half and half, onion, parsley sprigs and anchovy paste 15 seconds. With motor running, add cheese, a cube at a time through opening in top. Continue **GRIND**ing until smooth. Makes about 1½ cups dip.

GUACAMOLE

Mexico's favorite appetizer

3 medium-sized ripe avocados, peeled and cubed
1 medium tomato, cubed
1 small onion, sliced
2 tablespoons lemon or lime juice
½ teaspoon salt
Dash hot pepper sauce

GRIND all ingredients 30 seconds or until smooth, stopping motor to push ingredients to blades, if necessary. Serve with toasted tortillas or corn chips. Makes about 2 cups.

CHILI CON QUESO

A simple, but spicy, dip from South-of-the-Border

1 pound sharp process Cheddar cheese, cubed
1 cup milk
1 (4-ounce) can green chili peppers
2 tablespoons flour

GRIND all ingredients about 30 seconds or until smooth, stopping motor to push ingredients to blades, if necessary. Pour into saucepan or chafing dish; cook and stir over low heat until smooth and thick. Serve with toasted tortillas. Makes 3½ cups.

CHEESE DUO DIP

Top a fresh fruit salad with a spoonful of this dip

1 (8-ounce) package cream cheese, cubed
8 ounces blue cheese, cubed
½ cup evaporated milk
¾ teaspoon celery seed
1 clove garlic, peeled

GRIND all ingredients 45 seconds, stopping motor to push ingredients to blades, if necessary. Makes 3 cups.

SUNSHINE DIP

Try dollops of this dip on tomato slices or over hot, cooked vegetables

3 hard-cooked eggs, peeled and diced
1 (3-ounce) package cream cheese, cut in cubes
2 tablespoons half and half (half milk, half cream)
2 tablespoons mayonnaise
2 tablespoons prepared mustard
1 tablespoon coarsely chopped green pepper
1 teaspoon vinegar

GRIND all ingredients 15 seconds or until smooth. Makes 1½ cups dip.

PINEAPPLE-BLUE CHEESE DIP

Also good as a salad dressing, especially for fruits

1 (8-ounce) package cream cheese, cubed
1 (8¾-ounce) can crushed pineapple
1 (5-ounce) package blue cheese, cubed
1 tablespoon chopped chives

GRIND all ingredients 30 seconds or until smooth, stopping motor to push ingredients to blades, if necessary. Chill. Makes about 3 cups.

HOT ORANGE MARMALADE DIP

1 jar (12-ounce) thick orange marmalade
¼ cup catsup
2 (⅛-inch) slices unpeeled lemon, quartered
1 tablespoon soy sauce
¼ teaspoon ginger
1 small clove garlic, sliced

CHOP ingredients 25 seconds or until lemon peel is coarsely chopped. Pour into electric fondue pot or small saucepan. Simmer gently over very low heat until thickened, 8 to 10 minutes; stir frequently. Serve warm as a dip for cocktail franks or small meat balls. Makes about 1¼ cups sauce.

HE-MAN GARLIC DIP

⅓ cup milk
2 tablespoons Worcestershire sauce
1 tablespoon paprika
1 or 2 cloves garlic, peeled
1 teaspoon vinegar
1 (8-ounce) package cream cheese, cubed

GRIND milk, Worcestershire sauce, paprika, garlic and vinegar 10 seconds. With motor running, add cheese, a cube at a time, through opening in top. Continue **GRIND**ing until smooth. Makes about 1½ cups dip.

APPLE-STUFFED EDAM

1 (1-pound) Edam cheese
1 medium apple, cored and cubed
⅓ cup half and half (half milk, half cream)
1 teaspoon lemon juice
⅛ teaspoon salt

Cut top off cheese, using zig-zag strokes with knife. Cut out center of cheese, leaving ½-inch shell and red cover intact. Cube cheese from center and top and **GRIND** with all remaining ingredients 30 to 45 seconds, stopping motor to push ingredients to blades, if necessary. Pile blended mixture into cheese shell and chill. Makes about 1¼ cups spread.

SHRIMP IN BEER

1 cup beer or ale
3 tablespoons cooking oil
2 tablespoons lemon juice
2 (⅛-inch) slices onion, quartered
1 (⅛-inch) slice unpeeled lemon, quartered
2 tablespoons flour
½ teaspoon salt
¼ teaspoon thyme
⅛ teaspoon paprika
2 dashes hot red pepper sauce
1½ pounds cooked, shelled, deveined, washed shrimp
2 teaspoons finely chopped parsley, optional
1 pimiento, diced, optional

Combine ¼ cup beer or ale and next 9 ingredients in blender container. **GRATE** until onion and lemon are finely chopped, 3 to 5 seconds. Pour into large saucepan or blazer pan of chafing dish. Stir in remaining beer. Heat, stirring constantly until sauce thickens. Fold in shrimp; heat. Sprinkle with finely chopped parsley and pimiento, if desired. Serve hot as appetizer. Makes 12 to 18 servings.

CORNED BEEF DIP

½ of 12-ounce can corned beef, cubed
⅔ cup Blender Mayonnaise (page 154)
1 package (3 ounce) room temperature cream cheese, cubed
2 teaspoons horseradish
1 teaspoon prepared mustard
1 (2-inch) sweet pickle, quartered
1 (⅛-inch) slice onion, quartered, optional
½ teaspoon seasoned salt
½ teaspoon Worcestershire sauce
¼ teaspoon celery salt, optional

CRUMB corned beef, ½ at a time, until coarsely chopped, switching motor on and off as needed; turn into bowl. Combine remaining ingredients in container in order listed. **CRUMB** until well mixed, 3 to 5 seconds; add to meat and mix. Chill. Serve with crackers, chips, or use as a sandwich spread. Makes about 2 cups.

EASY SWISS FONDUE

1 cup milk, scalded
1 small clove garlic, sliced
1 pound natural Swiss cheese, in ½-inch cubes
2 tablespoons flour
¼ teaspoon salt
¼ teaspoon nutmeg
Dash cayenne
½ cup dry white wine
2 tablespoons kirsch
French bread, cubed

Pour hot milk into container; add garlic. Turn speed to **GRATE** and add cheese cubes through top opening, one at a time, blending until smooth. Add flour, salt, nutmeg, cayenne and wine. **GRATE** until smooth, 5 to 10 seconds. Stop motor as needed and push ingredients into blades with rubber spatula. Cook in fondue pot on low heat, stirring constantly until thickened. Stir in kirsch. Twirl cubes of bread in cheese mixture; drain, cool and eat. Makes about 3⅓ cups.

HAM FONDUE: STIR 1 cup cubed (½-inch) fully-cooked ham, ¼ cup at a time, switching motor on and off, until ham is coarsely chopped. Stir into Easy Swiss Fondue before adding kirsch. Heat. Omit kirsch, if desired.

FRANKS FONDUE: STIR 4 fully-cooked wieners or franks (½-inch slices), ⅓ cup at a time, switching motor on and off, until franks are coarsely chopped. Proceed as directed for Ham Fondue above.

SHRIMP FONDUE: STIR 1 or 2 cans (4½-ounce) shrimp, drained, ⅓ cup at a time, switching motor on and off, until shrimps are coarsely chopped. Proceed as directed for Ham Fondue above.

PIZZA FONDUE: STIR ¼ cup catsup and ¼ to ½ teaspoon oregano into fondue before heating. Omit nutmeg and kirsch.

SALAMI PIZZA FONDUE: STIR 1 cup diced (½-inch) cotto or hard salami, ¼ cup at a time, switching motor on and off, until sausage is coarsely chopped. Omit nutmeg and kirsch. Proceed as directed for Ham Fondue above.

Easy Swiss Fondue

BEVERAGES BY THE DOZEN

Frosty sparklers, soda fountain specials, fruit juices for breakfast, steaming mugs of hot chocolate and cool, cool cocktails are all crowd pleasers, doubly welcome when the fixing is fast and easy.

Zesty pick-ups are ready to sip and enjoy in seconds when a multi-speed electric blender is available. Try the easy-to-do recipes on the following pages for real crowd pleasing drinks. There's a drink for most every occasion, all tempters for thirsty days.

PARTY PUNCH FOR MANY

1 can (6-ounce) frozen orange juice concentrate partially defrosted
1 can (6-ounce) frozen limeade concentrate, partially defrosted
1 can (6-ounce) frozen pineapple juice concentrate, partially defrosted
1 tablespoon instant tea
5 cups ice water
1 cup peach or apricot nectar
⅓ cup grenadine, optional
4 cups crushed ice
1 pint light rum, optional

BEAT first 4 ingredients and 1 cup ice water, switching motor on and off until well mixed, 5 to 8 seconds. Cover; refrigerate until serving time. Just before serving, pour juices into punch bowl. Stir in nectar and grenadine. Add remaining 4 cups of ice water, ice and rum; stir gently. Makes about 14 cups, 28 servings.

HOLIDAY EGGNOG

Rich and creamy! A necessity for any winter get-together

6 eggs, separated
1 pint brandy or whiskey
⅓ cup dark rum
2 cups cold milk
¾ cup sugar
2 cups heavy cream

BEAT egg yolks 5 seconds. Pour in brandy and rum and **BEAT** 5 seconds longer. Add milk and **BEAT** 10 seconds. Pour into chilled punch bowl. With electric or rotary beater, beat egg whites until foamy. Gradually add sugar and beat to stiff peaks. **WHIP** cream 20 seconds or until stiff. Fold egg whites and cream into milk mixture. Sprinkle with nutmeg. Makes 24 servings.

DOUBLE GINGER PUNCH

1 (approximately 1-x-2-inch) piece candied ginger, cubed
2 (6-ounce) cans frozen lemonade concentrate
2 (6-ounce) cans frozen limeade concentrate
4 cups cold water
1 quart ginger ale, chilled

GRIND candied ginger, lemonade concentrate, limeade concentrate and water 30 seconds. Chill. Pour into punch bowl and gently mix in ginger ale. Garnish with slices of lemon and lime. Makes 20 servings.

MINT PUNCH

Remember this recipe for showers or other celebrations

6 sprigs fresh mint
2 cups sugar
2 cups water
2 cups lemon juice
¼ teaspoon salt
Green food coloring
1 quart ginger ale, chilled

BLEND mint, sugar and water 15 seconds. Simmer 5 minutes. Strain, then add lemon juice, salt and a few drops green food coloring. Chill thoroughly. Gently mix with ginger ale to serve. Garnish with additional mint sprigs. Makes about 1½ quarts.

SPARKLING FRUIT PUNCH

1 can (6-ounce) frozen orange juice concentrate, partially defrosted
⅓ cup defrosted frozen pineapple juice concentrate
⅓ cup defrosted frozen lemonade concentrate
1 cup crushed ice
1 cup cold water
2 tablespoons sugar
2 bottles (10-ounce) chilled ginger ale
10 to 15 washed strawberries, sliced, optional

BEAT first 6 ingredients until well mixed, 5 to 8 seconds. Prepare additional punch as needed. Pour into chilled punch bowl and add ginger ale; stir gently. Float strawberries on punch, if desired. Makes about 5½ cups, 10 to 12 servings.

QUICK FIX FRUIT JUICES

Empty contents of 1 can (6-ounce) frozen concentrated fruit juice or fruitade (orange, tangerine, grape juice, lemonade or limeade) into container. Add amount of water called for on label. **BEAT** until well mixed, 3 to 5 seconds.

PEACH SPLASH

1 package (12-ounce) frozen sliced, sweetened peaches, partially defrosted and broken apart
2 tablespoons sugar
¼ teaspoon salt
¼ teaspoon nutmeg or cinnamon
2 cups chilled milk
½ cup whipped cream or dessert topping, optional
Mint sprigs, optional

BLEND first 4 ingredients and 1 cup milk until smooth, 10 to 15 seconds. Stop motor as needed and push ingredients into blades with rubber spatula. Add remaining milk. **WHIP** until smooth, 2 or 3 seconds. Pour into glasses. Garnish with a dollop of whipped cream or dessert topping and mint, if desired. Makes about 3½ cups, 3 or 4 servings.

TROPICAL FLOATS

2 cups chilled milk
½ cup undrained canned crushed pineapple
1 or 1½ pints orange sherbet
Mint sprigs, optional

BEAT milk, pineapple and ½ pint sherbet until well mixed, about 5 seconds. Pour into 4 tall glasses; top with remaining sherbet. Garnish glasses with mint sprigs, if desired. Makes about 5 cups, 4 servings.

SUNNY SIPPER

2 cups unsweetened pineapple juice, chilled
1 medium carrot, sliced
1 orange, peeled and quartered
1 tablespoon seedless golden raisins

LIQUEFY all ingredients 2 minutes. Pour over ice cubes to serve or add 3 ice cubes and **LIQUEFY** a few seconds longer. Makes 2 to 3 servings.

LIME FREEZE

Add 4 jiggers of rum for a rapid Daiquiri

1 (6-ounce) can frozen limeade concentrate
5 to 6 cups crushed ice
Green food coloring

GRIND limeade concentrate and ice until slushy, stopping motor several times to push ice to blades. Tint with a few drops green food coloring. Spoon into 6 tall chilled glasses and serve at once. Makes 6 servings.

LIME LIFT

1 envelope lemon-lime flavored drink powder
¾ cup sugar
2 limes, peeled and quartered
2 cups unsweetened pineapple juice, chilled
4 cups cold water

GRIND drink powder, sugar, limes and pineapple juice 30 seconds or until smooth. Pour into punch bowl or large pitcher and stir in water. Float block of ice in punch bowl and pour Lime Lift over ice. Makes 10 servings.

PINEAPPLE-MINT WHIP

2 cups cold milk
1 cup drained canned pineapple chunks, chilled
1 sprig fresh mint

LIQUEFY all ingredients 2 minutes. Makes 2 to 3 servings.

SHAKES AND MALTS

1 cup milk
Malted Milk Powder, if desired
Flavoring
1½ cups vanilla ice cream,
    serving consistency

Put milk, powder and flavoring into container, cover and process at **STIR** until thoroughly blended. Stop and add ice cream, spooning it into the container by tablespoonfuls. Cover and process 1 cycle at **GRATE**. Makes 2 servings.

THICK MOCHA SHAKE

2 cups chilled milk
1 pint chocolate ice cream, cubed
¼ cup chocolate syrup
1 tablespoon instant coffee
Whipped cream or dessert topping, optional

BEAT all ingredients except whipped cream until well mixed, about 10 seconds. Pour into 4 tall glasses. Top with whipped cream or dessert topping, if desired. Makes about 4 cups, 4 servings.

DOUBLE CHOCOLATE FLOATS

2½ cups chilled milk
1 to 1½ pints chocolate ice cream
½ cup chocolate syrup

Combine milk, ½ pint ice cream, cubed, and syrup. **BEAT** until well mixed, 5 to 10 seconds. Pour into tall glasses; top each with a scoop of ice cream. Makes about 3¾ cups, 3 to 4 servings.

RASPBERRY FIZZ

1 cup fresh raspberries
¼ cup orange juice
2 teaspoons lime juice
1 tablespoon sugar
1 cup crushed ice
1 quart carbonated water, chilled

GRIND raspberries, orange and lime juice and sugar 5 seconds. Add ice and **GRIND** 10 seconds longer. Pour into 4 tall chilled glasses and fill with carbonated water. Garnish with whole raspberries and sprigs of fresh mint, if desired. Makes 4 servings.

CHOCOLATE PEPPERMINT OR COFFEE FLOATS: Follow recipe for Double Chocolate Floats (above); substitute peppermint or coffee for chocolate ice cream. Makes about 3¾ cups, 3 to 4 servings.

TAFFY PEPPERMINT SMOOTHIE

2 cups chilled milk
¼ cup molasses
¼ cup finely chopped peppermint stick candy
⅛ teaspoon salt
1 pint vanilla ice cream, cubed
Peppermint sticks to garnish glasses, if desired

BEAT first 4 ingredients and ½ of the ice cream until thick and smooth, 8 to 10 seconds. Stop motor as necessary and push ingredients into blades. Add remaining ice cream and **BEAT** until ice cream is blended in, 5 to 8 seconds. Makes about 4 cups, 3 to 4 servings.

GELATIN PICK-ME-UP

Helps in dieting and in strengthening fingernails

1 envelope unflavored gelatin
¾ cup cold or hot liquid (orange, tomato or other juice, milk, water, broth or bouillon)

GRIND gelatin and liquid 10 seconds, if liquid is cold; 40 seconds, if liquid is hot. Drink at once. Makes 1 serving.

MOCHA FLOAT

1 quart cold milk
3 tablespoons sugar
1½ tablespoons instant coffee powder
⅛ teaspoon almond extract
½ pint chocolate ice cream
½ pint vanilla ice cream

BLEND milk, sugar, coffee and almond extract 10 seconds. Pour into 6 chilled glasses. Top each glass with a spoonful of chocolate and vanilla ice cream. Makes 6 servings.

CHOCO-MINT FLOAT

2 peppermint sticks (about 5 inches long), broken into short pieces
1 quart milk
Red food coloring
1 pint chocolate ice cream

GRIND peppermint sticks and milk 10 seconds. Add a drop or two of red food coloring, if desired. Pour into 4 tall glasses and top each with a scoop of ice cream. Makes 4 servings.

DOUBLE RASPBERRY SODA

A perfect bridge party refresher, photo page 24.

1 (10-ounce) package frozen raspberries, partially thawed
1 quart carbonated water or lemon-lime carbonated beverage, chilled
1 pint raspberry sherbet

MINCE raspberries 10 seconds; strain, if desired. Pour about ½ cup raspberry purée into each of 4 or 5 tall chilled glasses. Pour in carbonated water and top with scoop of raspberry sherbet. Makes 4 to 5 servings.

STRAWBERRY-BANANA MILK SHAKE

Photo page 24

2 cups milk
2 scoops vanilla ice cream
1 banana, peeled and sliced
½ cup fresh strawberries, hulled

LIQUEFY all ingredients 45 seconds. Pour into 2 tall chilled glasses. Makes 2 milk shakes.

CHERRY-VANILLA FLOAT

1 (4-ounce) jar maraschino cherries and syrup
1 quart cold milk
1 pint vanilla ice cream

Reserve 4 cherries for garnish. **STIR** remaining cherries, syrup and milk 15 seconds. Pour into 4 tall chilled glasses and top each with scoop of ice cream and reserved cherry. Makes 4 servings.

BEST BANANA MILK SHAKE

1 cup cold milk
1 banana, peeled and sliced
4 ice cubes
1 tablespoon honey

LIQUEFY all ingredients 1 minute. Sprinkle with nutmeg. Makes 2 servings.

PINEAPPLE-ORANGE FROST

Photo page 24

1 quart cold milk
½ pint pineapple sherbet
1 orange, peeled and quartered

BLEND all ingredients 1 minute or until smooth. Garnish with candy orange slice and fresh or canned pineapple chunks if desired. Makes 4 servings.

Orange Frappé   Apricot Shake   Carrot Cocktail

CHERRY WHIZ

Try Bing cherries, when in season, instead of tart cherries

2 cups unsweetened pineapple juice, chilled
1 cup pitted red tart cherries, fresh or canned
1 slice lime
Dash salt

LIQUEFY all ingredients 2 minutes. Pour over cracked ice to serve or add 3 ice cubes and **LIQUEFY** a few seconds longer. Makes 2 to 3 servings.

APRICOT SHAKE

See photo at left.

2 cups cold milk
½ cup dried apricots
2 tablespoons sugar
½ teaspoon vanilla

GRIND all ingredients 1½ minutes. Pour into chilled glasses. Garnish with dried or canned apricots, if desired. Makes 2 to 3 servings.

STRAWBERRY FROST

1 cup fresh or frozen strawberries
1 cup orange juice
2 tablespoons sugar
1 cup crushed ice

WHIP all ingredients 1 to 1½ minutes or until smooth. Makes 2 to 3 servings.

ORANGE FRAPPÉ

See photo at left.

1 (6-ounce) can frozen orange juice concentrate, partially thawed
3 cups crushed ice
3 ounces bourbon, gin or vodka (optional)

GRIND all ingredients about 1 minute or until slushy. Mound in glasses and serve at once. Makes 4 servings.

ORANGE GLOW

1 cup cold milk
½ cup orange juice
1 orange, peeled and quartered
1 lemon, peeled and quartered
1 tablespoon sugar
4 ice cubes

LIQUEFY all ingredients about 45 seconds or until smooth. Makes 3 to 4 servings.

FRESH RHUBARB COCKTAIL

1½ cups unsweetened pineapple juice, chilled
1 cup diced raw rhubarb
⅓ to ½ cup honey
1 cup crushed ice

LIQUEFY all ingredients 2 minutes. Makes 2 to 3 servings.

CARROT COCKTAIL

See photo at left.

2 cups unsweetened pineapple juice, chilled
3 carrots, sliced

LIQUEFY all ingredients 2 minutes. Add 3 ice cubes and **LIQUEFY** a few seconds longer. Makes 2 to 3 servings.

FOUR FRUIT WHIZ

2 cups unsweetened pineapple juice, chilled
1 orange, peeled and quartered
½ apple, cored and sliced
½ pear, cored and sliced

LIQUEFY all ingredients 2 minutes. Pour over ice cubes to serve or add 3 ice cubes and **LIQUEFY** a few seconds longer. Makes 3 servings.

FRUIT-NUT MILK SHAKE

2 cups cold milk
1 canned peach half
1 banana, peeled and sliced
2 pitted dates
2 tablespoons almonds

LIQUEFY all ingredients 2 minutes. Pour into chilled glasses. Makes 2 servings.

PINK PEPPERMINT VELVET

2 cups chilled milk
1 pint peppermint stick ice cream, cubed
Few drops red food coloring
Peppermint stick candy, optional
Mint sprigs, optional

BEAT first 3 ingredients until well mixed, about 5 to 10 seconds. Pour into 4 tall glasses. Garnish with peppermint sticks or mint sprigs or both, as desired. Makes about 3¾ cups, 4 servings.

HOT CHOCOLATE

1½ squares (1½ ounces) unsweetened chocolate
3 cups hot (scalded) milk
¼ to ⅓ cup sugar
1 teaspoon vanilla
Dash of salt

Cut chocolate into small pieces; add to container. Cover; turn to **BEAT** switching motor on and off as needed to chop chocolate very fine. Add remaining ingredients; **BEAT** just until well mixed, about 5 seconds. Makes about 3 cups, 3 to 4 servings.

BRAZILIAN CHOCOLATE: Follow recipe for Hot Chocolate (above); add ½ teaspoon instant coffee with sugar and vanilla.

Double Raspberry Soda Page 21, Pineapple-Orange Frost Page 21, Strawberry-Banana Milk Shake Page 21, Slush Cup Page 106.

MOSCOW HOT CHOCOLATE

1½ cups hot water
1 (1-ounce) square unsweetened chocolate
¼ cup sugar
⅛ teaspoon salt
2 cups hot coffee
1 cup milk
1 teaspoon vanilla

GRIND hot water, chocolate, sugar and salt 30 seconds. Pour into electric fondue pot or saucepan along with remaining ingredients and heat until piping hot (do not boil). Stir before serving. Makes 5 cups.

CALYPSO CHOCOLATE: Follow recipe for Hot Chocolate (page 24). Add ½ teaspoon pumpkin pie spice with sugar. Top servings with whipped cream, if desired. Makes about 3½ cups, 4 to 5 servings.

AFTER-DINNER MOCHA

3 cups hot (scalded) milk
½ cup chocolate syrup
3 tablespoons sugar
1 tablespoon instant coffee
¼ teaspoon salt
Whipped cream or dessert topping, optional
Chocolate curls, optional

Combine first 5 ingredients in container. **BEAT** until well mixed, 5 seconds. Serve in small cups. If desired garnish with whipped cream and a chocolate curl. Makes about 3½ cups, 6 to 8 servings.

HOT BUTTERSCOTCH TODDY

½ cup butterscotch bits
¼ cup semi-sweet chocolate bits
3 cups hot (scalded) milk
Dash of salt
1 teaspoon vanilla
½ teaspoon maple flavoring
Whipped cream or marshmallows, optional

GRATE first 2 ingredients and 1 cup hot milk 5 seconds or until bits are melted. Stop motor. Add remaining milk, salt and flavorings; **STIR** 5 seconds. Top each serving with whipped cream or marshmallows, if desired. Use electric fondue pot to keep toddy warm. Makes about 3⅔ cups, about 4 servings.

HOT COCOA

3 cups hot (scalded) milk
3 tablespoons cocoa (not instant)
⅓ cup sugar
1 teaspoon vanilla
Dash of salt
Whipped cream or marshmallows, optional

Combine first 5 ingredients in container; **BEAT** until well mixed, about 5 seconds. Garnish servings with whipped cream or marshmallows, if desired. Makes about 2¼ cups, 2 or 3 servings.

PEANUT BUTTERSCOTCH TODDY: Follow recipe for Hot Butterscotch Toddy (above) and add ¼ cup peanut butter with butterscotch and chocolate bits.

HOT PEANUT CHOCOLATE TODDY: Follow recipe for Hot Butterscotch Toddy (above); substitute semi-sweet chocolate bits for butterscotch bits and add ¼ cup peanut butter with bits.

QUICK COCOA

2 cups hot (scalded) milk
½ cup instant cocoa mix
¼ cup miniature marshmallows
1 teaspoon vanilla
Whipped cream or marshmallows, optional

Combine first 4 ingredients in container; **BEAT** until well mixed, about 5 seconds. Garnish servings with whipped cream or marshmallows, if desired. Makes about 2¼ cups, 2 to 3 servings.

MINTED ICE TEA

Fresh and true flavors. Bet you'll make this all summer long

4 sprigs mint
1 lemon, peeled and quartered
1 (1-inch) strip lemon peel
2 tablespoons sugar
1½ quarts hot tea

GRATE mint, lemon, peel and sugar 30 seconds. Pour hot tea over and let steep 20 minutes. Strain into pitcher and chill thoroughly. Makes 1½ quarts.

EMERALD FIZZ

1 jigger gin
1 jigger lemon juice
1 egg white
1 teaspoon green crème de menthe
1 teaspoon sugar
2 ice cubes

GRIND all ingredients 30 seconds. Strain, if desired. Makes 1 serving.

COMMODORE COCKTAIL

1 jigger bourbon
1 jigger crème de cacao
1 jigger lemon juice
2 ice cubes

GRIND all ingredients 30 seconds. Strain, into champagne glass. Makes 1 serving.

FROZEN DAIQUIRI

Practice will tell you the amount of ice to use

2 to 3 cups crushed ice
5½ jiggers rum
1½ jiggers lime juice
1 tablespoon powdered sugar

GRIND all ingredients about 30 seconds or until slushy. Serve at once. Makes 4 servings.

TOM OR RUM COLLINS

1 jigger gin or rum
1 jigger lime or lemon juice
1 tablespoon powdered sugar
2 ice cubes
Carbonated water, chilled

GRIND gin or rum, lime or lemon juice, sugar and ice 15 seconds. Strain into a tall chilled glass. Fill with carbonated water. Garnish with lime or lemon slice and maraschino cherry, if desired. Makes 1 serving.

BLOODY MARY

½ cup chilled tomato juice
3 jiggers vodka
¼ cup lemon juice
¼ teaspoon Worcestershire sauce
¼ teaspoon salt
½ cup crushed ice

Combine ingredients in blender container. **BLEND** until ice melts, 10 to 15 seconds. Makes 2 servings.

SILVER FIZZ

1 jigger gin
1 jigger lemon juice
1 egg white
1 teaspoon sugar
1 to 2 ice cubes
Carbonated water, chilled

GRIND gin, lemon juice, egg white, sugar and ice 15 seconds. Strain into highball glass and fill with carbonated water. Makes 1 serving.

STINGER

5 jiggers brandy
2 jiggers white crème de menthe
1 jigger lime juice
½ cup crushed ice

GRIND all ingredients 15 seconds. Strain, if desired. Makes 4 servings.

GRASSHOPPER

4 jiggers white crème de cacao
4 jiggers green crème de menthe
1 jigger cream or half and half (half milk, half cream)
2 ice cubes

MIX all ingredients 15 seconds. Strain, if desired. Makes 4 servings

BACARDI

4 jiggers light rum
2 jiggers grenadine
1½ jiggers lime juice
4 to 6 ice cubes

MIX all ingredients 15 seconds. Strain, if desired. Makes 4 servings.

SLOE GIN FIZZ

4 jiggers sloe gin
3 jiggers lemon juice
2 tablespoons sugar
1 cup crushed ice
8 ice cubes
Chilled carbonated water
Mint sprigs, optional

Pour first 4 ingredients into container. **CREAM** 8 to 10 seconds. Strain, if desired; pour into 4 tall 10-ounce glasses. Add 2 ice cubes to each glass; fill with carbonated water and stir gently. Garnish glasses with mint sprigs, if desired. Makes 4 tall drinks.

Whiskey Sour

WHISKEY SOUR

Frosty-cold and frothy from the blender

5 jiggers whiskey
2 jiggers lemon juice
2 tablespoons sugar
2 ice cubes

GRIND all ingredients 20 seconds. Strain into cocktail glasses. Garnish with orange slice and maraschino cherry, if desired. Makes 4 servings.

SHERRY FLIP

Use brandy instead of sherry, if you wish

1 egg yolk
1 jigger sherry
1 teaspoon sugar

GRIND all ingredients 10 seconds. Serve in a wineglass. Sprinkle top with nutmeg. Makes 1 serving.

ALEXANDER

5 jiggers gin or brandy
1½ jiggers crème de cacao
1 jigger cream or half and half (half milk, half cream)
2 ice cubes

GRIND all ingredients 15 seconds. Strain, if desired. Makes 4 servings.

PINK LADY

4½ jiggers gin
2 egg whites
1 jigger apple brandy
1 jigger lemon juice
½ jigger grenadine
2 ice cubes

GRIND all ingredients 15 seconds. Strain, if desired. Makes 4 servings.

ORANGE BLOSSOM

4½ jiggers gin
2½ jiggers orange juice
1 tablespoon lime juice
½ tablespoon sugar
2 ice cubes

GRIND all ingredients 15 seconds. Strain, if desired. Makes 4 servings.

BREADS

BREADS, SO EASY-MADE AND SO GOOD!

Hot, fragrant fresh baked breads, no aroma quite so tempting, no food so good!

How long since you've taken a whiff of luscious, fresh-from-the-oven bread or rolls? Too difficult to make? Not at all! You'll find your multi-speed blender saves time and steps galore when preparing yeast or quick breads, muffins, popovers or crispy waffles.

Banana Wheat Germ Bread is always a favorite with the men folks, but try Old Fashioned Gingerbread, Cinnamon Swirl Bread, Stollen and Tutti-Fruitti Rolls. They're all so delicious they will make any meal extra-special.

Try the interesting bread recipes that follow. They're all easy-made, all are baking creations!

BANANA WHEAT GERM BREAD

2 cups sifted flour
1 cup sugar
1 teaspoon soda
1 teaspoon salt
½ cup wheat germ
2 eggs
⅓ cup cooking oil
⅓ cup milk
1 teaspoon vanilla
2 cups sliced bananas (2 large)
½ cup pecan halves

Combine first 4 ingredients; sift into mixing bowl. Stir in wheat germ. **CREAM** eggs, oil, milk, vanilla and ½ of the banana pieces until smooth, about 10 seconds. Add remaining banana pieces; **CREAM** until smooth, about 15 seconds. Add pecan halves; **CREAM** until pecan halves are coarsley chopped, about 10 seconds. Pour over dry ingredients and mix just until dry ingredients are moistened. Pour into greased 9 x 5 x 3-inch loaf pan. Bake in moderate oven (350°F.) until done, 60 to 70 minutes. Cool in pan 5 minutes. Remove from pan and finish cooling on rack. Makes a 9 x 5 x 3-inch loaf.

ORANGE NUT BREAD

3 cups sifted flour
4 teaspoons baking powder
1¼ teaspoons salt
1 cup walnut halves
Peel of 1 (3-inch) orange, (thin orange colored portion only, cut into thin strips)
Fruit of 1 orange, quartered
¾ cup milk
½ cup molasses
1 egg
½ cup light brown sugar (firmly packed), broken up
¼ cup room temperature butter or margarine, sliced

Combine first 3 ingredients; sift into mixing bowl. **BLEND** walnuts, ⅓ cup at a time, switching motor on and off until coarsely chopped. Stir into dry ingredients. Combine remaining ingredients in blender container. **GRIND** 30 seconds. (Mixture may appear curdled.) Pour over dry ingredients; stir just until dry ingredients are moistened. Pour into greased 9 x 5 x 3-inch loaf pan. Bake in moderate oven (350°F.) until done, about 50 minutes. Cool in pan 5 minutes. Remove from pan and finish cooling on rack. Makes a 9 x 5 x 3-inch loaf.

CRANBERRY NUT BREAD

1 cup pecan or walnut halves
1 cup cranberries, cut in half
2 cups sifted flour
2½ teaspoons baking powder
1¼ teaspoons salt
1 egg
¼ cup soft butter or margarine, sliced
4 (1-inch) squares orange peel, cut in thin strips
⅓ cup orange juice
⅓ cup water
1 cup sugar

CHOP nuts, ¼ cup at a time, by switching motor on and off until nuts are very coarsely chopped. Pour nuts into mixing bowl. Repeat until nuts are chopped. Add cranberries to nuts. Combine flour, baking powder and salt; sift into mixing bowl. Mix gently. Combine remaining ingredients in blender container. **GRATE** until orange rind is finely chopped, 20 to 25 seconds. Stop motor and push ingredients in blades with rubber spatula as needed. Pour over dry ingredients and mix just until dry ingredients are moistened. Pour into greased and floured loaf pan (9 x 5 x 3-inch). Bake in moderate oven (350°F.) until done, about 1 hour. Cool in pan 5 minutes; remove from pan and finish cooling on rack. Makes one 9 x 5 x 3-inch loaf.

OLD FASHIONED GINGERBREAD

2¾ cups sifted flour
1½ teaspoons ginger
1 teaspoon soda
1 teaspoon cinnamon
¾ teaspoon salt
2 eggs
1 cup molasses
1 cup buttermilk
½ cup soft butter or margarine, sliced
½ cup sugar

Combine first 5 ingredients; sift into mixing bowl. Add remaining ingredients to blender container in order listed. **PURÉE** until smooth, 25 to 30 seconds. Stop motor and push ingredients into blades with rubber spatula as needed. Add to dry ingredients; stir just until dry ingredients are moistened. Pour into greased and floured 13 x 9 x 2-inch baking pan. Bake in moderate oven (350°F.) until done, 35 to 40 minutes. Serve warm or cool in pan on rack. Cut into squares. Makes one 13 x 9 x 2-inch gingerbread, 16 to 20 servings.

Date Corn Bread, Country Kitchen Muffins Page 33; Luscious Yeast Rolls, Cinnamon Swirl Bread, Whole-Grain Wheat Bread Page 31.

WHOLE-GRAIN WHEAT BREAD

See photo at left.

1½ cups whole grains of wheat
2 cups milk
2 envelopes active dry yeast
4 cups all-purpose flour (approximately)
½ cup butter or margarine, softened
2 eggs
¼ cup sugar
2 teaspoons salt
Melted butter or margarine, as needed

SHRED grains of wheat 40 seconds in container. Pour ground wheat into large mixing bowl. Heat milk and cool to lukewarm. Let yeast and lukewarm milk stand in blender container 5 minutes. Mix 3¾ cups flour with ground wheat. **GRIND** butter, eggs, sugar and salt with yeast and milk 20 seconds. Pour over flour and mix with wooden spoon until all dry ingredients are moistened. Turn out on floured surface and knead until smooth, adding small amounts of flour as needed. Return to bowl; brush top with melted butter. Cover and let rise in warm place until doubled, about 1½ hours. Knead dough down and divide in half. On lightly floured surface, roll half of dough to 10 x 12-inch rectangle. Fold in thirds, starting at long side; fold ends under. Place in buttered 9 x 5 x 3-inch pan, seam-side down, and brush with melted butter. Repeat with remaining dough. Cover and let rise in warm place until doubled, 45 to 60 minutes. Bake in a moderate oven (375°F.) 40 to 45 minutes, or until golden brown and loaf sounds hollow when tapped. Turn out of pans onto wire rack to cool. Do not slice until completely cooled. Makes 2 (9 x 5 x 3-inch) loaves.

CINNAMON SWIRL BREAD

See photo at left.

Prepare one recipe Luscious Yeast Rolls (at right). Combine and mix ½ cup sugar and 1 tablespoon cinnamon; set aside. Turn dough onto lightly floured board; roll into 8 x 16-inch rectangle. Sprinkle surface with 3 tablespoons of cinnamon-sugar mixture. Roll tightly, starting at a narrow side. Moisten edge; press together. Place sealed edge down, in well greased 9 x 5 x 3-inch loaf pan. Cover, place in warm draftless area; let double in size. Bake in moderate oven (375°F.) until done and browned, 40 to 45 minutes. Cool in pan 5 minutes, turn out of pan. Brush entire outside of loaf using 3 tablespoons melted butter or margarine; roll loaf in remaining cinnamon-sugar mixture; cool on rack. Makes one 9 x 5 x 3-inch loaf.

LUSCIOUS YEAST ROLLS

See photo at left.

1 envelope active dry yeast
¼ cup warm water
1 cup milk, scalded
¼ cup butter or margarine
3 tablespoons sugar
1 teaspoon salt
1 egg
3 to 3½ cups all-purpose flour
Melted butter or margarine, as needed

STIR yeast and warm water 5 seconds. Combine milk, butter, sugar and salt; cool to lukewarm. Add to blender container along with egg and **GRIND** 10 seconds. Add 1 cup flour; **GRIND** 20 seconds. Pour into large mixing bowl. Add flour to make soft dough. Turn out onto lightly floured surface and knead until dough is smooth and elastic. Place in buttered bowl, brush with melted butter; cover and let rise in warm place until doubled. Shape as desired.

CINNAMON PECAN ROLLS: Divide dough in half. On lightly floured surface roll each half to 8 x 18-inch rectangle. **GRATE** 1 cup brown sugar, ½ cup pecans, ¼ cup melted butter or margarine and 1½ teaspoons cinnamon 20 seconds. Spread ½ the mixture over each rectangle. Roll lengthwise as for jelly roll. Cut 1½-inch slices and place, cut side up, in buttered muffin tins. Brush with melted butter. Cover and let rise in warm place until doubled. Bake in moderate oven (375°F.) 20 to 25 minutes. Cool on rack. Makes 2 dozen rolls.

GOLDEN CHEESE BREAD

3 cups all-purpose flour
¾ cup milk, scalded
3 tablespoons sugar
2 tablespoons butter or margarine
1 teaspoon salt
¼ cup warm water
1 envelope active dry yeast
1 egg
¾ cup sharp Cheddar cheese, cubed
½ tablespoon poppy seed

Sift flour into large bowl. Combine milk, sugar, butter and salt; cool to lukewarm. **STIR** water and yeast 5 seconds; add egg and milk mixture and **GRIND** 30 seconds, adding cheese through opening in top while motor is running. Pour over flour and mix well. Turn out onto floured surface and knead 10 minutes, adding flour if needed. Replace in bowl; cover and let rise in warm place until doubled, about 1¼ hours. Knead down and roll out on lightly floured surface to 10 x 12-inch rectangle. Fold in thirds, starting at long side; fold ends under. Place in buttered 9 x 5 x 3-inch loaf pan, seam-side down and brush with melted butter. Sprinkle with poppy seed. Cover and let rise in warm place until doubled. Bake in moderate oven (375°F.) 30 to 35 minutes. Cool on rack. Makes 1 loaf.

TUTTI-FRUITTI ROLLS

1 recipe Luscious Yeast Rolls (page 31)
1 cup pecan or walnut halves
½ cup currants or seedless raisins
3 tablespoons soft butter or margarine
2 tablespoons milk
¼ cup brown sugar
1 teaspoon vanilla

Prepare dough; while it's rising prepare filling. **BLEND** nuts, ¼ cup at a time, switching motor on and off until coarsely chopped. Turn into bowl. Add currants or raisins; mix and save. Combine remaining ingredients in blender container in order listed. **PURÉE** until well mixed, 10 to 12 seconds. Stop motor; push ingredients into blades as needed. Stir into nut-fruit mixture. Turn dough onto lightly floured board; roll into a 15 x 9-inch rectangle. Spread nut-fruit mixture evenly over dough. Roll up tightly starting at wide side. Seal well by pinching edges together. Stretch roll as needed to shape into an even roll 18 inches long. Cut into 18 1-inch slices; place each slice in a well greased muffin cup or arrange slices in a well greased 13 x 9 x 2-inch pan. Cover; place in warm draftless area; let double in size. Bake in moderate oven (375°F.) until done and browned, 25 to 30 minutes. Cool in pan 5 minutes; remove from pan and frost while warm with Confectioners' Sugar Frosting (page 53). Makes 1½ dozen rolls.

STOLLEN

⅔ cup blanched almonds, cut in half
⅓ cup candied cherries, quartered
½ cup currants or raisins
½ cup diced mixed candied fruit
1 recipe Luscious Yeast Roll Dough (page 31)
3 tablespoons soft butter or margarine
Candied fruit, optional
Toasted blanched almonds, optional

CHOP blanched almonds in blender container, ⅓ cup at a time, switching motor on and off until coarsely chopped. Pour into bowl; repeat. Add next 3 ingredients to bowl; mix. Prepare dough as directed in recipe, except add nuts and fruit to mixture before first flour is added. After dough has risen turn onto lightly floured board; shape or roll into an oval 12 inches long and 8 inches wide. Spread dough with 2 tablespoons butter or margarine; fold dough in half starting at longer side. Transfer to greased baking sheet; shape into a crescent. Melt remaining 1 tablespoon butter or margarine; brush top and sides of crescent. Cover; place in warm draftless area; let double in size. Bake in moderate oven (375°F.) until done and browned, 30 to 35 minutes. Serve plain, dust with confectioners' sugar or frost while warm with a Confectioners' Sugar Frosting (page 53). Decorate as desired with candied cherries and citron and toasted blanched almonds. Makes 1 large stollen.

Stollen

BUTTERMILK CORN BREAD

1 cup sifted flour
1 cup yellow corn meal
2 tablespoons sugar
1½ teaspoons baking powder
1 teaspoon salt
½ teaspoon soda
2 eggs
¼ cup cooking oil or melted shortening
1 cup buttermilk

Combine first 6 ingredients; sift into mixing bowl. **GRATE** eggs, oil or shortening and buttermilk until well mixed, about 5 seconds. Add ½ of the dry ingredients. **GRATE** until mixed, about 5 seconds. Pour blended buttermilk mixture over dry ingredients in bowl. Stir just until dry ingredients are moistened. Pour into greased 8 x 8 x 2-inch pan. Bake in hot oven (425°F.) until done, 20 to 25 minutes. Makes 8 x 8 x 1½-inch bread.

CHEESE BUTTERMILK CORN BREAD: Follow Buttermilk Corn Bread (above) and add 1 cup diced (½-inch) Cheddar cheese and 1 (⅛-inch) slice onion (2-inch diameter) to egg, oil and buttermilk mixture before processing. Makes 8 x 8 x 1½-inch bread.

CORN MUFFINS: Follow Buttermilk Corn Bread (above) and increase sugar to ¼ cup. Fill greased muffin pans (2½ x 1¼-inch) ⅔ full. Bake in hot oven (425°F.) until done, 15 to 18 minutes. Makes 12 muffins.

DATE CORN BREAD

See photo page 30.

¾ cup sifted flour
½ cup yellow corn meal
3 teaspoons baking powder
½ teaspoon salt
¾ cup milk
1 egg
3 tablespoons sugar
3 tablespoons cooking oil
10 pitted dates

Combine first 4 ingredients; sift into mixing bowl. **BEAT** milk, egg, sugar and oil 10 seconds. Add dates. **CHOP** 25 seconds or until dates are coarsely chopped. Stop motor; push ingredients into blades with rubber spatula as needed. Pour over dry ingredients. Stir just until dry ingredients are moistened. Pour into greased 8 x 8 x 2-inch pan. Bake in hot oven (425°F.) until done, 18 to 20 minutes. Makes 8 x 8 x 1½-inch bread.

CORN STICKS: Pour Date Corn Bread batter into hot well-greased cornstick pans. Bake in hot oven (425°F.) 15 to 18 minutes. Makes about 18 sticks.

COUNTRY KITCHEN MUFFINS

See photo page 30

2 cups sifted flour
3 teaspoons baking powder
1 teaspoon salt
1 egg
1 cup milk
¼ cup melted butter or margarine
⅓ cup sugar

Sift first 3 ingredients into bowl. **CREAM** remaining ingredients 10 seconds, or until smooth. Pour over dry ingredients. Stir just until dry ingredients are moistened. Fill greased muffin pans (2½ x 1¼-inch) ⅔ full. Bake in hot oven (400°F.) 20 to 25 minutes. Makes 12 muffins.

APRICOT MUFFINS: Fold ⅔ cup diced cooked dried apricots into Country Kitchen Muffin batter (above) before filling pans.

BACON MUFFINS: Prepare as for Apricot Muffins (above). Substitute ½ cup crisp bacon bits for apricots.

BLUEBERRY MUFFINS: See photo page 34. Prepare same as Apricot Muffins (above). Substitute ¾ to 1 cup fresh or well drained canned blueberries for apricots.

OATMEAL MUFFINS: Follow Country Kitchen Muffins (above) and reduce flour to 1¾ cups and add ½ cup uncooked rolled oats to dry ingredients. Sprinkle tops of unbaked muffins with mixture of 1 tablespoon sugar and ¼ teaspoon cinnamon.

PRUNE OR DATE MUFFINS: Prepare as for Apricot Muffins (above). Substitute ½ cup diced pitted prunes or dates for apricots.

WHOLE WHEAT MUFFINS: Prepare as for Country Kitchen Muffins (above). **SHRED** ½ cup whole grains of wheat 40 seconds. Substitute for ⅔ cup flour and increase milk to 1¼ cups.

BANANA MUFFINS: Add to Country Kitchen Muffins 1 banana, pealed and broken into pieces, to egg mixture before **LIQUEFY**ing.

WHEAT GERM BANANA MUFFINS

Prepare as for Country Kitchen Muffins (page 33). Substitute ¾ cup wheat germ for 1 cup of flour and 3 tablespoons brown sugar for ¼ cup granulated sugar. Add 1 small banana, peeled and broken into pieces, to egg mixture before processing.

BANANA BRAN MUFFINS

1 cup sifted flour
3 teaspoons baking powder
½ teaspoon salt
1 cup whole bran cereal
1 egg
1½ cups sliced ripe banana (about 2 medium)
¼ cup milk
¼ cup melted shortening or cooking oil
⅓ cup sugar
1 teaspoon vanilla

Combine first 3 ingredients; sift into mixing bowl. Stir in bran cereal. **CREAM** remaining ingredients in container until smooth, about 5 seconds. Stop motor and push ingredients into blades with rubber spatula as needed. Pour over dry ingredients; mix just until dry ingredients are moistened. Fill greased muffin pans (2½ x 1¼-inch) ¾ full. Bake in hot oven (400°F.) until done and golden brown, about 20 minutes. Makes 12 muffins.

BRAN NUT MUFFINS: Fold ½ cup coarsely chopped pecans into Banana Bran Muffin batter (above) just before filling pans. See directions for chopping nuts on page 7.

SPEEDY-MADE MUFFINS FROM A MIX

Follow directions given on package label. Combine eggs and liquid ingredients in blender container. Add dry ingredients; **BLEND** until well mixed, 10 to 15 seconds. Stop motor and push ingredients into blades as needed. Bake as directed on package.

POPOVERS

1 cup milk
3 eggs
2 teaspoons butter or margarine
½ teaspoon salt
1 cup sifted flour

Combine ingredients in container in order listed. **MIX** until smooth, about 40 seconds. Stop motor; push ingredients into blades with rubber spatula as needed. Fill well-greased 5-ounce custard cups or muffin pans half full. Bake in hot oven (400°F.) until brown and crisp, 35 to 40 minutes. Makes 8 popovers.

34

Blueberry Muffins Page 33, Banana Bran Muffins

HERB POPOVERS: Follow recipe for Popovers (at left) and add ¾ teaspoon fines herbes blend with dry ingredients.

PARMESAN POPOVERS: Follow recipe for Popovers (at left) and add ¼ cup grated Parmesan cheese with dry ingredients.

SPICE POPOVERS: Follow recipe for Popovers (at left) and add 1 tablespoon sugar, ¾ teaspoon cinnamon and ¼ teaspoon nutmeg with dry ingredients.

FIX-AHEAD POPOVERS

Prepare batter using recipe for Popovers (at left) 4 to 6 hours before serving time. Fill well-greased 5-ounce custard cups or muffin pans half full. Store in freezer. At serving time bake frozen batter in a hot oven (425°F.) until popovers are crisp and browned, 35 to 40 minutes.

YORKSHIRE PUDDING

Prepare Popovers batter (at left). Pour 2 to 3 tablespoons roast drippings or melted butter or margarine into 9 x 9 x 2-inch square baking pan. Increase oven temperature to 425°F., and heat pan in oven while preparing batter. Pour batter into hot pan. Bake until crisp and brown, 25 to 30 minutes. Cut into squares and serve at once. Makes 8 servings.

CRISPY WAFFLES

2 egg yolks
1¼ cups milk
⅓ cup cooking oil or melted shortening
3 tablespoons sugar
1 teaspoon salt
1½ cups sifted flour
2 teaspoons baking powder
2 egg whites, stiffly beaten

Combine first 5 ingredients in blender container. **PURÉE** until well mixed, 2 to 3 seconds. Add flour and baking powder; **CREAM** until smooth, 8 to 10 seconds. Stop motor and push ingredients into blades with rubber spatula as needed. Do not overbeat. Pour into mixing bowl; fold in beaten egg whites. Pour ⅓ of batter into preheated waffle iron. Bake. Makes three square 9-inch waffles.

CHEESE WAFFLES: Follow Crispy Waffles recipe and add 1 cup diced (½-inch) Cheddar cheese to egg yolk mixture and decrease sugar to 2 tablespoons.

SPICY APPLE WAFFLES: Follow Crispy Waffles recipe and add 1 teaspoon cinnamon and ¼ teaspoon nutmeg to sifted dry ingredients. Add 1 cup coarsely blender-chopped peeled apple to egg yolk mixture and increase sugar to ¼ cup.

CHOCOLATE CHIP WAFFLES: Fold ½ cup semisweet chocolate bits into Crispy Waffles batter just before folding in egg whites. Bake as directed for Crispy Waffles. Serve with syrup, sundae or fruit sauce or top with ice cream or whipped cream.

NUT WAFFLES: Fold ½ cup chopped nuts, peanuts, pecans or walnuts, into Crispy Waffles batter just before folding in egg whites. Bake as directed. Serve with syrup, or as a dessert topped with ice cream, fruits or favorite sundae sauce.

PINEAPPLE WAFFLES: Fold ½ cup well-drained crushed pineapple into Crispy Waffles batter just before folding in egg whites. Bake as directed. Serve with syrup or as a dessert topped with whipped cream or ice cream.

PANCAKES

1¼ cups milk
1 egg
2 tablespoons melted shortening or cooking oil
2 tablespoons sugar
¾ teaspoon salt
2½ teaspoon baking powder
1¼ cups sifted flour

Combine ¾ cup milk and remaining ingredients in container. **MIX** just until ingredients are blended, about 20 seconds. Stop motor; push ingredients into blades with rubber spatula as needed. Add remaining ½ cup milk. **MIX** until smooth, about 15 seconds. For each pancake pour ¼ cup batter onto lightly greased griddle. Cook until edges are dry, top is full of bubbles and underside is brown. Turn and brown second side. Makes 8 pancakes.

APPLE PANCAKES: Follow Pancake recipe (above) and add 1 cup thinly sliced peeled raw apple to batter during the last 5 seconds of mixing time and **MIX** until apple is coarsely chopped, 5 to 10 seconds. Makes about 10 pancakes.

BANANA PANCAKES: Follow Pancake recipe (above) and add ½ cup sliced ripe banana to batter with the remaining ½ cup milk. Makes about 10 pancakes.

BUTTERMILK PANCAKES: Follow Pancake recipe (above) and substitute buttermilk for the sweet milk called for in recipe, add ½ teaspoon soda and decrease baking powder to 1½ teaspoons. Makes about 8 pancakes.

ORANGE PECAN PANCAKES: Follow Pancake recipe (page 35) and add one ¼-inch slice unpeeled orange, quartered, to batter with the dry ingredients. Add ¾ cup pecan halves during the last 5 seconds of mixing time and **MIX** until pecans are coarsely chopped, about 5 seconds. Makes about 10 pancakes.

BLUEBERRY PANCAKES: Prepare Pancakes (page 35) and carefully fold ¾ cup fresh or well-drained canned blueberries into batter just before baking. Serve with syrup or top with sour cream and brown sugar.

BACON OR HAM HOT CAKES: Prepare Pancakes (page 35) and fold ½ cup crisp bacon bits or finely chopped fully-cooked ham into batter just before baking.

WHOLE GRAIN WHEAT PANCAKES

From grains to batter in the blender container

1 cup sifted all-purpose flour
2½ teaspoons baking powder
1 teaspoon salt
¾ cup whole grains of wheat
1¾ cups milk
3 eggs
¼ cup salad oil

Sift flour, baking powder and salt together. **SHRED** wheat 60 seconds. Add milk, eggs and salad oil and **LIQUEFY** 10 seconds. Add half the flour mixture; **GRIND** 40 seconds, adding remaining flour through opening in top while motor is running. If necessary, STOP BLENDER, use rubber spatula to keep mixture around processing blades. Cover and continue to process at **GRIND** until smooth. Pour ¼ cup onto hot buttered griddle for each pancake. Bake until brown on both sides. Makes 12 pancakes.

POTATO PANCAKES

Try these topped with applesauce for a Sunday evening supper, or serve with Sauerbraten (page 82)

1½ cups pared potatoes, cubed
¼ cup milk
2 eggs
1 slice onion
4 parsley sprigs
½ teaspoon salt
¼ cup all-purpose flour
¼ teaspoon baking powder

PURÉE ½ cup potatoes, milk, eggs and onion 20 seconds. Add parsley and another ½ cup potatoes. **PURÉE** 20 seconds. Add flour and baking powder and **PURÉE** 20 seconds, adding last ½ cup of potatoes through opening in top while motor is running. Pour ⅓ cup of batter on hot buttered griddle for each pancake. Bake until brown on both sides. Makes 8 pancakes.

PANCAKES FOR CRÊPES AND BLINTZES

1 cup milk
2 eggs
1 tablespoon melted butter or margarine
1 teaspoon baking powder
½ teaspoon salt
1 cup sifted flour

Combine ingredients in container in order listed. **MIX** until smooth, about 30 seconds. Stop motor as needed and push ingredients into blades with rubber spatula. Pour 2 tablespoons batter into hot, greased 6-inch fry pan; tilt and rotate pan quickly to spread batter evenly over bottom of pan. Cook until top is set and underside lightly browned; turn and brown second side. Pancakes for blintzes are browned on one side only. Makes 16 thin pancakes.

BERRY CRÊPES

See photo at right.

1 (10-ounce) package frozen berries, thawed and drained (reserve syrup)
2 tablespoons sugar
1 tablespoon cornstarch
1 (2-inch) piece lemon peel
8 Dessert Crêpes
1 cup fresh berries (sliced, if strawberries)
¼ cup butter or margarine, softened
½ cup water
⅓ cup sugar
1 teaspoon cornstarch
¼ cup brandy, rum or whiskey

GRATE thawed berries, sugar, cornstarch and lemon peel 10 seconds. Empty into saucepan and cook and stir over low heat until thick, about 5 minutes. Spread over crêpes. Roll crêpes or fold in quarters. At serving time, heat reserved berry syrup, fresh berries, butter, water, sugar and cornstarch in electric chafing dish or electric skillet, stirring gently, until bubbly. Place crêpes in hot sauce and simmer several minutes, spooning sauce over crêpes until heated through. Add liquor and ignite. Serve flaming. Makes 4 servings.

Pancakes for Crêpes

BUTTERS

DISTINCTIVE SWEET BUTTERS

Wonderful butters, all easy-made in the blender! All add a distinctive flavor when spread on French or hot toast, English muffins, hot biscuits, rolls or muffins, coffee cakes and fancy breads or pancakes and waffles.

CINNAMON BUTTER

½ cup (1-stick) soft butter or margarine, sliced
½ cup granulated or confectioners' sugar
½ teaspoon cinnamon

Combine ingredients in blender container in order listed. **BLEND** until smooth, 40 to 60 seconds. Stop motor and push ingredients into blades with rubber spatula, as needed. Makes about 1 cup.

HONEY BUTTER

½ cup honey
½ cup (1-stick) soft butter or margarine, sliced

Combine ingredients in blender container in order listed. **BLEND** until smooth, 40 to 60 seconds. Stop motor and push ingredients into blades with rubber spatula, as needed. Chill. Makes about 1 cup.

MAPLE BUTTER: Follow Honey Butter recipe (above) and substitute maple syrup for honey Makes about 1 cup.

CINNAMON HONEY BUTTER: Add ¼ to ½ teaspoon cinnamon to Honey Butter ingredients (above) before processing. Makes about 1 cup.

ORANGE MARMALADE BUTTER

⅔ cup thick orange marmalade
½ cup (1-stick) soft butter or margarine, sliced

Prepare as directed for Honey Butter (above). Makes about 1¼ cups.

SWEET FRUITY BUTTER: Follow recipe for Orange Marmalade Butter (above); substitute thick apricot, peach or raspberry preserves for orange marmalade. Makes about 1¼ cups.

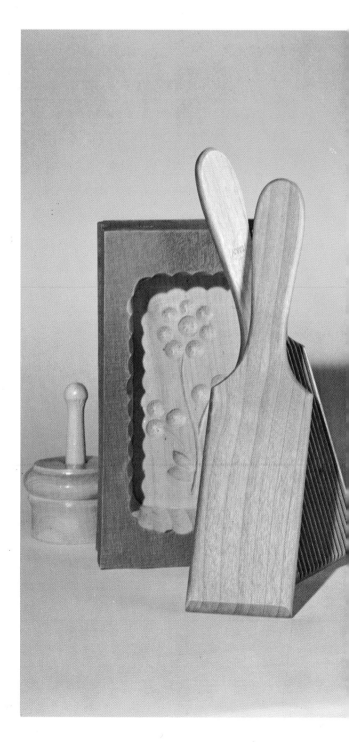

STRAWBERRY BUTTER

½ cup (1 stick) soft butter or margarine, sliced
¼ cup confectioners' sugar
2 teaspoons kirsch or cream
8 to 10 strawberries, washed, hulled and halved

Combine first 3 ingredients in blender container. **BLEND** until smooth, 20 to 30 seconds. Stop motor; push ingredients into blades with rubber spatula as needed. Add ½ of the berries at a time; **BLEND** as directed above until strawberries are coarsely chopped, 15 to 20 seconds. Add remaining strawberries; **BLEND** until finely chopped, 10 to 15 seconds. Delicious on waffles, pancakes and English muffins. Makes about 1 cup.

TOFFEE BUTTER

½ cup pecan halves
1 stick (½-cup) room temperature butter or margarine, sliced
⅔ cup (packed) brown sugar, broken up
¼ teaspoon maple flavoring

CHOP pecans, ¼ cup at a time, switching motor on and off until chopped medium fine; empty into bowl. Combine next 3 ingredients in blender container; **BLEND** until smooth, 50 to 60 seconds. Stop motor; push ingredients into blades with rubber spatula as needed. Add to nuts; mix well. Great on French toast, toasted English muffins, pancakes or waffles. Makes about 1⅓ cups.

CHURNED BUTTER

1 cup heavy cream, sweet or sour
Salt, to taste
Herbs, optional

Pour cream into blender container, cover and process at **WHIP** until butter forms. Pour into strainer to drain off liquid, then put butter into small bowl and press with a spatula to remove as much liquid as possible. Add salt while kneading butter. Try adding 1 tablespoon dried herbs (parsley, tarragon, savory or a garlic clove) per cup of cream for a delightful herb butter. Makes ⅔ cup.

HOMEMADE NUT BUTTERS

2 tablespoons salad oil
1½ cups salted nuts

For filbert, pecan, English or black walnut, or almond butters, put vegetable oil into blender container. Add nuts and process at **SHRED** until a crunchy or smooth consistency is reached. If necessary, STOP BLENDER, use rubber spatula to keep mixture around processing blades. Cover and continue to process at **SHRED**. If unsalted nuts are used, add salt for flavor. Makes ¾ cup.

GARLIC BUTTER

1 cup (2 sticks) room temperature butter or margarine, sliced
1 clove garlic, quartered
2 to 3 small sprigs parsley (no stems)

CRUSH ingredients until garlic is very finely chopped, about 40 seconds. Stop motor and push ingredients into blades with rubber spatula, as needed. Spread on French or Italian bread before heating or on hot steaks or burgers before serving. Makes about 1 cup.

ONION BUTTER: Follow Garlic Butter recipe (above); substitute 1 thin (⅛-inch) slice onion, quartered, or 1 (5-inch) green onion, cut in ½-inch lengths, for garlic. Delicious spread on sizzling steaks and burgers. Makes about 1 cup.

HERB BUTTER: Follow Garlic or Onion Butter recipe (above) and add ¾ teaspoon seasoned salt, and ¾ teaspoon fines herbes blend, dill weed, oregano, savory or chervil to ingredients before processing. Fine on hot crusty breads, steaks, burgers or broiled fish. Makes about 1 cup.

MUSTARD BUTTER: Follow Garlic Butter recipe (above). Substitute ¼ cup prepared mustard and ¾ teaspoon horseradish for garlic. Delicious spread on bread used for making corned beef or ham sandwiches. Makes about 1 cup.

LEMON PARSLEY BUTTER: Follow Garlic Butter recipe (above) and change as follows: Omit garlic. Increase parsley to 4 sprigs, add two dashes hot red pepper sauce, ¼ cup lemon juice and 1 inch square of lemon peel (white trimmed off), cut in strips, before processing. Delicious on fish, seafood or vegetables. Makes about 1 cup.

CURRY BUTTER: Follow recipe for Garlic Butter (above) and change as follows: Omit garlic; add 1 teaspoon curry powder and ⅓ cup well drained chutney or 2 pieces preserved ginger before processing. Delicious on fish, ham or chicken. Makes about 1 cup.

PEANUT BUTTER

1½ cups salted peanuts

Put peanuts into blender container, cover and process at **SHRED** to the desired consistency. If necessary, STOP BLENDER, use rubber spatula to keep mixture around processing blades. Cover and continue to process at **SHRED**. Makes ¾ cup.

CAKES

Scrumptious rich cakes, made from a modern cake mix or favorite home recipe can be whipped up in seconds with the help of a multi-speed blender with a 6-cup container. If container is a 4 or 5-cup capacity, prepare ½ box of cake mix or ½ cake recipe at a time.

To assure successful blender-made cakes, select one of the cake recipes that follow. Be sure to read the recipe carefully and follow it exactly. Don't improvise! Once acquainted with the technique of making cakes the blender way, old favorite cake recipes can easily be adapted for blender preparation.

Always use standard measuring cups and spoons and measure ingredients carefully.

Don't try making angel food and real sponge cakes or beating egg whites in blender! When stiffly beaten egg whites are required beat them with hand or electric beater.

Be sure to use the blender for chopping nuts, dried fruits, chocolate, coconut, citrus rind and the mixing of liquid and semiliquid ingredients. It will save time and effort.

CAKE MIXES

Prepare favorite white, yellow, chocolate or other cake mix, except angel food, sponge, chiffon or pound cake. Use ingredients called for on package label. Combine liquid, eggs and ½ of the dry mix in blender container; mix with rubber spatula. **GRATE** 8 to 10 seconds. Stop motor; scrape down sides and push ingredients into blades with rubber spatula as necessary. Add remaining dry ingredients; **GRATE** about 20 seconds. Stop motor; scrape down sides and push ingredients into blades with rubber spatula. **PURÉE** until smooth, 10 to 12 seconds. Stop motor, scrape down sides and push ingredients into blades as necessary. Bake as directed on package label. Cool and frost as desired.

SPICED BANANA CAKE

See photo page 45.

2¼ cups sifted flour
1 teaspoon baking powder
1 teaspoon soda
1 teaspoon salt
1 teaspoon cinnamon
½ teaspoon nutmeg
2 eggs
¾ cup soft shortening
½ cup buttermilk or sour milk
1 teaspoon vanilla
1½ cups sugar
1½ cups sliced bananas (2 medium)

Combine first 6 ingredients; sift into mixing bowl. **BLEND** eggs, shortening, buttermilk or sour milk, vanilla and sugar until creamy, about 30 seconds. Stop motor; push ingredients into blades with rubber spatula as needed. Add banana pieces, pushing pieces down into mixture with small rubber spatula. **BLEND** until smooth, about 50 seconds. Stop motor; push ingredients into blades with rubber spatula as needed. Add to dry ingredients; stir until dry ingredients are moistened and batter smooth. Pour into 2 greased and floured 8-inch layer pans. Bake in moderate oven (350°F.) until done, 30 to 35 minutes. Cool in pans 5 minutes; remove from pans and cool on rack. Fill and frost layers with favorite lemon, orange or confectioners' sugar frosting (pages 53 and 55). Makes a 2 layer 8-inch cake.

BANANA NUT CAKE: Follow recipe for Spiced Banana Cake (recipe above) and add ½ cup pecan halves to batter after bananas are mashed. **BLEND** until nuts are coarsely chopped, 3 to 5 seconds. Fill and frost layers with a favorite fluffy white frosting mix. Makes a 2 layer 8-inch cake.

FLUFFY PRUNE CAKE WITH LEMON FROSTING

2 cups sifted flour
3 teaspoons baking powder
½ teaspoon salt
¾ teaspoon ground cinnamon
¾ teaspoon ground cloves
3 eggs, separated
½ cup milk
¾ cup soft shortening
1 cup (packed) brown sugar, broken-up
1 cup pitted cooked prunes

Combine first 5 ingredients; sift into mixing bowl. Combine egg yolks, milk, shortening and sugar in container. **PURÉE** until smooth, about 50 seconds. Stop motor as needed and push ingredients into blades with rubber spatula. Add prunes and **PURÉE** until well mixed, about 30 seconds. Combine with dry ingredients; mix just until dry ingredients are moistened. Fold in stiffly beaten egg whites. Pour into 2 well greased 8-inch layer pans. Bake in moderate oven (350°F.) until done, 25 to 30 minutes. Cool; put layers together and frost top and sides with Creamy Lemon Frosting (page 55). Makes a 2 layer, 8-inch cake.

ORANGE SPICE CAKE

This fragrant cake is glazed with orange while still warm

2 cups sifted all-purpose flour
1½ teaspoons baking powder
1 teaspoon soda
1 teaspoon cinnamon
½ teaspoon salt
½ teaspoon ground cloves
½ teaspoon nutmeg
1 cup raisins
1 cup water
1 cup sugar
½ cup shortening
1 egg
½ cup nuts
1 small orange (thin orange portion of peel and fruit only)
½ cup sugar

Sift together flour, baking powder, soda, cinnamon, salt, cloves and nutmeg. **BLEND** raisins, water, sugar, shortening and egg 20 seconds. Add nuts and **GRATE** 20 seconds. Pour into bowl with flour and mix well. Pour into greased 9 x 13 x 2-inch pan and bake in moderate oven (350°F.) 30 to 35 minutes, or pour into greased 9-inch square pan and bake 40 to 45 minutes. **PURÉE** orange and peel and sugar 20 seconds. Pour over cake as soon as it comes from oven. Cool cake in pan. Makes 9 servings.

Regal Cheese Cake

REGAL CHEESE CAKE

See photo at left.

2 tablespoons butter or margarine
1 (8-ounce) package zwieback
½ cup sugar
¼ cup butter or margarine, softened
5 eggs
2½ pounds cream cheese, softened
¼ cup heavy cream
Yellow portion of peel of ½ lemon
Orange portion of peel from ½ orange
1¾ cups sugar
½ teaspoon vanilla
2 egg yolks
3 tablespoons flour

Butter sides and bottom of 9-inch spring form pan. Break 2 zwieback into blender container and **CRUMB** 30 seconds, breaking 6 more zwieback through opening in top while motor is running. Empty crumbs into large bowl. Repeat until all zwieback is crumbed. Add sugar and butter and mix well. Press over bottom and up sides of pan. **STIR** 2 eggs, 1 pound cream cheese, half of the heavy cream, lemon and orange peel 20 seconds. Scrape down sides of container with rubber spatula. **GRIND** 30 seconds, adding ⅓ of the sugar through opening in top while motor is running.* Empty into large mixing bowl. **STIR** 3 eggs, 1 pound cream cheese and vanilla 20 seconds. Scrape down sides of container with rubber spatula. **GRIND** 30 seconds, adding ⅓ of sugar through opening in top while motor is running.* Add to bowl. **STIR** 2 egg yolks, ½ pound cream cheese, flour and remaining heavy cream 20 seconds.* **GRIND** 30 seconds, adding last ⅓ of sugar through opening in top while motor is running.* **GRIND** until smooth.* Add to bowl and mix thoroughly. Carefully spoon cheese mixture into prepared pan. Bake in very slow oven (275°F.) 1 hour. Turn oven off; leave cake in oven 1 hour. Cool slowly to room temperature, then chill. Top with Strawberry Glaze; chill to set Glaze. Remove from pan to serve. Makes 16 to 18 servings.

STRAWBERRY GLAZE: GRIND ½ cup washed, hulled strawberries, ½ cup water, ½ cup sugar and 1½ tablespoons cornstarch 5 seconds. Cook and stir until clear and thick. Add 1½ cups washed, hulled, sliced strawberries and spoon over top of cheese cake.

If necessary, STOP BLENDER, use rubber spatula to keep mixture around processing blades. Cover and continue to process at GRIND.

LEMONY-LIGHT CHEESE CAKE

2 envelopes unflavored gelatin
¼ lemon (thin yellow portion of peel and fruit only)
½ cup hot milk
⅓ cup sugar
2 egg yolks
1 (8-ounce) package cream cheese, cubed and softened
½ cup heavy cream
1 heaping cup crushed ice

SHRED gelatin, lemon peel and fruit and hot milk 40 seconds. Add sugar, egg yolks and cream cheese and **GRIND** 30 seconds.* **GRIND** 20 seconds, adding cream and ice through opening in top while motor is running. **GRIND** until smooth.* Immediately pour into 9-inch layer cake pan. Sprinkle with 2 or 3 tablespoons blender-made graham cracker crumbs (page 8). Chill until firm. Makes 6 servings.

ORANGE CHEESE CAKE

Fresh orange flavor with no hand grating!

16 to 18 zwieback
2 tablespoons sugar
¼ cup butter or margarine, melted
1 pound cream-style cottage cheese
1 cup milk
4 eggs
¼ small orange (thin orange portion of peel and fruit only)
½ cup sugar
2 tablespoons flour
¼ teaspoon salt

Break 2 zwieback into blender container and **CRUMB** 10 seconds, breaking 2 more zwieback into container through opening in top while motor is running. Empty into measuring cup. Repeat until you have 1½ cups crumbs. Combine crumbs, sugar and butter and mix well. Reserve ¾ cup mixture, pat remainder over bottom of 9-inch square pan. Chill. **GRIND** cottage cheese and all remaining ingredients 40 seconds.* Pour into crumb-lined pan; sprinkle with reserved crumbs. Bake in slow oven (325°F.) 1 hour. Chill. Makes 9 servings.

YELLOW CAKE

2½ cups sifted cake flour
4 teaspoons baking powder
1 teaspoon salt
½ cup shortening
1½ cups sugar
2 eggs
1 teaspoon vanilla
1 cup milk

Sift flour, baking powder and salt into large bowl.
BLEND shortening and ½ cup sugar 30 seconds. Add
1 cup sugar, eggs and vanilla and **BLEND** 60 seconds.
Add milk and **STIR** 20 seconds. Add to flour; mix
until smooth, 150 strokes. Pour into 2 greased and
floured 9-inch layer cake pans. Bake in moderate
oven (375°F.) 30 minutes. Cool in pans 10 minutes.
Turn out; cool. Frost with French Butter Cream (page
52).

VARIATIONS

Follow above recipe and change as follows:

CUP CAKES: Fill paper-lined muffin pans ⅔ full of
batter. Bake in moderate oven (375°F.) until done,
about 15 minutes. Cool and frost. Makes about 36
cup cakes.

MOCHA SPICE CAKE: Add 1½ teaspoons cinnamon,
1 teaspoon nutmeg and ½ teaspoon allspice to dry
ingredients before sifting. Frost with favorite coffee
or mocha frosting (pages 52 and 53).

PECAN OR WALNUT CAKE: Substitute ¼ teaspoon
almond extract for ½ teaspoon of the vanilla. Fold 1
cup moderately fine blender chopped pecans or walnuts into batter just before pouring into pans. See
directions for chopping nuts page 7. Frost cooled
cake layers with favorite chocolate or butterscotch
frosting (page 52); decorate with chopped nuts.

CHERRY NUT CAKE

Blender chop ⅓ cup pecan or walnut halves (see
chopping directions page 7); save. **BLEND** ½ cup
maraschino cherry halves, switching motor on and
off until finely chopped; save. Fold nuts and chopped
cherries into favorite white cake mix batter (see recipe page 41 before filling pans. Bake, cool and frost
layers with favorite fluffy white frosting mix tinted
pale pink with a few drops of red food color. Garnish
top with well drained maraschino cherry quarters, if
desired. Makes a 2 layer 8-inch cake.

FEATHERY FUDGE CAKE

2¼ cups sifted flour
3 teaspoons baking powder
¼ teaspoon salt
3 eggs, separated
½ cup cocoa
¾ cup room temperature butter or margarine, sliced
1 cup cold water
1½ cups sugar
1½ teaspoons vanilla
½ teaspoon red food color

Sift first 3 ingredients into mixing bowl. Combine
egg yolks, cocoa, butter or margarine, ½ cup water, ½
cup sugar, vanilla and red color in blender container.
BLEND until smooth, 60 to 70 seconds. Stop motor;
scrape down sides as needed and push ingredients
into blades with rubber spatula. Add remaining ½
cup water and ½ cup sugar; **BLEND** until smooth, 40
to 50 seconds. Stop motor as needed and push ingredients into blades with rubber spatula. Whip egg
whites with hand or electric beater until fluffy; add
remaining ½ cup sugar, 1 tablespoonful at a time, and
beat until glossy after each addition. Make a well in
center of dry ingredients. Empty chocolate mixture
into well; stir gently until dry ingredients are moistened and batter smooth. Fold in egg whites. Pour
into 2 greased and floured 9-inch round pans. Bake
in slow oven (300°F.) until done, 35 to 40 minutes.
Cool in pans 5 minutes; turn layers onto racks to cool.
Frost with favorite chocolate frosting (page 52), and
sprinkle chopped nuts over top. Makes 2 9-inch layers.

CHOCOLATE CARAMEL CAKE

Prepare Red Devil's Food Cake (page 45). Frost top
and sides of cake with Butterscotch Frosting (page
52) and sprinkle with blender chopped toasted almonds or walnuts (see chopping directions page 7).

DOUBLE RICH DEVIL'S FOOD CAKE

Prepare Red Devil's Food Cake (page 45) and bake in
13 x 9 x 2-inch pan. Frost top and sides with Black
Satin Chocolate Frosting (page 52). If desired, sprinkle
top with coarsely chopped nuts or peppermint stick
candy (see chopping directions page 6).

RED DEVIL'S FOOD CAKE

2¼ cups sifted flour
2½ teaspoons baking powder
¼ teaspoon soda
1 teaspoon salt
3 squares (1-ounce) unsweetened chocolate, cut into small pieces
½ cup boiling water
½ cup soft shortening
1¾ cups sugar
3 eggs
½ teaspoon red food color, optional
1 cup buttermilk or sour milk
1½ teaspoons vanilla

Sift first 4 ingredients into mixing bowl. Add chocolate pieces to blender container. **BLEND** 8 to 10 seconds or until chocolate is finely chopped. Add boiling water to chocolate. **BLEND** 10 to 15 seconds, or until smooth. Add remaining ingredients to container in order listed. **BLEND** until smooth, about 45 seconds. Stop motor; push ingredients into blades with rubber spatula as needed. Make a well in center of dry ingredients; pour chocolate mixture into well, stirring during addition and just until dry ingredients are moistened and batter smooth. Pour into greased and floured 13 x 9 x 2-inch pan. Bake in moderate oven (350°F.) until done, 35 to 40 minutes. Cool in pan 5 minutes. Remove from pan and finish cooling on rack. Frost. Makes 1 cake 13 x 9 x 1¾-inches.

WHEAT AND APPLE NUT CAKE

¾ cup whole grains of wheat
½ cup sifted all-purpose flour
1 teaspoon baking powder
1 teaspoon baking soda
¼ teaspoon salt
¼ cup buttermilk
2 eggs
1 cup sugar
½ cup butter or margarine, softened
1 teaspoon vanilla
1 small green apple, cored and sliced
¼ cup pecans

SHRED half the wheat 60 seconds. STOP MOTOR, scrape down sides of container with rubber spatula and **SHRED** 60 seconds longer. Empty into mixing bowl. Repeat with remaining wheat. Add flour, baking powder, soda and salt to wheat and sift together. **GRIND** buttermilk, eggs, sugar, butter and vanilla 30 seconds. STOP MOTOR, scrape down sides of container with rubber spatula. **GRIND** 15 seconds, adding apple and pecans through opening in top while motor is running. **GRIND** 5 seconds longer. Pour over flour mixture and blend well. Pour into 2 greased and floured 8-inch layer cake pans or 1 8-inch square pan. Bake in moderate oven (375°F.) 25 to 35 minutes. Cool in pans 5 minutes. Turn out onto racks and cool completely. Frost with thin confectioners' sugar icing. Each piece (2 x 2½ x 1½-inches) has approximately 223 calories.

Spiced Banana Cake Page 41. Whipped Cream Frosting Page 53.

SPICY APPLESAUCE CAKE

2 cups sifted flour
2 teaspoons baking powder
1 teaspoon cinnamon
1 teaspoon nutmeg
½ teaspoon ground cloves
½ teaspoon soda
1 cup pecan or walnut halves
1 cup seedless raisins
2 eggs
½ cup room temperature butter or margarine, sliced, or soft shortening.
1 cup thick applesauce, canned (or recipe page 78)
1¼ cups (packed) brown sugar, broken up
1 teaspoon vanilla

Sift first 6 ingredients into mixing bowl. **BLEND** nuts, ⅓ cup at a time, switching motor on and off, until coarsely chopped. Pour into dry ingredients. Stir raisins into dry ingredients. Combine remaining ingredients in blender container in order listed. **BLEND** until mixture is smooth. Stop motor; push ingredients into blades with rubber spatula as needed. Pour into flour mixture; stir until dry ingredients are moistened. Pour into well greased and floured 13 x 9 x 2-inch baking pan. Bake in moderate oven (350°F.) until done, 35 to 40 minutes. Cool in pan 10 minutes; turn out of pan and cool on cake rack. Serve warm topped with whipped cream or vanilla ice cream or frost with Lemon or Orange Frosting (pages 53 and 55). Makes one 13 x 9 x 1¾-inch cake.

LAST MINUTE HOLIDAY FRUIT CAKE

See photo at right

Assemble the following in large mixing bowl, 2 cups (packed) quartered dried apricots, 2 cups red candied cherries (whole), 1 cup light seedless raisins, 2 cups pecan halves and ½ pound each of red, white and green candied pineapple slices, cut in ½-inch wedges. Mix. Prepare a (17½ to 19½-ounce) white or yellow cake mix as directed in recipe for cake mixes, page 41. Increase eggs to 4; substitute orange juice for ½ of the liquid. Add eggs, liquids and a 1-inch square of orange rind (no white), cut in strips, to blender container. **BLEND** until rind is finely chopped, 4 to 5 seconds. Proceed as directed for preparing cake mixes. Pour batter over fruits and mix. Pack tightly into a greased 10-inch tube pan lined with brown paper or foil and greased again. Bake in very slow oven (275°F.) until done, about 2 hours. Cool in pan 10 to 15 minutes; remove from pan and cool on rack. Remove paper or foil. Makes one 10-inch tube cake 3½ to 4 inches high.

CARROT CAKE

This cake is best if made a day or two in advance

3 cups sliced carrots
4 eggs
1¼ cups oil
2 cups sugar
2 cups sifted all-purpose flour
2 teaspoons baking powder
2 teaspoons soda
1 teaspoon cinnamon
1 teaspoon salt
½ teaspoon nutmeg
1 cup golden raisins
1 cup confectioners' sugar
Milk

PURÉE ½ cup carrots 10 seconds. Empty into large bowl and repeat until all carrots are grated. **BEAT** eggs 5 seconds. Add oil and sugar and **BLEND** 30 seconds, stopping motor to push ingredients to blades, if necessary. Sift together flour, baking powder, soda, cinnamon, salt and nutmeg. Add to carrots along with raisins. Mix well so carrots and raisins are coated with flour. Pour ingredients from blender container over carrots and mix well. Pour into 9 x 13 x 2-inch pan and bake in moderate oven (350°F.) 45 to 50 minutes. Cool, then refrigerate. **GRIND** confectioners' sugar with enough milk to make thin frosting. Spread over cake. Makes 12 servings.

BROILED APRICOT CAKE

Prepare 1 package favorite white cake mix batter (recipe page 41). Bake in well greased and floured 13 x 9 x 2-inch pan in moderate oven (350°F.) until done, 35 to 40 minutes. While cake is baking combine ¾ cup thick apricot preserves, ¼ cup maraschino cherry quarters, and 1⅓ cups flaked coconut. Mix and fold in 1 cup miniature marshmallows. Spread over top of hot cake; broil 3 to 4 inches from heat source until marshmallows and coconut are lightly browned, 2 to 4 minutes. Cool before serving. Makes one 13 x 9 x 1¾-inch cake.

Last Minute Holiday Fruit Cake

HOT MILK SPONGE CAKE

1¼ cups sifted cake flour
1½ teaspoons baking powder
½ teaspoon salt
2 eggs
1 cup sugar
1 teaspoon vanilla
½ cup milk, scalded
2 tablespoons butter or margarine

Sift flour, baking powder and salt into a large bowl. **BEAT** eggs 20 seconds. Add sugar and vanilla and **GRIND** 30 seconds. Add flour mixture and **STIR** 20 seconds. Empty into bowl. Combine milk and butter and pour into flour mixture. Stir only until mixed. Pour into a 9-inch layer cake pan lined with 2 layers of waxed paper. Bake in moderate oven (350°F.) 30 to 35 minutes. While warm, top with Broiled Nutty Chocolate Frosting, page 55.

CHOCOLATE CREAM CAKE: Double recipe and bake in 2 9-inch layer cake pans. Split each layer. Spread with filling from Chocolate Angel Torte (page 50).

PEACH CHIFFON PARTY CAKE

4 egg whites
¼ teaspoon cream of tartar
¼ cup sugar
½ cup pecans
1 cup sifted cake flour
1½ teaspoons baking powder
¾ teaspoon salt
3 egg yolks
6 tablespoons water
¼ cup salad oil
½ cup brown sugar, firmly packed
½ teaspoon vanilla
½ teaspoon almond extract
2 (10-ounce) packages frozen sliced peaches, thawed
1 cup heavy cream, whipped

Beat egg whites and cream of tartar with rotary or electric beater until foamy. Gradually add ¼ cup sugar and continue beating until stiff. **GRATE** pecans 10 seconds. Add to egg whites. Sift together flour, baking powder and salt. **STIR** egg yolks and water 5 seconds. Add oil, brown sugar, vanilla and almond extract and **BEAT** 25 seconds. Add to flour. Mix until smooth. Pour over egg whites and pecans and fold until thoroughly blended. Pour into waxed paper-lined jelly roll pan (10½ x 15½ x 1-inches). Bake in moderate oven (375°F.) 15 to 20 minutes. Turn out onto cake rack or bread board. Carefully remove paper. Cool cake. Cut crosswise in half to form 2 layers 7 x 5-inches each. Drain 1 package of peaches and **PURÉE** 5 to 10 seconds. Turn into bowl with half of the whipped cream, folding carefully to mix. Spread on one piece of the cake. Top with second piece of cake and spread with remaining whipped cream. Drain the remaining package of peaches and arrange peach slices on top of cake. Refrigerate until dessert time. Makes 10 to 12 servings.

BANANA CHIFFON CAKE

2½ cups sifted cake flour
1 tablespoon baking powder
1 cup egg whites (7 or 8 whites)
½ teaspoon cream of tartar
2 medium bananas, peeled
5 egg yolks
⅓ cup cold water
½ cup salad oil
1½ cups sugar
1 teaspoon salt
1 teaspoon vanilla

Sift together flour and baking powder. Beat egg whites and cream of tartar with rotary or electric beater until soft peaks form. **BLEND** bananas 20 seconds. Add egg yolks, water, oil, sugar, salt and vanilla and **BLEND** 30 seconds. STOP MOTOR, scrape down sides of blender container with rubber spatula. **BLEND** 10 seconds longer or until smooth. Pour into bowl with flour and stir until smooth. Fold flour mixture into egg whites until smooth. Turn into 10-inch tube pan. Bake in slow oven (325°F.) for 55 minutes, then at 350° 10 to 15 minutes longer. Invert and cool. Frost with favorite icing or sifted confectioners' sugar. Makes 12 servings.

BLUEBERRY FUNNY CAKE

¾ cup sugar
1 (10-ounce) package frozen blueberries, thawed
2 (1-inch) pieces lemon peel
½ lemon, peeled
1 tablespoon butter or margarine, softened
2 teaspoons cornstarch
1¼ cups sifted cake flour
1 teaspoon baking powder
½ teaspoon salt
¾ cup sugar
¼ cup shortening
½ cup milk
1 egg
1 teaspoon vanilla
1 (9-inch) unbaked Nut Pastry Shell (page 119)
Blueberries and whipped cream for garnish

WHIP ¾ cup sugar, blueberries, lemon peel and fruit, butter and cornstarch 10 seconds. Empty into saucepan and cook and stir until smooth and thick. Cool to lukewarm. Sift together flour, baking powder and salt. **BEAT** sugar, shortening, milk, egg and vanilla 60 seconds. Pour over flour mixture and beat until smooth. Pour batter into pastry shell. Pour blueberry mixture gently over batter. Bake in moderate oven (350°F.) 1 hour. Cool. Serve with additional blueberries and whipped cream. Makes 6 servings.

Graham Cracker Torte

GRAHAM CRACKER TORTE

You can use whipped dessert mix for a filling

27 single graham crackers
1 cup nuts
2 tablespoons flour
2 teaspoons baking powder
¼ teaspoon salt
½ cup shortening, butter or margarine, softened
1 cup sugar
3 eggs
¾ cup milk
1 cup heavy cream, whipped
Chopped candied ginger for garnish

Break 2 graham crackers into blender container and **GRATE** 10 seconds, breaking 4 more crackers through opening in top while motor is running. Empty into measuring cup. Repeat until you have 2 cups crumbs. Put all crumbs in large bowl. **GRATE** nuts 10 seconds and add to crumbs. Add flour, baking powder and salt; mix thoroughly. **WHIP** shortening, sugar and eggs 30 seconds, adding milk through opening in top while motor is running. Add to dry ingredients and stir until moistened. Pour into 2 buttered and floured 8-inch layer cake pans. Bake in moderate oven (350°F.) 30 minutes. Cool 10 minutes in pan, then turn out on racks and cool. Fill and frost with whipped cream. Garnish with chopped candied ginger. Makes 10 to 12 servings.

TORTE ELEGANTE

3 eggs
1¼ cups sugar
⅔ cup hot milk
1 tablespoon butter or margarine
1½ cups sifted cake flour
1¼ teaspoons baking powder
⅛ teaspoon salt
½ teaspoon vanilla

BLEND eggs, sugar, hot milk and butter 10 seconds. Sift together flour, baking powder and salt. **STIR** 30 seconds, adding flour through opening in top while motor is running. Add vanilla, STOP MOTOR and scrape down sides of container with rubber spatula. **STIR** 10 seconds. Spread evenly in paper-lined jelly roll pan (10½ x 15½ x 1-inch). Bake in moderate oven (375°F.) 10 to 12 minutes. Cool slightly. Turn out on rack and remove paper. Cut crosswise into fourths. Frost each section with French Butter Cream, page 52. Stack layers and frost sides and ends of torte. Garnish with shaved chocolate, if you wish. Chill. Makes 8 servings.

NOTE: You may turn baked cake out onto towel covered with sifted confectioners' sugar, remove paper and roll up as for jelly roll. Cool, then unroll. Fill, reroll and chill.

QUICK AND EASY DOBOS TORTE

1 package (4-ounce) chocolate pudding and pie filling
  (not instant)
1 12-ounce pound cake (7 x 3½ x 2½-inches)
¾ cup room temperature butter or margarine
1 cup sifted confectioners' sugar
½ teaspoon vanilla
1 cup semi-sweet chocolate bits

Prepare pudding and pie filling as directed on package
label; cool, stirring often. While pudding is cooling
slice cake lengthwise into 6 even layers. Pour cooled
pudding into container; add ½ cup butter or margarine, ½ cup sugar and vanilla. **BLEND** until smooth,
50 to 60 seconds. Stop motor; push ingredients into
blades with rubber spatula as needed. Add remaining
sugar. **BLEND** until smooth as directed above, about
20 to 30 seconds. Spread tops of 5 cake slices with
frosting; restack layers quickly and top with remaining
cake slice. Plunge 2 long wood or metal skewers
through cake to hold layers together. Chill. Combine
remaining ¼ cup butter or margarine and chocolate
bits in small heavy saucepan. Cover; place over low
heat until chocolate melts; stir until smooth. Remove
skewers. Spread chocolate over top and sides of cakes
quickly. If mixture thickens too rapidly return to heat
and stir in 1 teaspoon butter or margarine. Chill until
serving time. Slice very thin. Yields: One 7½ x 4½ x
2¾-inch torte, 20 to 24 slices.

CHOCOLATE NUT TORTE

1 cup pecan or walnut halves
1 package chocolate cake mix
1 pint (2 cups) whipping cream
1 tablespoon sugar
½ teaspoon vanilla

CHOP nuts in container, ½ cup at a time, switching
motor on and off until coarsely chopped, 5 to 6 times.
Save. Mix and bake cake mix as directed in recipe for
cake mixes (page 41). Cool layers; cut each layer
into 2 even layers. Whip cream; fold in sugar and
vanilla. Restack cake layers, spreading top of each
cake layer with whipped cream. Spread top and sides
of cake with cream; sprinkle with chopped nuts.
Store in refrigerator until served. Makes 1 8-inch cake,
10 to 12 servings.

CHOCOLATE ANGEL TORTE

*Use Chocolate Cream filling for jelly roll or for Chocolate
Cream Cake, page 48.*

1 large angel food cake, sliced crosswise into 4 layers

CHOCOLATE CREAM FILLING:
2⅓ cups milk
½ cup sugar
½ cup flour
⅓ cup cocoa
1 cup butter or margarine, softened
1 cup confectioners' sugar
2 teaspoons vanilla
1½ cups walnuts

BEAT milk, sugar, flour and cocoa 10 seconds. Pour
into saucepan and cook and stir over medium heat
until very thick, about 5 to 10 minutes. Cover and
cool to room temperature. **BEAT** butter 10 seconds.
Add confectioners' sugar and vanilla and **GRIND** 20
seconds. Add cooled mixture from saucepan, ½ cup
at a time, **GRIND**ing 10 seconds after each addition.
STOP MOTOR, scrape down sides of container with
rubber spatula. **GRIND** 20 to 30 seconds longer or
until smooth. Spread each layer of cake with filling.
Rinse blender container and **GRATE** ½ cup nuts.
Sprinkle over the cake layers. Repeat with remaining
nuts. Stack layers and chill. Makes 12 servings.

MODERN-MADE BLITZ TORTE

2 layers (8 or 9-inch) yellow cake (made from
  mix, page 41, or Yellow Cake, page 44)
⅔ cup toasted almonds
1 package (3½-ounce) vanilla pudding and pie filling
  (not instant)
1½ cups half and half (half milk, half cream)
1 package favorite fluffy white frosting mix
1½ to 2 teaspoons rum flavoring

Prepare cake layers; cool. While cake is baking chop
almonds. Add ⅓ cup almonds at a time to blender
container. **CHOP**, switching motor on and off until
nuts are coarsely chopped. Pour into bowl after each
chopping. Prepare pudding as directed on package
label, except use 1½ cups half and half instead of
milk called for. Cool, stirring often to keep crust from
forming on pudding. Prepare frosting mix as directed
on package label; substitute rum flavoring for vanilla.
Place 1 cake layer on serving plate; spread with ½
of filling, sprinkle ½ of nuts over filling and spread
with ½ of frosting mix. Cover with second cake layer;
spread with remaining pudding, frosting and nuts.
Makes one 9-inch 2 layer torte.

CAKE FROSTINGS

A luscious frosting makes a cake! Even the simplest cake becomes a treat when frosted attractively with a delicious frosting. Try the recipes for Black Satin, Chocolate Butter Cream, Lady Baltimore, Coconut Pecan or Creamy Lemon Frostings on the following pages. All are easily made and are real winners for flavor.

CREAMY FROSTING MIXES

(Not egg white or fluffy frostings). See package directions for ingredients used. Combine water and soft butter or margarine in container. Cover and set speed at **BLEND**. Start motor and add dry ingredients gradually, a small amount at a time through top opening. Stop motor often and scrape down sides of container and push ingredients into blades with rubber spatula.

CHOCOLATE BUTTER CREAM FROSTING

½ cup milk
⅓ cup butter or margarine
1 teaspoon salt
3 cups sifted confectioners' sugar
2 packages (6-ounce) semi-sweet chocolate bits
2 teaspoons vanilla

Combine milk, butter or margarine, salt and ½ cup sugar in saucepan; bring to scalding stage. Pour into blender container; add chocolate bits and **PURÉE** 15 to 20 seconds, or until smooth. Stop motor as needed and push ingredients into blades with rubber spatula. Add remaining sugar and vanilla and **MINCE** until smooth, 20 to 30 seconds. Stop motor as needed and scrape down sides and push ingredients into blades with rubber spatula. Makes about 2 cups frosting. Will frost top, sides and between layers of a double layer 8-inch cake. Use ½ recipe for a 13 x 9 x 2-inch cake.

VARIATIONS

BUTTERSCOTCH FROSTING: Substitute butterscotch bits for semi-sweet chocolate ones. Decrease milk to ¼ cup, confectioners' sugar to 2 cups and butter or margarine to 3 tablespoons. Substitute 1 teaspoon maple flavoring for vanilla. Makes about 1½ cups.

CHOCOLATE MINT FROSTING: Substitute mint flavored chocolate bits for semi-sweet chocolate ones and ¼ to ½ teaspoon mint or peppermint extract for vanilla. Makes about 2 cups.

MILK CHOCOLATE FROSTING: Substitute milk chocolate bits for semi-sweet chocolate ones. Makes about 2 cups.

MOCHA FROSTING: Add ½ to 1 teaspoon instant coffee to milk; reduce vanilla to 1 teaspoon. Makes about 2 cups.

QUICK BLACK SATIN FROSTING

Follow recipe for Black Satin Chocolate Frosting (at right) and substitute 1½ cups semi-sweet chocolate bits for unsweetened chocolate and reduce sugar to ⅓ cups. Makes 2 cups.

BLACK SATIN CHOCOLATE FROSTING

See photo page 54.

4 squares (1-ounce) unsweetened chocolate, cut into small pieces
1 cup boiling water
1 cup sugar
¼ cup cornstarch
¼ teaspoon salt
⅓ cup cold water
2 teaspoons vanilla

BLEND chocolate pieces, switching motor on and off until coarsely chopped. Add hot water; **BLEND** 10 to 15 seconds or until smooth. Add sugar; **BLEND** 10 seconds or until mixed. Combine cornstarch, salt and cold water in saucepan. Add chocolate mixture; mix. Cook over low heat, stirring constantly, until thick. Remove from heat; stir in vanilla. Cool, stirring frequently. Makes 2 cups.

CHOCOLATE ICING

3 to 5 tablespoons hot milk
2 tablespoons butter or margarine, softened
2 (1-ounce) squares unsweetened chocolate, each square cut in 6 or 8 pieces.
1 teaspoon vanilla
3 cups confectioners' sugar
½ teaspoon salt
1 (3-ounce) package cream cheese (optional)

SHRED 3 tablespoons of the hot milk, butter, chocolate and vanilla 40 seconds. STOP MOTOR, scrape down sides of container with rubber spatula. Add 1 cup sugar and salt. **GRIND** 60 seconds. Add 1 tablespoon milk if mixture is too heavy. If necessary, STOP BLENDER, use rubber spatula to keep mixture around processing blades. Cover and continue to process at **GRIND**. Continue adding sugar, scraping down sides of container and **GRIND**ing until all sugar is added and icing is of spreading consistency. It may be necessary to empty frosting into bowl and mix in last amounts of sugar by hand. Enough to fill and frost 2 (8 x 9-inch) layers.

FRENCH BUTTER CREAM

1 (6-ounce) package regular or mint-flavored semi-sweet chocolate pieces
¼ cup boiling water or hot strong coffee
4 egg yolks
½ cup butter or margarine, softened
¼ cup confectioners' sugar
1 teaspoon vanilla

SHRED chocolate 10 seconds. STOP MOTOR, scrape down sides of container with rubber spatula. Add water or coffee and **GRIND** 5 seconds. Add egg yolks, butter, sugar and vanilla and **GRIND** 15 seconds or until smooth. Chill frosting, if necessary, until of spreading consistency. Enough frosting to fill and frost 2 (8 or 9-inch) layers.

SNOWY CAKE ICING

1 egg
⅓ cup butter or margarine, softened
1 tablespoon milk
1 tablespoon vanilla
3½ cups confectioners' sugar

GRIND egg, butter, milk, vanilla and 1 cup sugar 30 seconds. Empty into a mixing bowl. Gradually add remaining sugar and mix by hand until of spreading consistency. Enough frosting to fill and frost 2 (8 or 9-inch) layers.

CONFECTIONERS' SUGAR

If you run out of confectioners' sugar at a crucial moment, just add ½ cup granulated sugar to the container, cover and process at **LIQUEFY** until finely pulverized. Let stand, without removing cover, until sugar settles. (This is pulverized sugar rather than a true confectioners' sugar and we do not recommend the use of more than a half cup with commercial confectioners' sugar.)

CONFECTIONERS' SUGAR FROSTING

3 tablespoons milk or cream
2 teaspoons vanilla
¼ teaspoon salt
½ cup room temperature butter or margarine, sliced
3 cups sifted confectioners' sugar

Combine first 4 ingredients in blender container in order listed. **BLEND** until smooth, 15 to 20 seconds. Stop motor as needed and push ingredients into blades with rubber spatula. Add sugar, ¼ cup at a time, and **PURÉE** until mixed. Stop motor as needed to scrape down sides and push ingredients into blades with rubber spatula. Repeat process. If mixture becomes too thick at last and motor labors, turn mixture into bowl and stir in last of sugar by hand. Makes about 1⅓ cups. Will frost a 12 x 9 x 2-inch cake.

VARIATIONS

CHERRY FROSTING: Reduce vanilla to 1 teaspoon and add ¼ cup well drained maraschino cherry halves with sugar. Makes about 1½ cups.

COFFEE FROSTING: Substitute hot water for milk or cream; omit vanilla and add 1 teaspoon instant coffee with water. Makes about 1⅓ cups.

LEMON FROSTING: Omit vanilla; add 1 1-inch lemon rind square (no white) cut in strips with butter or margarine. **BLEND** until rind is finely chopped. Substitute lemon juice for milk or cream. Makes about 1⅓ cups.

ORANGE FROSTING: Prepare same as Lemon Frosting except substitute 2 orange rind squares for lemon rind and use orange instead of lemon juice. Makes about 1⅓ cups.

PEANUT BUTTER FROSTING. Add ¼ cup creamy style peanut butter with butter or margarine when processing. Makes about 1½ cups.

WHIPPED CREAM FROSTING

See photo page 45

1 cup heavy cream
½ envelope unflavored gelatin
2 tablespoons cold water
¼ lemon (thin yellow portion of peel and fruit only)
2 tablespoons confectioners' sugar
⅛ teaspoon salt

Reserve 2 tablespoons heavy cream, then **WHIP** remainder as directed on page 9. Scald 2 tablespoons cream and **GRIND** with gelatin and water 40 seconds. Add lemon, sugar and salt and **LIQUEFY** 20 seconds. Pour into a bowl and chill until the consistency of unbeaten egg white. Fold chilled gelatin into whipped cream until smooth. Chill frosted cake until service. Enough frosting to fill and frost 2 (8 or 9-inch) round layers.

LADY BALTIMORE FROSTING

See photo page 54

3 or 4 macaroons
¼ cup walnuts
½ cup maraschino cherries
1⅔ cups sugar
½ cup water
⅓ cup light corn syrup
2 egg whites
¼ teaspoon salt
1 teaspoon vanilla
Whole drained maraschino cherries
Walnut halves

Break macaroons into container and **CRUMB** 10 seconds. Empty into measuring cup. Repeat, if necessary, until you have ¼ cup crumbs. **GRATE** walnuts 5 seconds. Empty into bowl. **GRATE** cherries 10 seconds and add to bowl with nuts. Combine sugar, water and corn syrup in saucepan. Cook and stir over low heat until boiling. Boil 2 to 3 minutes or to soft ball stage (240°). Remove from heat. Beat egg whites with rotary or electric beater until foamy. Add salt and continue beating until stiff. Pour syrup in fine stream over egg whites, beating constantly until frosting stands in stiff peaks. Add vanilla. Fold ⅓ of frosting into chopped cherries and nuts along with macaroon crumbs. Spread over 1 layer yellow or white cake. Place second layer on top. Spread remaining frosting over top and sides of cake. Garnish with whole cherries and walnut halves. Makes about 2½ cups, enough for 2 8-inch layers.

PEPPERMINT FROSTING

See photo at left

Omit vanilla in Confectioners' Sugar Frosting (page 53) and add ¼ teaspoon peppermint extract. Add 1 or 2 drops red food color with milk and sprinkle frosted cake or cakes with blender chopped peppermint stick candy (see chopping directions on page 6). Makes 1⅓ cups.

COCONUT PECAN FROSTING

1⅓ cups pecan or walnut halves
1 cup undiluted evaporated milk
1 cup sugar
3 egg yolks
½ cup butter or margarine
1 teaspoon vanilla
1⅓ cups flaked coconut

CHOP nuts, ⅓ cup at a time, switching motor on and off until coarsely chopped. Pour into bowl. Save. Combine next 5 ingredients in blender container. **WHIP** until well mixed, 3 to 5 seconds. Pour into saucepan; cook slowly until thickened, 10 to 12 minutes, stirring constantly. Cool slightly; stir in nuts and coconut. Stir until cool and spreading consistency. Delicious on chocolate cake. Makes about 2½ cups, enough for 2 8-inch layers.

BROILED COCONUT FROSTING

¼ cup nuts
¼ cup coconut
½ cup butter or margarine, softened
¾ cup light brown sugar, firmly packed
¼ cup half and half (half milk, half cream)

GRATE nuts and coconut 5 seconds. Empty into saucepan. Add remaining ingredients and heat until blended. Spread on warm cake and broil until coconut is browned. Cool slightly before cutting. Enough frosting to top a 9-inch cake.

BROILED NUTTY CHOCOLATE FROSTING

½ cup nuts
¼ cup butter or margarine, softened
½ cup brown sugar, firmly packed
¼ cup cocoa
2 tablespoons milk

GRATE nuts 5 seconds. Empty into bowl. **GRIND** butter and brown sugar 20 seconds. STOP MOTOR, scrape down sides of container with rubber spatula. Add cocoa and milk and **LIQUEFY** 20 seconds. Add to nuts and mix. Spread over warm cake and broil about 2 minutes. Cool cake slightly. Enough frosting to top a 9-inch cake.

BERRY CREAM FILLING

1 cup milk
5 tablespoons all-purpose flour
¼ cup sugar
½ cup butter or margarine, softened
½ cup fresh or frozen strawberries, blackberries, raspberries or chopped peaches
½ cup confectioners' sugar
2 teaspoons vanilla

GRIND milk, flour and sugar 10 seconds. Pour into saucepan and cook and stir over medium heat until thick, about 5 to 10 minutes. Cover; cool. **GRIND** butter, berries, sugar and vanilla 20 seconds. Scrape down sides of container; **GRIND** 10 seconds more. Add cooked mixture; **GRIND** 15 seconds. Scrape down sides of container; **GRIND** 5 seconds longer. Use to fill and frost cakes or torte.

MARSHMALLOW FROSTING

8 large marshmallows, quartered
¼ cup milk
2 tablespoons butter or margarine
¼ teaspoon salt
1½ teaspoon vanilla
2 cups sifted confectioners' sugar

Combine all ingredients except vanilla and sugar in saucepan. Place over low heat and melt marshmallows. Pour into blender container; add vanilla and ⅓ cup sugar at a time. **GRATE** until smooth. Stop motor and push ingredients into blades with rubber spatula as needed. Continue processing until all sugar is added. Wonderful topping for cup cakes. Makes about ¾ cup frosting.

CREAMY LEMON FROSTING

⅓ cup room temperature butter or margarine, sliced
2 (1-inch) squares lemon rind, cut into strips
2¼ cups sifted confectioners' sugar
¼ cup lemon juice

BLEND butter or margarine and lemon rind until rind is finely chopped. Add ½ cup of confectioners' sugar at a time and **BLEND** until smooth. Add lemon juice after first addition of sugar. Stop motor as needed and push ingredients into blades with rubber spatula. Makes about 1½ cups frosting, enough for spreading between layers and on top and sides of 2 layer 8-inch cake.

DELICIOUS CAN'T-FAIL
CANDIES AND CONFECTIONS

Candy making has always been a fun time, and in grandma's day the results were successful when an experienced cook was in charge. Now, the beginning cook can turn out great rich, creamy-smooth candies the very first time.

Fudge, panoche and pralines have always been top favorites with candy lovers of all ages. Today's candy recipes use convenience foods, chocolate and butter-scotch bits, marshmallows, peanut butter and dried fruits to cut down the long cooking and beating time and assure success. And, the modern multi-speed blender takes care of all of the tedious chopping of nuts and fruits easily and in seconds!

Try the simple candy recipes that follow. All are made with the help of the blender. Make plenty, for all of the candies make fine gifts to ship to servicemen or students and are great for money raisers at bazaars. Keep plenty on hand so the candy dishes can be kept filled for snackers.

BLENDER-MADE ALMOND PASTE

½ pound blanched almonds, about 1½ cups
¾ cups sugar
2 tablespoons water
1 tablespoon lemon juice
⅛ teaspoon salt

Pour ¼ cup almonds into container. **CHOP** until finely chopped, 8 to 10 seconds. Empty container into coarse sieve over bowl; shake nuts through sieve. Return any large pieces to container. Repeat process until all nuts are chopped. Combine remaining ingredients in small saucepan. Heat slowly, stirring constantly until syrup comes to a full boil to center of pan. Remove from heat. Pour over finely chopped almonds; mix well. Cool slightly, about 5 minutes. Knead until paste holds together and can be formed into a roll. Wrap tightly in aluminum foil or pack in a Mini-Blend container and cover tightly. Let ripen in refrigerator about 1 week before using for preparing macaroons, marzipan, fillings for coffee cakes and cookies, etc. Makes about ¾ pound.

RUM BALLS

See photo page 59

1½ cups pecan halves
⅓ cup rum, bourbon or brandy
1 teaspoon vanilla
Dash of salt
¼ cup room temperature butter or margarine, sliced
2 squares (1-ounce) unsweetened chocolate, melted
1 box (1-pound) confectioners' sugar

BLEND pecans, ⅓ cup at a time, switching motor on and off until nuts are coarsely chopped. Empty into measuring cup. Place next 5 ingredients in container in order listed. **CREAM** until smooth, about 15 seconds. **MIX**, adding confectioners' sugar ¼ cup at a time. Stop motor as needed and push ingredients into blades with rubber spatula. If mixture becomes very stiff and motor labors, turn mixture into bowl and stir last of sugar in by hand. Stir in ½ cup of the chopped pecans. Shape into small balls using a rounded teaspoonful of mixture for each ball. Roll balls in remaining pecans. Store in air-tight container to mellow. Makes about 4 dozen.

PEANUT BUTTER PANOCHE

See photo page 59

1 cup salted peanuts
2 cups (packed) brown sugar
1 cup granulated sugar
1 cup undiluted evaporated milk
2 tablespoons butter or margarine
¼ teaspoon salt
2 cups miniature marshmallows
1 cup peanut butter
1 tablespoon vanilla

BLEND peanuts, ⅓ cup at a time, switching motor on and off until coarsely chopped. Save. Combine sugars, milk, butter or margarine and salt in heavy saucepan; mix. Place over moderate heat and bring to a full rolling boil. Boil, stirring constantly, 2 minutes. Remove from heat. Stir in marshmallows, peanut butter and vanilla; beat until smooth. Stir in ⅔ of the chopped peanuts. Beat just until mixture begins to lose its gloss. Pour into buttered 13 x 9 x 2-inch pan. Sprinkle remaining chopped peanuts over top and press into candy. Cool. Cut into 1-inch squares. Makes about 8 dozen pieces.

QUICK CHOCOLATE PECAN FUDGE

See photo page 59

1½ cups pecan halves
1 package (3¾-ounce) chocolate pudding and pie filling (not instant)
1 cup sugar
½ cup undiluted evaporated milk
1 package (6-ounce) semi-sweet chocolate bits
1 cup miniature marshmallows
1½ teaspoons vanilla

BLEND pecan halves, ⅓ cup at a time, switching motor on and off until coarsely chopped. Combine next 3 ingredients in heavy saucepan. Cook over moderately high heat, stirring constantly until mixture is bubbling rapidly to center of pan. Boil 1 minute, stirring vigorously. Remove from heat; stir in chocolate bits, marshmallows and vanilla. Beat until chocolate and marshmallows are melted; stir in chopped pecans. Stir until mixture begins to lose its gloss. Pour into buttered 8 x 8 x 2-inch pan at once and spread evenly. Cool; cut in squares. Makes 25 pieces.

CHOCOLATE ANGEL CONFECTION

1⅓ cup salted peanuts
3 packages (6-ounce) semi-sweet chocolate bits
¼ teaspoon salt
2 teaspoons vanilla
4 cups miniature marshmallows

BLEND peanuts, ⅓ cup at a time, switching motor on and off, until coarsely chopped. Melt chocolate bits in top of double boiler over hot water. Remove from heat; stir in salt and vanilla. Stir in miniature marshmallows; mix well. Sprinkle ¼ of the chopped peanuts over surface of a sheet of heavy aluminum foil; turn candy out onto chopped nuts. Roll candy up in foil and shape into a log. Unwrap and spoon off teaspoonfuls of log and shape into 1¼-inch balls. Roll balls in remaining peanuts. Chill until firm. Makes about 3½ dozen.

QUICK PRALINES

1½ cups pecan halves
1 package (3¾-ounce) butterscotch pudding and pie
   filling (not instant)
1 cup granulated sugar
½ cup (packed) brown sugar
½ cup undiluted evaporated milk
1 tablespoon butter or margarine

BLEND pecans, ⅓ cup at a time, switching motor on
and off until coarsely chopped. Combine pudding
mix, sugars, milk and butter or margarine in heavy
saucepan. Place over moderately high heat and cook,
stirring constantly, until sugar dissolves. Cook to soft
ball stage (234°F.), stirring often. Remove from heat;
stir in pecans. Beat until mixture thickens and begins to lose its gloss. Spoon tablespoonfuls of mixture onto buttered baking sheet. Cool. Makes about
2 dozen pralines.

BURNT SUGAR PRALINE SQUARES

2 cups pecan halves
3¾ cups sugar
1 can (13-ounce) undiluted evaporated milk
3 teaspoons vanilla
3 tablespoons butter or margarine

BLEND pecan halves, ⅓ cup at a time, switching
motor on and off until coarsely chopped. Combine
2½ cups of the sugar and evaporated milk in large
heavy saucepan. Place over low heat. Cook, stirring
often. While mixture is cooking, pour remaining 1¼
cups sugar into a large heavy fry pan. Cook over low
heat until sugar melts, stirring constantly. Pour cara-
melized sugar into the sugar-milk mixture very slowly,
stirring vigorously while adding. Cook to firm ball
stage (244°F.). Remove from heat; stir in vanilla and
butter. Stir until mixture thickens; stir in pecans.
Continue stirring until mixture begins to lose its gloss.
Pour into buttered 9 x 9 x 2-inch pan; spread evenly.
Cool; cut into squares. Makes 36 squares.

PRALINE CLUSTERS: Instead of pouring Burnt Sugar
Praline Squares into pan, spoon rounded tablespoonfuls of candy onto buttered baking sheets. Makes
about 4 dozen pieces.

DATE PECAN ROLLS

1½ cups pecan halves
1 cup undiluted evaporated milk
1 package (8-ounce) pitted dates
3 cups sugar
¼ cup light corn syrup
2 tablespoons butter or margarine
¼ teaspoon salt
1 teaspoon vanilla

BLEND pecans, ½ cup at a time, switching motor on
and off until coarsely chopped, pour into bowl; save.
BEAT evaporated milk and ½ of the dates until
coarsely chopped, about 10 seconds. Add remaining
dates and **BEAT** until coarsely chopped, about 10 seconds. Pour mixture into large heavy saucepan. Add
sugar, syrup, butter and salt; stir. Bring to boil slowly,
stirring constantly. Cook to soft ball stage (234 to
240°F.). Remove from heat. Stir in vanilla and pecans.
Beat until a spoonful of mixture dropped onto waxed
paper will hold its shape. Spoon an equal amount of
mixture onto two 12-inch lengths of aluminum foil
which are well buttered. When lukewarm, shape into
2 rolls 10-inches long. Roll in foil; chill. Cut into
¼-inch slices. Makes about 80 slices.

APRICOT COCONUT BALLS

⅔ cup pecan or walnut halves
¼ cup light corn syrup
1 egg
1 cup quartered dried apricots
½ cup red candied cherries, cut in half
½ cup blender-crumbed vanilla wafer crumbs (page
   8), about 12 wafers
¾ cup flaked or shredded coconut

CHOP pecan or walnut halves in container, ⅓ cup at
a time, switching motor on and off until coarsely
chopped, pour into bowl; save. Combine next 4 ingredients in blender container in order listed. **BEAT**
until apricots are coarsely chopped. Stop motor and
push ingredients into blades as needed. Pour into
saucepan; cook over low heat, stirring constantly
until thickened, about 1 minute. Remove from heat;
stir in nuts and crumbs. Cool slightly. Shape into balls,
using 1 rounded teaspoonful of mixture for each. Roll
balls in coconut. Chill. Makes 2½ to 3 dozen balls.

APRICOT PECAN BALLS: Follow recipe for Apricot
Coconut Balls (above) and change as follows: Use
pecans in mixture and roll balls in coarsely chopped
pecans instead of coconut. Makes 2½ to 3 dozen
balls.

A. Apricot Coconut Balls; B. Quick Pralines page 58; C. Peanut Butter Panoche page 57
D. Quick Chocolate Pecan Fudge; E. Rum Balls page 57

COOKIES

Delicious cookies galore are made-easy with the help
of the blender. Just use one of the tested recipes that
follow and you're on your way. Soon you'll be able
to adapt your own as well as an endless variety of new
cookie recipes so they, too, can be prepared with the
blender.

The expert cookie maker relies on the blender to take
most of the tedious work out of cookie making. Use
it to chop nuts, dried fruits, fruit rind, chocolate and
the like, and mix the liquids, eggs, fat and sugar.

When making cookies the blender-way for the first
time select a recipe for an old favorite like Chocolate
Chip Drops, Molasses Drops, Brownies or Mincemeat
Bars. Follow the recipe exactly. You'll be delighted
with the results and the speed with which plain and
fancy cookies can be prepared with a blender.

Chocolate Chip Drops, Molasses Drops page 61

CHOCOLATE CHIP DROPS

See photo at left

1¼ cups sifted flour
½ cup granulated sugar
½ teaspoon baking powder
½ teaspoon salt
½ cup pecan halves
½ cup semi-sweet chocolate bits
1 egg
1 teaspoon vanilla
1 tablespoon water
⅓ cup (packed) brown sugar, broken up
½ cup room temperature butter or margarine, sliced

Sift first 4 ingredients into mixing bowl. **BLEND** pecan halves, switching motor on and off until coarsely chopped. Stir pecans and chocolate bits into dry ingredients. **BEAT** egg, vanilla, water, brown sugar and ½ of the butter until smooth, 10 to 15 seconds. Add remaining butter; **BEAT** until smooth, about 10 seconds. Stop motor as needed and push ingredients into blades with rubber spatula. Add to dry ingredients; mix well. Drop level tablespoonfuls onto ungreased baking sheet. Bake in moderate oven (350°F.) until done and lightly browned, 12 to 15 minutes. Makes about 3 dozen cookies.

FROSTED CHOCOLATE DROPS

See photo page 63

1½ cups sifted flour
¼ teaspoon soda
1 egg
½ cup room temperature butter or margarine, sliced
1 teaspoon vanilla
1 cup (packed) brown sugar, broken up
½ cup buttermilk
2 squares (1-ounce) unsweetened chocolate, melted
1¼ cups walnut halves

Sift flour and soda into mixing bowl. **BEAT** egg, butter, vanilla, brown sugar, buttermilk and chocolate until smooth, 25 seconds. Stop motor as needed and push ingredients into blades with rubber spatula. Add ½ of the walnuts; **BEAT** until coarsely chopped, 2 to 3 seconds. Repeat with remaining walnuts. Add to dry ingredients; mix well. Chill dough well, about 1 hour. Drop rounded tablespoonfuls onto lightly greased baking sheet. Bake in moderate oven (350°F.) until done, about 10 minutes. Cool and spread, if desired, with half recipe of Chocolate Butter Cream Frosting (page 52). Makes about 3 dozen cookies.

MOLASSES DROPS

See photo at left

3 cups sifted flour
3 teaspoons baking powder
1 tablespoon cinnamon
2 teaspoons ginger
½ teaspoon salt
1 cup seedless raisins
1½ cups bran flakes
¾ cup molasses
2 eggs
1 cup (packed) brown sugar, broken up
1 cup shortening

Sift first 5 ingredients into mixing bowl. Stir in raisins and cereal. **BEAT** molasses, eggs and brown sugar until smooth, about 20 seconds. Add shortening. **BEAT** until smooth, about 50 seconds. Stop motor as needed and push ingredients into blades with rubber spatula. Add to dry ingredients; mix well. Drop rounded tablespoonfuls onto lightly greased baking sheet. Bake in moderate oven (350°F.) about 12 minutes or until done and lightly browned. Makes about 4½ dozen cookies.

PECAN-RAISIN BRAN DROPS

2 cups sifted flour
1 cup granulated sugar
2 teaspoons baking powder
1 teaspoon salt
½ teaspoon cinnamon
½ teaspoon nutmeg
1½ cups walnut or pecan halves
1½ cups bran flakes
2 eggs
3 teaspoons vanilla
1 cup (packed) brown sugar, broken up
1 cup room temperature butter or margarine, sliced
1 cup seedless raisins

Sift first 6 ingredients into mixing bowl. **BLEND** walnut or pecan halves, about ⅓ cup at a time, switching motor on and off, until coarsely chopped. Stir nuts and cereal into dry ingredients. **BEAT** eggs, vanilla, brown sugar and ½ of the butter until smooth, about 20 seconds. Add remaining butter; **BEAT** until smooth, about 15 seconds. Stop motor as needed and push ingredients into blades with rubber spatula. Add ½ of raisins. **BEAT** until coarsely chopped, about 15 seconds. Add remaining raisins; repeat process. Add to dry ingredients; mix well. Chill dough about 1 hour. Drop rounded tablespoonfuls onto lightly greased baking sheet. Bake in moderate oven (375°F.) until done and lightly browned, 10 to 12 minutes. Makes 4½ dozen cookies.

MINCEMEAT OAT DROPS

2 cups sifted flour
2 teaspoons baking powder
½ teaspoon salt
1¾ cups rolled oats, quick or regular
1 package (9-ounce) dry mincemeat, broken into chunks
1 cup boiling water
1 cup room temperature butter or margarine, sliced
1 cup (packed) brown sugar, broken up
1 egg

Sift first 3 ingredients into mixing bowl. Stir in rolled oats. **CHOP** mincemeat and water until well mixed, about 20 seconds. Add butter, sugar and egg. **GRATE** until evenly mixed, 10 to 12 seconds. Stop motor as needed and push ingredients into blades with rubber spatula. Turn into dry ingredients. Mix well. Drop level tablespoonfuls onto well-greased baking sheet. Bake in moderate oven (375°F.) until done and lightly browned, about 12 minutes. Makes about 5½ dozen cookies.

PUMPKIN SPICE BRAN DROPS

See photo at right

2½ cups sifted flour
1 teaspoon soda
½ teaspoon salt
1 teaspoon cinnamon
1 teaspoon ginger
½ teaspoon ground cloves
1 cup whole bran cereal
1 egg
½ cup molasses
¾ cup room temperature butter or margarine, sliced
1 cup (packed) brown sugar, broken up
1 cup seedless raisins
1 cup canned pumpkin

Sift first 6 ingredients into mixing bowl. Stir in cereal. **BEAT** egg, molasses, butter and ½ of the brown sugar until smooth, about 30 seconds. Add remaining brown sugar and raisins; **BEAT** until smooth, about 20 seconds. Stop motor as needed and push ingredients into blades with rubber spatula. Add to dry ingredients. Add pumpkin; mix well. Drop rounded tablespoonfuls onto greased baking sheet. Bake in moderate oven (350°F.) until done, 12 to 15 minutes. Makes about 4½ dozen cookies.

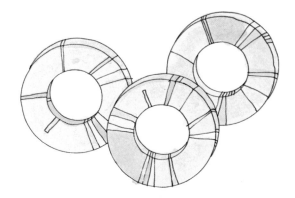

PINEAPPLE NUT DROPS

2 cups sifted flour
1 teaspoon baking powder
½ teaspoon salt
1 cup walnut halves
1 egg
2 tablespoons milk
2 teaspoons vanilla
½ cup soft shortening
1 cup (packed) brown sugar, broken up
2 squares (1-inch) orange rind, cut in slivers
1 can (13¼-ounce) crushed pineapple, drained (1 cup)

Sift first 3 ingredients into mixing bowl. **BLEND** walnut halves, ⅓ cup at a time, switching motor on and off until nuts are coarsely chopped. Stir into dry ingredients. **GRATE** egg, milk, vanilla, shortening, brown sugar and orange rind until smooth, about 25 seconds. Add pineapple; **GRATE** about 10 seconds or until well mixed. Add to dry ingredients; mix well. Drop rounded tablespoonfuls onto lightly greased baking sheet. Bake in moderate oven (375°F.) until done, about 15 minutes. Makes 4 dozen cookies.

CHOCOLATE ALMOND CRISPS

¾ cup sifted flour
1 package (6-ounce) semi-sweet chocolate bits
2 eggs
1 cup toasted blanched almonds
1 cup sugar
1½ teaspoons vanilla
¼ teaspoon salt

Combine flour and chocolate bits in mixing bowl. **BLEND** remaining ingredients, switching motor on and off until nuts are finely chopped. Stop motor as needed and push ingredients into blades with rubber spatula. Add to flour mixture and mix well. Chill 1 hour. Drop level tablespoonfuls onto well-greased baking sheet. Bake in moderate oven (350°F.) until done, about 10 minutes. Makes about 3½ dozen cookies.

A. Pumpkin Spice Bran Drops; B. Mincemeat Bars page 64
C. Chocolate Chip Drops; D. Frosted Chocolate Drops (unfrosted) page 61

CHOCOLATE NUT MACAROONS

½ cup pecan or walnut halves
2 cups moist flaked coconut
⅔ cup sweetened condensed milk
½ cup semi-sweet chocolate bits
1 teaspoon vanilla

BEAT nuts, switching motor on and off until coarsely chopped, 3 to 4 seconds. Empty into bowl. **BEAT** ½ of the coconut at a time until fine, about 10 seconds; add to nuts. Add remaining ingredients; mix well. Drop tablespoonfuls onto well-greased baking sheet. Bake in slow oven (300°F.) until done and a delicate brown, about 18 minutes. Remove from baking sheet at once. Cool on rack. Makes about 2 dozen cookies.

CHERRY COCONUT MACAROONS

¼ cup blanched almonds
2 cups moist flaked coconut
½ cup sweetened condensed milk
12 red candied cherries
1 teaspoon almond extract

BEAT almonds until very fine; turn into bowl. **BEAT** ½ of the coconut until fine, about 10 seconds. Turn into bowl. **BEAT** remaining coconut, sweetened condensed milk, cherries and extract until finely chopped, 10 to 12 seconds. Combine ingredients; mix well. Drop tablespoonfuls onto well-greased baking sheet. Bake in slow oven (300°F.) until done and a delicate brown, about 18 minutes. Remove from baking sheet at once; cool on rack. Makes about 1½ dozen cookies.

BROWNIES

See photo at right

¾ cup sifted all-purpose flour
½ teaspoon baking powder
½ teaspoon salt
1 cup pecans
2 (1-ounce) squares semi-sweet chocolate, each square cut in 6 or 8 pieces
2 eggs
1 cup sugar
⅓ cup shortening
½ teaspoon vanilla

Sift flour, baking powder and salt into large mixing bowl. **GRATE** ½ cup nuts 5 seconds. Add to flour. Repeat with remaining nuts. **SHRED** chocolate 40 seconds. Add eggs and **LIQUEFY** 10 seconds. Add sugar, shortening and vanilla and **GRIND** 20 seconds. STOP MOTOR, scrape down sides of container with rubber spatula. **GRIND** 30 seconds or until ingredients are thoroughly mixed. Add to flour mixture and mix well. Spread evenly in lightly greased 8-inch square pan. Bake in moderate oven (350°F.) 15 minutes. Makes 24 brownies.

BEST-EVER BLENDER BROWNIES

1 cup sifted flour
½ teaspoon baking powder
1 teaspoon salt
1 cup walnut halves
2 eggs
1 cup sugar
⅔ cup cooking oil
2 squares (1-ounce) unsweetened chocolate, melted
2 teaspoons vanilla

Sift first 3 ingredients into mixing bowl **BLEND** walnut halves, ⅓ cup at a time, switching motor on and off until coarsely chopped. Stir nuts into dry ingredients. **PURÉE** remaining ingredients until well blended, 25 to 30 seconds. Add to dry ingredients; mix well. Spread into greased 9 x 9 x 2-inch square pan. Bake in moderate oven (350°F.) until done, 20 to 25 minutes. Cool. Serve plain or frost with favorite chocolate or mint frosting and cut in squares or bars. Makes 25 brownies.

MINCEMEAT BARS

See photo page 63

1 package (9-ounce) condensed mincemeat
1 cup undiluted evaporated milk
¼ cup granulated sugar
½ cup pecan halves
1½ cups sifted flour
1 teaspoon baking powder
½ teaspoon salt
½ cup room temperature butter or margarine, sliced
1 teaspoon vanilla
½ cup (packed) brown sugar, broken up

Break mincemeat into small pieces. Combine with evaporated milk and granulated sugar in small saucepan. Cook, stirring often, until very thick, about 5 minutes. **BLEND** pecans, switching motor on and off until coarsely chopped. Stir into mincemeat mixture. Cool. Combine flour, baking powder and salt; sift into mixing bowl. **BEAT** butter, vanilla and ¼ cup of brown sugar until smooth, about 30 seconds. Stop motor as needed, and push ingredients into blades with rubber spatula. Add remaining brown sugar; **BEAT** until smooth, about 30 seconds. Add to dry ingredients and mix with pastry blender until mixture is crumbly. Save ½ cup crumb mixture for top. Press remaining crumb mixture on bottom of greased 9 x 9 x 2-inch square pan. Spread mincemeat mixture over crust. Sprinkle reserved crumbs over top. Bake in moderate oven (350°F.) until done and lightly browned, about 30 minutes. Cool. Cut in bars, 1 x 3 inches. Makes about 27 bars.

Mexican Wedding Cakes page 67   Butter Chews page 66   Brownies page 64

RICH APRICOT SQUARES

¾ cup dried apricots
¼ cup warm water
1 cup sifted all-purpose flour
½ cup butter or margarine, softened
¼ cup granulated sugar
⅓ cup sifted all-purpose flour
½ teaspoon baking powder
¼ teaspoon salt
½ cup nuts
2 eggs
1 cup light brown sugar, firmly packed
½ teaspoon vanilla
Confectioners' sugar

Combine apricots and warm water; set aside. Put 1 cup flour in a bowl. **BLEND** butter and granulated sugar 30 seconds. Add to bowl with flour and mix thoroughly. Pack into bottom of 9-inch square pan. Bake in slow oven (325°F.) 25 minutes. Sift ⅓ cup flour, baking powder and salt into bowl. **GRATE** nuts 5 seconds and add to bowl with flour. **BEAT** eggs 10 seconds. Add brown sugar, vanilla and apricots and **BLEND** 40 seconds. STOP MOTOR, scrape down sides of container with rubber spatula and **BLEND** 20 seconds. Pour into bowl with flour and nuts; mix thoroughly. Spread over baked layer and bake at 325° 35 minutes. Top will be soft. Cool several hours. Sprinkle with confectioners' sugar. Cut into 16 squares.

FRUIT TREASURES

¾ cup sifted all-purpose flour
½ teaspoon baking powder
½ teaspoon cinnamon
¼ teaspoon soda
¼ teaspoon salt
¼ teaspoon ground cloves
2 cups walnuts
½ cup golden raisins
½ cup dark raisins
⅓ cup butter or margarine, softened
¼ cup brown sugar, firmly packed
1 egg
1½ cups pitted dates
1 teaspoon vanilla
½ cup coconut

Sift together flour, baking powder, cinnamon, soda, salt and cloves. **GRATE** ½ cup walnuts and golden raisins 10 seconds. Empty into bowl with flour. Repeat with remaining walnuts and dark raisins. **GRIND** butter, sugar and egg 20 seconds. Add dates and vanilla; **GRIND** 10 seconds. STOP MOTOR, scrape down sides of container with rubber spatula. Add remaining nuts and **GRIND** 20 seconds, carefully pushing ingredients to center of container with rubber spatula while motor is running. Pour into bowl with flour. Add coconut. Mix thoroughly. Drop by teaspoonfuls onto greased baking sheet. Bake in moderate oven (350°F.) 12 minutes.

FRUIT SQUARES

1½ cups dried apricots
¾ cup walnut halves
1½ cups sifted flour
⅔ cup room temperature butter or margarine, sliced
⅓ granulated sugar
2 eggs
1 teaspoon vanilla
¼ teaspoon salt
1⅔ cups (packed) brown sugar, broken up
Confectioners' sugar, optional

Rinse apricots. Place in saucepan, cover with cold water and bring to a boil, then reduce heat and simmer 10 minutes. Drain and cool. **BLEND** walnuts, about ⅓ cup at a time, switching motor on and off until nuts are coarsely chopped. Add 3 tablespoons flour to chopped walnuts; mix and set aside. **CRUMB** butter and granulated sugar until well blended, about 40 seconds. Stop motor as needed and push ingredients into blades with rubber spatula. Add to remaining flour; mix well. Spread evenly over bottom of greased 9 x 9 x 2-inch pan. With tines of fork, rough surface of mixture. Bake in moderate oven (350°F.) until lightly browned, about 25 minutes. **BEAT** eggs, vanilla and salt 10 seconds. Add brown sugar, ⅓ at a time and **PURÉE** 10 seconds after each addition. Add apricots, ⅓ at a time; **PURÉE** until fairly smooth after each addition, 15 to 20 seconds. Add to walnut mixture; mix well. Spread over hot baked cookie base. Reduce temperature to slow oven (325°F.) and bake until done, about 45 minutes. If desired, sprinkle with confectioners' sugar while warm. Cut in squares. Makes 25 squares.

BUTTER CHEWS

See photo page 65

1 cup nuts
1½ cups sifted all-purpose flour
3 tablespoons sugar
¾ cup butter or margarine, melted
3 egg whites
¼ cup brown sugar, firmly packed
3 egg yolks
1¾ cups brown sugar, firmly packed
¾ cup coconut

GRATE nuts 5 seconds. Empty into a bowl. **SHRED** flour and 3 tablespoons sugar 20 seconds, adding butter through opening in top while motor is running. Pack into bottom of 9-inch square pan. Bake in moderate oven (375°F.) 15 minutes. Beat egg whites with rotary or electric beater until foamy. Gradually add ¼ cup brown sugar and continue beating until stiff. **GRIND** egg yolks and 1¾ cups brown sugar 10 seconds. Pour into bowl with egg whites. Add nuts and coconut and fold in until smooth. Pour over baked layer and spread evenly. Bake at 375° 25 to 30 minutes longer. Cool. Cut in 16 squares.

CHINESE CHEWS

¾ cup sifted flour
1 teaspoon baking powder
¼ teaspoon salt
1 cup walnut or pecan halves
2 eggs
1 cup granulated sugar
1 teaspoon vanilla
1 cup pitted dates, cut into quarters
Confectioners' sugar

Sift first 3 ingredients into bowl. **BLEND** nuts, ⅓ cup at a time, switching motor on and off until coarsely chopped. Stir into dry ingredients. **BEAT** eggs, sugar and vanilla until smooth, about 10 seconds. Add dates. **BEAT** until dates are coarsely chopped, 20 to 25 seconds. Stop motor as needed and push ingredients into blades with rubber spatula. Add to dry ingredients; mix well. Spread evenly into greased 9 x 9 x 2-inch square pan. Bake in slow oven (325°F.) until done, about 40 minutes. Sift confectioners' sugar over warm cookies before cutting into bars or cut warm cookies into bars and roll each in confectioners' sugar. Makes 2 dozen bars.

LINZER BARS

¾ cup walnuts
1¼ cups sifted all-purpose flour
½ cup butter or margarine, softened
½ cup sugar
1 egg yolk
⅓ cup raspberry jam
2 egg whites
¼ cup sugar

GRATE ½ cup nuts 10 seconds. Pour into measuring cup. Repeat with remaining nuts. **GRIND** butter, sugar and egg yolk 20 seconds. STOP MOTOR, scrape down sides of container with rubber spatula and **GRIND** 20 seconds. Empty into bowl with flour and mix until moistened. Pack into bottom of 8-inch square pan. Prick with fork. Bake in moderate oven (350°F.) 15 to 20 minutes or until golden. Remove from oven and spread jam over top. Beat egg whites with rotary or electric beater until foamy. Gradually add ¼ cup sugar and continue beating until stiff. Fold chopped nuts into egg whites and spread over jam. Bake at 350° 25 minutes longer. Cool in pan. Cut into 16 cookies.

YUMMY FROSTED BARS

1 cup nuts
1 cup raisins or dates
2 cups sifted all-purpose flour
1½ teaspoons baking powder
¼ teaspoon salt
¼ teaspoon soda
¼ cup shortening
½ cup sugar
1 egg
¼ cup dark molasses
¼ cup dark corn syrup
½ cup milk
1 teaspoon vanilla

CHOP nuts 5 seconds. Empty into a bowl. **CHOP** raisins 5 seconds and add to nuts. Sift together flour, baking powder, salt and soda. **MIX** shortening and sugar 20 seconds. STOP MOTOR, scrape down sides of container with rubber spatula. Add egg, molasses and syrup. **STIR** 30 seconds. Add milk and vanilla and **STIR** 20 seconds. Combine nuts and raisins with flour and mix. Add contents of blender container and stir. Pour into buttered 13 x 9½ x 2-inch pan. Bake in moderate oven (350°F.) 25 minutes. When cool frost with Confectioners' Sugar Frosting, page 53. Makes 2 dozen 2-inch bars.

SHORTBREAD CRUMB COOKIES

1¼ cups sifted flour
½ teaspoon soda
¼ teaspoon salt
1½ teaspoons cinnamon
⅔ cup walnut halves
1 cup finely crushed shortbread cookie crumbs (about 14 shortbread cookies, 1¾ inches square, page 8)
1 egg
⅓ cup milk
¼ cup room temperature butter or margarine, sliced
1 cup (packed) brown sugar, broken up
1 teaspoon vanilla

Sift first 4 ingredients into mixing bowl. **BLEND** walnut halves, ⅓ cup at a time, switching motor on and off until coarsely chopped. Stir walnuts and cookie crumbs into dry ingredients. **BEAT** egg, milk, butter, brown sugar and vanilla until smooth, 25 to 30 seconds. Add to dry ingredients; mix well. Drop rounded tablespoonfuls onto lightly greased baking sheet. Bake in moderate oven (350°F.) until done and lightly browned, 12 to 15 minutes. Makes 2½ dozen cookies.

MEXICAN WEDDING CAKES

See photo page 65

1 cup nuts
2 cups sifted all purpose flour
¼ teaspoon salt
1 cup butter or margarine, softened
¼ cup sugar
2 teaspoons vanilla
Confectioners' sugar

GRATE ½ cup nuts 5 seconds. Empty into mixing bowl. Repeat with remaining nuts. Add flour and salt to nuts. **GRIND** butter, sugar and vanilla 60 seconds. If necessary, STOP BLENDER, use rubber spatula to keep mixture around processing blades. Cover and continue to process at **GRIND**. Pour into bowl with nuts and flour. Mix until smooth. Shape by teaspoonful into crescents or small balls. Bake in slow oven (325°F.) 20 minutes. Cool. Put ½ cup confectioners' sugar in small clean paper bag. Add about 6 cookies and shake gently. Put sugared cookies in cookie jar. Repeat with remaining cookies. Makes 6 or 7 dozen.

DESSERTS

Desserts, simple or elegant, are fun to eat, fun to think about, fun to make when an electric blender is available.

Fabulous molded desserts, pretty parfaits, old-fashioned puddings, ice creams and quick-made packaged puddings are just a few of the desserts that can be whizzed up with ease the blender-way. Count on the blender to chop nuts, grate coconut and chocolate, crumb cookies, chop fruits and take care of scores of other hard-to-do jobs.

Try the dessert recipes on the following pages. Some are fine for topping off a family meal, others are just right to serve after a festive dinner party, at informal parties, to tote to a bazaar, tempt an invalid or please teen-ages.

CHOCOLATE NUT FONDUE WITH ORANGE SAUCE

½ cup pecan or walnut halves
1 cup milk
1 tablespoon butter or margarine
2 squares (1-ounce) unsweetened chocolate, cut in small pieces
⅔ cup sugar
¼ teaspoon salt
2 teaspoons vanilla
3 eggs, separated
1 cup soft bread crumbs (see page 8 for preparation directions)
Orange Sauce (see recipe page 172)

CHOP nuts, ¼ cup at a time, switching motor on and off until coarsely chopped. Empty into bowl. Repeat. Combine milk and butter or margarine in saucepan; scald. **CHOP** chocolate, switching motor on and off until finely chopped. Add hot milk; **BLEND** until chocolate melts. Add ⅓ cup sugar, salt, vanilla and egg yolks; **BLEND** until well mixed, 5 to 6 seconds. Pour over nuts. Add bread crumbs; mix. Beat egg whites until fluffy with electric or hand beater. Add remaining ⅓ cup sugar, 1 tablespoonful at a time, and beat well after each addition. Beat until stiff and glossy. Fold into chocolate mixture. Pour into an 8 x 4 x 3-inch loaf pan or baking dish. Bake in slow oven (300°F.) until set, 40 to 45 minutes. Serve warm with Orange Sauce. Makes 6 servings.

PEACH PECAN CRISP

16 to 20 graham crackers, broken in half
½ cup (packed) brown sugar
3 tablespoons melted butter or margarine
½ cup pecan halves
2 cups fresh or drained canned or frozen peach slices
Whipped cream or vanilla ice cream, optional

CRUMB 8 to 10 graham cracker halves at a time, switching motor on and off until crumbs are moderately fine. Pour into bowl. Repeat. Add sugar and butter or margarine to crumbs; mix well with forks or pastry blender. **CHOP** nuts, ¼ cup at a time, switching motor on and off until coarsely chopped. Pour into crumbs; repeat. Mix nuts into crumbs. Spread peaches over bottom of buttered shallow baking dish, 10 x 6 x 2-inches. Sprinkle crumbs evenly over fruit. Bake in moderate oven (350°F.) until lightly browned and bubbly around edges, 25 to 30 minutes. Serve warm or cold, plain or topped with whipped cream or ice cream, as desired. Makes 6 servings.

ALMOND DESSERT CREAM

2 cups blanched almonds, cut in half
1 pint half and half (half milk, half cream)
1 cup light corn syrup
2 envelopes (2 tablespoons) unflavored gelatin
¾ cup sugar
1 teaspoon almond flavoring
½ teaspoon vanilla
½ teaspoon salt
Assorted drained canned fruit, to garnish or to serve with cream, as desired
Whipped cream or dessert topping

CHOP nuts ⅓ cup at a time, until very finely chopped; empty into bowl. Repeat as necessary. Combine 1½ cups half and half and syrup in saucepan; scald. Combine remaining ½ cup half and half and gelatin in container. **STIR** 1 second. Add scalded liquids and **STIR** until gelatin dissolves, 3 to 5 seconds. Add sugar, flavorings and salt; **STIR** until sugar dissolves, 2 to 4 seconds. Pour into bowl; chill until mixture becomes thick and syrupy. Stir in chopped nuts. Chill until mixture is consistency of egg whites, stirring frequently. Pour into tall oiled 8-cup mold. Chill until firm. Unmold on serving dish; garnish generously with colorful fruits and whipped cream or dessert topping. Makes 6 to 8 servings.

APRICOT CRÈME

A lovely light dessert to follow a heavy meal

1 (1-pound 13-ounce) can apricot halves
1 (3-ounce) package lemon-pineapple flavored gelatin
1 envelope unflavored gelatin
2 (2-inch) pieces lemon peel
¼ teaspoon salt
1 heaping cup crushed ice
1 cup heavy cream
Toasted coconut and mint sprigs for garnish

Drain apricots, reserving 1 cup syrup. Heat syrup to boiling. **GRIND** gelatins and hot syrup 40 seconds. Add apricots, lemon peel and salt; **MINCE** 10 seconds. Add ice and **GRATE** 20 seconds, adding cream through opening in top while motor is running. If necessary, STOP BLENDER, use rubber spatula to keep mixture around processing blades. Cover and continue to process at **GRATE**. Pour into oiled 1-quart or 8 individual molds and chill until firm. Unmold. Sprinkle toasted coconut over top and tuck mint sprigs in for garnish. Makes 8 servings.

PINEAPPLE CREAM

½ cup hot pineapple juice
2 envelopes unflavored gelatin
½ lemon, peeled
¼ cup maraschino cherry juice
⅓ cup sugar
½ cup heavy cream
12 maraschino cherries
2 heaping cups crushed ice

LIQUEFY pineapple juice, gelatin, lemon and maraschino cherry juice 60 seconds. Add sugar, cream and cherries and **BLEND** 5 seconds. Add ice and **SHRED** 60 seconds. Let stand 1 minute. Spoon into serving dishes.

BERRY CREAM: Substitute 1 (10-ounce) package frozen raspberries, partially thawed, for cherries and juice.

GINGER CREAM

¼ cup blanched salted almonds
½ cup milk, scalded
2 cups miniature marshmallows
¼ cup cold milk
1 envelope unflavored gelatin
½ cup candied ginger
2 tablespoons rum
1 cup half and half (half milk, half cream)

GRATE almonds 5 seconds. Empty into a bowl. **SHRED** scalded milk, marshmallows, cold milk, gelatin and ginger 40 seconds. STOP MOTOR, scrape down sides of container with rubber spatula. If marshmallows are not melted **LIQUEFY** 10 seconds longer. Pour into bowl and chill until mixture mounds when spooned. **WHIP** chilled mixture and rum 10 seconds, adding half and half through opening in top while motor is running. Pour into a 2 or 3-cup mold; chill until firm. Makes 6 servings.

LIME DIVINE

⅔ cup boiling water
2 envelopes unflavored gelatin
½ cup sugar
1 (6-ounce) can limeade or lemonade concentrate, thawed
2 heaping cups crushed ice

GRIND water and gelatin 60 seconds. Add sugar and **GRIND** 5 seconds. Add limeade and ice and **SHRED** 60 seconds or until ice is slushy. Let stand 1 minute. Spoon into serving dishes. Makes 6 to 8 servings.

ORANGE DIVINE: Follow recipe for Lime Divine (above), and substitute 1 can (6-ounce) orange juice concentrate for limeade and **MIX** one 2-inch strip orange peel, cut in strips, along with gelatin. Reduce sugar to ⅓ cup. Makes 6 to 8 servings.

MOCHA BAVARIAN CREAM

See photo at right

½ cup hot strong coffee
¼ cup cold water
2 envelopes unflavored gelatin
1 (6-ounce) package semi-sweet chocolate pieces
1 tablespoon sugar
2 egg yolks
1 heaping cup crushed ice
1 cup half and half (half milk, half cream)

STIR coffee, water and gelatin 20 seconds. Add chocolate and sugar; **BLEND** 25 seconds. **FRAPPÉ** 30 seconds, adding egg yolks, ice and half and half through opening in top while motor is running. STOP MOTOR, scrape down sides of container with rubber spatula. Pour in 1-quart mold, or individual serving dishes and chill. Serve with Mocha Sauce, page 171. Makes 6 servings.

STRAWBERRY BAVARIAN CREAM

1 (10-ounce) package frozen strawberries, thawed
2 envelopes unflavored gelatin
¼ cup cold milk
¼ cup sugar
2 egg yolks
1 heaping cup crushed ice
1 cup heavy cream

Drain berries, reserving ½ cup syrup. Heat syrup to simmering. **GRIND** gelatin, cold milk and hot syrup 40 seconds. Add sugar, berries and egg yolks and **GRIND** 15 seconds. **SHRED** 20 seconds, adding ice and cream through opening in top while motor is running. Turn into 1-quart mold and chill. Makes 6 servings.

DATE NUT ROLL

28 single graham crackers
1 cup nuts
½ cup half and half (half milk, half cream)
1 pound pitted dates
1 pound miniature marshmallows
1 cup heavy cream, whipped (see page 9)
Maraschino cherries for garnish

Break 3 crackers into blender container and **CRUMB** 10 seconds, breaking 2 more crackers through opening in top while motor is running. Empty into measuring cup; repeat until you have 2 cups crumbs. Place 1½ cups of the crumbs in large bowl. Set aside the other ½ cup crumbs. **GRATE** nuts 5 seconds and add to 1½ cups crumbs. **GRATE** 2 tablespoons half and half and ½ cup dates 10 seconds. Add to nuts. Repeat with remaining half and half and dates. Add marshmallows to bowl and mix. Shape into a roll on waxed paper. Roll in reserved ½ cup of crumbs. Chill several hours. Slice to serve. Top each serving with whipped cream and a maraschino cherry. Makes 8 to 10 servings.

Mocha Bavarian Cream

LEMON PUDDING

3 egg whites
¼ cup sugar
1¼ cups milk
1 cup sugar
3 egg yolks
¼ cup butter or margarine, softened
1 lemon (thin yellow portion of peel and fruit only)
½ cup flour

Beat egg whites with rotary or electric beater until foamy. Gradually add ¼ cup sugar; continue beating until stiff. **GRIND** milk, sugar, egg yolks, butter and lemon 30 seconds, adding flour through opening in top while motor is running. Pour over whites; fold in. Spoon into 8 buttered custard cups. Place cups in pan of hot water; bake in moderate oven (350°F.) 40 minutes. Cool, unmold and serve with Lemon Sauce, page 172. Makes 8 servings.

WHIPPED DESSERT TOPPING MIXES

Use ingredients called for in package directions. Be sure liquid used is very cold. Pour liquid into container; add dry mix, **WHIP** 5 to 10 seconds. STOP MOTOR, scrape down sides of container with rubber spatula. **STIR** 5 seconds longer or until soft peaks form. Watch carefully; stop motor every 5 seconds and examine. Don't overbeat!

STEAMED DATE PUDDING

A winter delight served with Hard Sauce

½ cup nuts
1 cup pitted dates
2 cups sifted all-purpose flour
1 teaspoon soda
1 teaspoon baking powder
¼ cup shortening
1 cup sugar
1 egg
1 cup milk
¼ lemon (thin yellow portion of peel and fruit only)

GRATE nuts 5 seconds. Empty into bowl or measuring cup. **GRATE** ½ cup dates 10 seconds. Empty into another bowl. Repeat with remaining dates. Sift flour, soda and baking powder into bowl with dates. **GRIND** shortening, sugar, egg and ½ cup milk 60 seconds. Add lemon and **GRIND** 10 seconds. Add remaining ½ cup of milk and **STIR** 5 seconds. Pour over flour and date mixture; add nuts. Stir until thoroughly blended. Pour into well-buttered 2-quart mold and cover tightly with lid or tie 2 thicknesses waxed paper over top. Place on rack in large deep pan and pour in enough water to make 2 inches deep. Cover pan tightly and simmer 2 hours, checking occasionally and adding more water if necessary. Serve hot or cold with Lemon Sauce or Hard Sauce, page 172. Makes 12 to 16 servings.

CHOCOLATE PUDDING

1½ cups skim milk
2 tablespoons cornstarch
2 tablespoons cocoa
1 teaspoon liquid sugar substitute
1 teaspoon vanilla
⅛ teaspoon almond extract

BLEND first 4 ingredients 20 seconds. Cook and stir over low heat until thick. Add remaining ingredients; mix. Chill. Makes 4 servings. Approximately 70 calories per serving.

CARAMEL RICE PUDDING

1 cup milk
1 egg
1 cup raisins
¼ cup brown sugar, firmly packed
⅛ teaspoon salt
1 cup cooked rice
Cinnamon

BLEND all ingredients except rice and cinnamon 40 seconds. Mix with rice. Spoon into 4 buttered custard cups. Sprinkle with cinnamon. Set cups in pan of hot water. Bake in moderate oven (350°F.) 30 minutes or until knife inserted in center comes out clean. Makes 4 servings.

APPLE DELIGHT PUDDING

1¼ cups sifted all-purpose flour
1¼ teaspoons soda
1 teaspoon cinnamon
½ teaspoon baking powder
¼ teaspoon each salt and ground cloves
¼ teaspoon nutmeg
4 medium tart apples, cored and sliced
1 egg
1 cup sugar
¼ cup butter or margarine, softened

Sift together flour, soda, cinnamon, baking powder, salt and spices. **PURÉE** 1 cup of apple slices 15 seconds. Empty into bowl with flour and repeat until all apples are grated. **BLEND** egg, sugar and butter 30 seconds or until smooth. Add to flour; mix until smooth. Spread in buttered 8-inch square pan. Bake in moderate oven (350°F.) 30 minutes. Serve with Butter Sauce, page 172. Makes 8 to 12 servings.

STRAWBERRY ICE CREAM DESSERT

See photo front cover

1½ cups boiling water
2 (3-ounce) packages wild strawberry-flavored gelatin
1 (10-ounce) package frozen sliced strawberries, partially defrosted
1 pint vanilla ice cream, cubed
Strawberry-Cranberry Sauce (page 172) for garnish
Whipped cream and fresh strawberries for garnish

GRIND boiling water and gelatin 10 seconds until gelatin is dissolved. Add strawberries and syrup; **GRIND** 20 seconds until strawberries are completely blended. Chill in container until mixture begins to set. Add ½ of the ice cream; **GRIND** 15 seconds. Add remaining ice cream; **GRIND** 45 to 60 seconds or until mixed. Stop motor as needed to scrape down sides and push ingredients into blades with rubber spatula. Pour into oiled 4-cup mold. Chill until firm. Garnish with Strawberry-Cranberry Sauce, whipped cream and fresh strawberries. Makes 6 to 8 servings.

QUICK CHOCOLATE POTS DE CRÈME

1 envelope (1-tablespoon) unflavored gelatin
¼ cup cold water
1 package (6-ounce) semi-sweet chocolate bits
2 tablespoons sugar
⅛ teaspoon salt
1 cup hot (scalded) milk
½ cup well drained crushed ice (see Blender Crushed Ice, page 9)
2 egg yolks
1 cup whipping cream
1½ teaspoons vanilla or 2 tablespoons crème de menthe

Combine gelatin and water in container; mix and let stand 2 to 3 minutes. Add chocolate bits, sugar and salt. Add hot milk; **BLEND** until chocolate is melted and mixture smooth, 15 to 20 seconds. Add ice, egg yolks, cream and vanilla or crème de menthe. **BLEND** until ice melts, about 20 seconds. Pour into 6 or 8 small sherbets or traditional cups for pots de crème. Makes 6 to 8 servings.

CUSTARD

3 eggs
2 cups milk
¼ to ⅓ cup sugar
¼ teaspoon salt
1 to 1½ teaspoons vanilla

Add ingredients to container in order listed. Set speed at **CREAM**; switch motor on and off 3 to 4 times or until ingredients are mixed. Fill 5 or 6 5-ounce custard cups to within ½-inch from top. Place cups in shallow pan. Place pan on oven rack; fill pan with hot water to 1-inch depth. Bake in moderate oven (325°F.) until firm. To test for doneness, insert blade of knife in center of custard, if it comes out clean custard is done. Serve warm or chilled, plain or with fruit or dessert sauce. Makes 5 to 6 servings.

INSTANT PUDDING MIXES

Pour milk or other liquid called for on package directions into container; add dry pudding mix. **STIR** just until mixed, 5 to 10 seconds. Pour into chilled dessert dishes; chill.

QUICK MAPLE POTS DE CRÈME: Follow recipe for Quick Chocolate Pots de Crème (above) and substitute butterscotch bits for semi-sweet chocolate ones and ½ teaspoon maple flavoring for vanilla or crème de menthe. Makes 6 to 8 servings.

ORANGE-PISTACHIO PARFAIT

¼ cup pistachio nuts
1 small orange (thin orange portion of peel and fruit)
¼ lemon (thin yellow portion of peel and fruit)
¾ cup sugar
½ cup water
3 eggs
2 tablespoons cold water
1 envelope unflavored gelatin
1 cup heavy cream

GRATE nuts 5 seconds. Empty into bowl. **SHRED** orange, lemon, sugar and water 20 seconds. Pour into saucepan; heat to boiling. **BEAT** eggs, water and gelatin 40 seconds, adding hot mixture through opening in top while motor is running. Empty into saucepan; cook and stir over low heat until slightly thickened. Pour into refrigerator tray; freeze until mushy. **GRIND** with cream 20 seconds. Add all but 1 tablespoon nuts. **GRIND** 5 seconds longer. Pour into refrigerator tray or sherbet dishes; freeze. Garnish with nuts. Makes 6 servings.

PARTY PARFAIT

Alternate layers of partially set, low calorie fruit-flavored gelatin and whipped nonfat dry milk in chilled parfait glasses. Garnish with a sprig of mint or a few graham cracker crumbs.

APRICOT OR PRUNE WHIP

1 cup water
⅔ cup sugar
½ thin (⅛-inch) slice unpeeled lemon, cut in thirds
2 cups quartered dried apricots or pitted prunes
1 cup whipped cream or dessert topping

Combine water, sugar and lemon in saucepan; bring to a boil. Add apricots or prunes. Cover; cook until fruit is tender, 15 to 20 minutes. Cool. Empty fruit into blender container; **BLEND** until fruit is finely chopped, 30 to 40 seconds. Stop motor as needed and push ingredients into blades with rubber spatula. Turn into bowl; chill; fold in cream or dessert topping. Spoon into serving dishes and chill. Serve plain or garnish with additional whipped cream as desired. Makes about 6 servings.

LEMON ICE

Tint a lemony yellow to match the photo at right

1 cup sugar
2 cups water
1 lemon (thin yellow portion of peel and fruit only)
½ teaspoon ginger or large piece candied ginger
⅛ teaspoon salt
Few drops yellow food coloring

Boil sugar and water 5 minutes. Remove from heat and set aside. **SHRED** lemon peel and fruit 20 seconds or until finely chopped. Add ginger, salt and food coloring. **STIR** 20 seconds, gradually adding hot sugar syrup through opening in top while motor is running. Pour into refrigerator tray and freeze about 2 hours or until slightly firm. Empty into container. **FRAPPÉ** 20 seconds. Return to refrigerator tray and freeze until firm. Makes 4 to 6 servings.

CHOCOLATE FREEZE

¼ cup sugar
½ cup water
1 (6-ounce) package regular or mint-flavored semi-sweet chocolate pieces
3 egg yolks
1½ cups heavy cream
1 teaspoon crème de menthe, optional

Boil sugar and water 3 minutes. **GRIND** chocolate pieces and sugar syrup 10 seconds or until chocolate is melted. Add egg yolks and **GRIND** 10 seconds. Cool to room temperature. **GRIND** 20 seconds, adding cream through opening in top while motor is running. Pour into 8 custard cups or sherbet dishes. Arrange on tray and cover dishes with foil or plastic wrap. Freeze until firm, about 2 or 3 hours. Garnish with whipped cream, flavored with 1 teaspoon crème de menthe, if you wish. Makes 8 servings.

STRAWBERRY ICE CREAM

1⅔ cup (1 14½-ounce can) evaporated milk
¼ cup sugar
½ cup water
2 tablespoons cornstarch
1 (10-ounce) package frozen strawberries, partially thawed

Freeze 1 cup evaporated milk until icy cold. **BEAT** ⅔ cup evaporated milk, sugar, water and cornstarch 10 seconds. Pour into saucepan and cook and stir over medium heat until thick. Chill thoroughly. **WHIP** icy cold evaporated milk 60 seconds or until stiff. Add chilled milk mixture and **BEAT** 20 seconds, carefully pushing mixture to center of container with rubber spatula while motor is running. Add strawberries and **GRIND** 5 seconds. Pour into freezer trays and freeze. Makes about 1 quart.

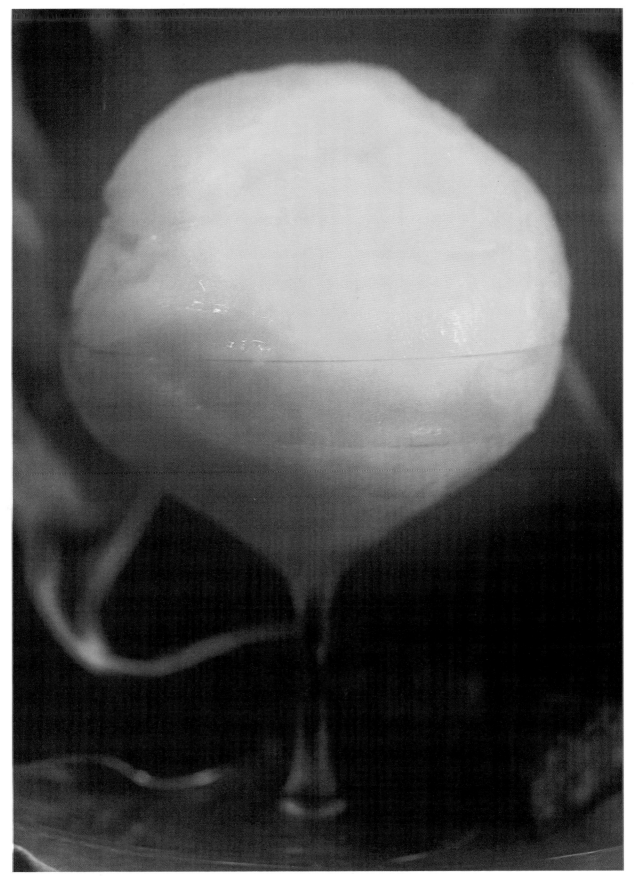

VANILLA CUSTARD ICE CREAM

2 cups half and half (half milk, half cream)
2 eggs
¾ cup sugar
2 tablespoons all-purpose flour
¼ teaspoon salt
2 cups half and half (half milk, half cream)
1½ tablespoons vanilla

STIR all ingredients, except last 2 cups half and half
and vanilla 20 seconds. Pour into 1-quart saucepan
and cook and stir over medium heat until thickened.
Cook 2 minutes longer. Put into blender container.
Add remaining half and half and vanilla and **BEAT** 10
seconds. If ice cream is to be made in ice cream
freezer, chill custard thoroughly, pour into freezer
and freeze as manufacturer directs. If frozen in refrigerator, pour custard from blender container into
3 or more refrigerator trays; and freeze until slushy.
Empty 1 tray at a time into blender container and
LIQUEFY 10 seconds. Return to tray and freeze. Cover
with plastic wrap. Makes about 1½ quarts.

VARIATIONS

Follow recipe for Vanilla Custard Ice Cream and
change as follows:

BANANA ICE CREAM: Reduce vanilla to 1 teaspoon.
BLEND 1 banana, peeled and sliced, and ½ of thin
lemon slice, peeled, with few drops yellow food coloring 20 seconds. Add to chilled ice cream mixture
before freezing.

MAPLE NUT ICE CREAM: Substitute 1 teaspoon maple
flavoring for vanilla. **CHOP** 1 cup nuts, ¼ cup at a
time, switching motor on and off until coarsely
chopped. Add to ice cream mix before freezing.

STRAWBERRY ICE CREAM: Reduce vanilla to 1 tablespoon. **CRUSH** 2 cups fresh washed and hulled strawberries and ¼ cup sugar 15 seconds. Stir into partially
frozen ice cream and continue freezing.

PEACH ICE CREAM: CRUSH 2 cups sliced peaches
and ½ cup sugar 15 seconds. Stir into partially frozen
ice cream and continue freezing.

ORANGE ICE BOX CAKE

32 lady fingers
1 cup nuts
1 cup sugar
½ cup water
2 envelopes unflavored gelatin
¼ cup water
¼ lemon (thin yellow portion of peel and fruit only)
Peel of ⅓ orange
1 orange, peeled and quartered
1 heaping cup crushed ice
2 cups heavy cream
8 ounces miniature marshmallows

Butter sides and bottom of 10-inch spring form or tube pan. Line sides with halved lady fingers. Break 4 lady fingers into blender container and **CRUMB** 5 seconds. Empty into large bowl. Repeat until all lady fingers have been crumbed. **GRATE** nuts 10 seconds and add to crumbs. Boil sugar and ½ cup water 2 minutes. **SHRED** gelatin, water, lemon, orange peel and fruit 20 seconds. Scrape down sides of container with rubber spatula. **GRIND** 40 seconds, adding hot sugar syrup through opening in top while motor is running. Add ice and **LIQUEFY** 20 seconds. Pour 2 cups orange mixture into measuring cup or bowl. **BLEND** orange mixture still in container 20 seconds, adding 1 cup cream through opening in top while motor is running. Pour into large bowl and add marshmallows. Pour 2 cups orange mixture from measuring cup back into blender container and **BLEND** 20 seconds, adding remaining cup of heavy cream through opening in top while motor is running. Add to bowl and fold in until marshmallows are melted and mixture is smooth. Combine lady finger crumbs and nuts and sprinkle ⅓ of mixture over bottom of pan; press firmly. Spoon half the orange mixture into pan. Sprinkle ⅓ of crumb mixture over and press into orange mixture. Spoon in remaining crumb mixture and cover with remaining crumbs. Press crumbs into orange mixture. Chill over night. To serve, remove side of spring form pan and cut wedges, or carefully loosen lady fingers from side of tube pan and invert cake onto serving plate. Garnish each slice with whipped cream and maraschino cherry, if you wish. Makes 12 to 16 servings.

MOCK DEVONSHIRE CREAM

1 cup dairy sour cream
1 package (3-ounce) room temperature cream cheese, cubed
3 tablespoons confectioners' sugar
½ teaspoon vanilla
1 cup whipping cream

Combine first 4 ingredients in container; **CREAM** until smooth, 40 to 60 seconds. Stop motor; push ingredients into blades as needed. Add cream. **CREAM** until fluffy and smooth, 5 to 8 seconds. Stop motor; push ingredients into blades as needed. Chill. Spoon over fresh berries or canned fruits. Makes about 2½ cups.

TORTONI SQUARES

½ cup toasted blanched almonds
1 cup fine blender-made vanilla wafer crumbs (page 8)
¼ cup melted butter or margarine
½ teaspoon almond extract
3 pints New York or vanilla ice cream
1 cup Apricot Dessert Sauce (page 170), or thick apricot preserves
Whipped cream or dessert topping, optional

Pour almonds into container. **BLEND** almonds, switching motor on and off until nuts are coarsely chopped. Combine first 4 ingredients in mixing bowl; mix well. Sprinkle ⅓ of the crumb mixture evenly over bottom of buttered aluminum foil-lined 8 x 8 x 2-inch pan. Spoon ½ of the ice cream over crumb mixture; spread ½ cup sauce or preserves over ice cream. Sprinkle with ½ of remaining crumb mixture; cover with remaining ice cream and preserves. Sprinkle with remaining crumb mixture. Freeze. To serve, cut into squares; top with whipped cream or dessert topping, if desired. Makes 9 to 12 servings.

FROZEN CHOCOLATE PEPPERMINT TORTE

6 to 8 peppermint sticks (about 4-inches long, ¼-inch diameter)
¾ cup room temperature butter or margarine
2 cups vanilla wafer crumbs (directions page 8)
3 eggs
¼ teaspoon salt
3 squares (1-ounce) unsweetened chocolate, melted
1½ cups sifted confectioners' sugar
1 teaspoon vanilla
4 cups miniature marshmallows
3 cups whipped cream or dessert topping

Line buttered 9 x 9 x 2-inch baking pan lengthwise and crosswise with strips of heavy aluminum foil leaving a 1-inch overhang over each side. Butter foil. Break candy sticks into ½-inch pieces. Add 8 to 10 candy pieces to container at a time; **BLEND** switching motor on and off until coarsely chopped. Empty into bowl; save. Melt ¼ cup butter or margarine; add wafer crumbs and mix with pastry blender. Press evenly over bottom of prepared pan. Add eggs, salt, remaining butter or margarine, chocolate and 1 cup sugar to container. **BLEND** until smooth and creamy, 40 to 60 seconds. Stop motor; push ingredients into blades with rubber spatula as needed. Add remaining sugar and vanilla. **BLEND** until smooth, 30 to 40 seconds. Spread in even layer over crumbs. Place in freezer. Fold marshmallows into whipped cream or dessert topping; spread in even layer over chocolate; sprinkle candy over cream. Freeze. When frozen lift torte from pan. Wrap and freeze or cut into 12 to 16 portions and serve. Makes 12 to 16 servings.

STRAWBERRY TRIFLE

1 package (3-ounce) vanilla pudding and pie filling
   (not instant)
1 pint strawberries, washed and hulled
¼ cup sugar
3 tablespoons orange liqueur, rum or orange juice
1 package (3-ounce) lady fingers (12 double)
2 cups sweetened whipped cream or dessert topping

Prepare pudding mix as directed on package label. Chill, stirring occasionally to keep it smooth. Select 16 pretty berries; reserve for garnishing dessert. Combine remaining strawberries, sugar and liqueur, rum or orange juice in blender container. **BLEND**, switching motor on and off until berries are finely chopped, about 30 seconds. Stop motor and push ingredients into blades with rubber spatula if needed. Stand 12 lady finger halves upright around edge of 1-quart compote or serving dish. Spoon ½ of pudding into dish; top with ½ of crushed berries. Cover with ½ of remaining lady finger halves. Repeat layers of pudding, fruit and lady fingers. Chill 2 to 4 hours. Just before serving top with whipped cream or dessert topping; garnish with reserved berries. Makes 6 to 8 servings.

APPLESAUCE

2 pounds cooking apples, peeled and quartered
⅓ to ½ cup sugar or ½ cup red cinnamon candies
½ cup water

Combine apples, sugar or cinnamon candies and water in covered saucepan. Cook until tender, 10 to 15 minutes. Place in container; **BLEND** to desired smoothness, about 10 seconds. Chill. Makes about 3 cups.

ALMOND STUFFED APPLES

¼ cup blanched almonds
2 tablespoons water
¼ cup sugar
¼ teaspoon almond extract
8 medium baking apples
Melted butter or margarine
Blender bread crumbs (see page 8)
Sugar
1 cup heavy cream, whipped (see page 9)

SHRED almonds 10 seconds. Empty onto piece of waxed paper. **BLEND** water, sugar and almond extract 10 seconds. Add ground almonds and **GRIND** 40 seconds, stopping motor once or twice to push ingredients to blades. Pare and core apples. Fill center of apples with almond paste. Roll apples in melted butter, then in crumbs and finally in sugar. Place in shallow, buttered baking dish and bake in hot oven (425°F.) 25 minutes or until tender. Serve with whipped cream. Makes 8 servings.

APRICOT CUSTARD

2 cups milk
½ cup dried apricots
⅓ cup sugar
3 eggs
¼ teaspoon salt

LIQUEFY all ingredients 60 seconds. Scrape down sides of container and **LIQUEFY** 60 seconds more. Scrape down sides of container again and **LIQUEFY** another 60 seconds. Pour into 6 or 8 buttered custard cups. Place cups in pan of hot water. Bake in moderate oven (350°F.) about 45 minutes or until knife inserted in center comes out clean. Cool cups on rack. Makes 6 to 8 servings.

BAKED CARAMEL CUSTARD

1 cup sugar
4 cups milk, scalded
6 eggs
2 teaspoons vanilla
½ teaspoon salt

Melt sugar in small heavy skillet over medium heat until it forms an amber-colored syrup. **WHIP** scalded milk, eggs, vanilla and salt 10 seconds, adding sugar syrup through opening in top while motor is running. Pour into shallow 1½-quart baking dish. Set baking dish in shallow pan on oven rack. Pour hot water into outer pan until 1 inch deep. Bake in moderate oven (350°F.) 1 hour or until knife inserted off center comes out clean. Remove from water and cool on rack. Makes 6 or 8 servings.

BANANA GLACÉ

1 egg white
¾ cup sugar
2 bananas, peeled and sliced
2 cups half and half (half milk, half cream)
⅓ cup cognac
⅛ teaspoon salt

Beat egg white with rotary or electric beater until foamy. Gradually add 2 tablespoons sugar and continue beating until stiff. **LIQUEFY** bananas 30 seconds or until smooth. **GRIND** 20 seconds, gradually adding remaining sugar, half and half, cognac and salt through opening in top while motor is running. Pour into bowl with egg white. Fold in until thoroughly blended. Spoon into refrigerator trays and freeze until firm. Makes 6 to 8 servings.

Quick Chocolate Pots de Crème page 73

ENTRÉES

Tasty, tempting but time-consuming dinner dishes become easy-to-fix when there's a blender to help.

Basic Meat Loaf, Sauerbraten, Beef Burgundy, Bombay Chicken Curry, Baked Macaroni and Cheese, Chicken Croquettes, and Quiche Lorraine all require a heap of fussy fixing. When a modern blender is available it takes over the tedious chopping of vegetables, etc., crumbing crackers and bread, grating cheese and the making of satin-smooth sauces for an endless array of plain and fancy main-dish foods, saving time and work aplenty.

Recipes for scores of luscious foreign favorites, marked with this symbol and familiar family dishes follow. Try a few and you will be tempted to make your own dinner favorites the blender way.

BASIC MEAT LOAF

2 pounds ground beef chuck
1 cup soft bread crumbs (page 8)
1 can (8-ounce) tomato sauce
2 eggs
2 teaspoons salt
½ teaspoon pepper
1 cup thin peeled carrot slices
1 cup (¾-inch) celery slices
1 medium (2-inch) onion, thinly sliced

Combine meat and crumbs in mixing bowl. Add next 4 ingredients to container. **BLEND** until mixed, about 5 seconds. Add sliced carrot. **BLEND,** switching motor on and off as needed to coarsely chop carrot, about 5 seconds. Add celery and onion slices. **BLEND,** switching motor on and off until vegetables are coarsely chopped, about 20 seconds. Add to meat mixture; mix well. Pack into greased 9 x 5 x 3-inch loaf pan. Bake in moderate oven (350°F.) until done, about 1 hour and 15 minutes. Cool in pan 10 minutes before turning out of pan. Makes 1 loaf, about 8 servings.

MINUTE MEAT LOAF

1½ pounds ground beef
½ pound ground lean pork
½ cup milk
⅓ cup uncooked rolled oats
1 egg
1 onion, sliced
1 stalk celery, sliced
1 clove garlic
4 parsley sprigs
1 teaspoon salt
⅛ teaspoon pepper

Put meat in a large mixing bowl. **SHRED** remaining ingredients 20 seconds. Add to meat; mix thoroughly. Shape into loaf in baking pan. Bake in moderate oven (350°F.) 1½ to 2 hours. Makes 8 servings.

FOR FROSTY TOP MEAT LOAF

Spread 2 cups instant mashed potatoes (page 193) on top of loaf during last ½ hour of baking. Grate 2 tablespoons cubed Cheddar cheese (page 6). Sprinkle over potatoes when meat loaf is removed from oven. Makes 6 to 8 servings.

MEAT AND 'TATER LOAF

2 eggs
¼ cup milk
1 clove garlic, sliced
2 cups diced (1-inch) raw potato
1 cup sliced (1-inch) celery
1 medium (2-inch) onion, sliced
1½ pounds ground beef
½ pound pork sausage meat
1 cup soft bread crumbs (page 8)
1 tablespoon Worcestershire sauce
2 teaspoons salt
¼ teaspoon pepper

CHOP eggs, milk, garlic and 1 cup potatoes, switching motor on and off until moderately fine. Add remaining potatoes; **CHOP** 5 seconds. Stop motor and push ingredients into blades with rubber spatula as needed. Add celery and onion; **CHOP** until vegetables are very fine, 8 to 10 seconds. Pour into mixing bowl; add remaining ingredients; mix. Pack into greased 9 x 5 x 3-inch loaf pan. Bake in moderate oven (350°F.) until done, 70 to 75 minutes. Makes a 9 x 5 x 3½-inch loaf.

STUFFED VEAL BREAST

1 tablespoon butter
2 medium onions, sliced
2 green peppers, seeded and coarsely chopped
1 cup sliced cabbage
3 stalks celery, sliced
1 slice white bread
½ pound mushrooms, sliced
3 teaspoons salt
½ teaspoon pepper
2 teaspoons paprika
1 breast of veal, with pocket for stuffing
1 (8-ounce) can tomato sauce

Melt butter in skillet. Place onions and green peppers in blender container; add enough water to cover. **GRATE** 5 to 10 seconds or just until coarsely chopped. Drain in sieve. Turn into skillet with butter. Repeat with cabbage and celery. Tear bread into container and **CRUMB** 10 seconds. Add to vegetables in skillet along with mushrooms, 1 teaspoon salt and ¼ teaspoon pepper. Cook and stir over low heat about 10 minutes. Stuff into pocket of veal breast and close with skewers or thread. Place on rack in roasting pan. Combine remaining salt, pepper and paprika and rub on meat. Pour tomato sauce over and cover loosely with foil. Bake in moderate oven (350°F.) 2 to 2½ hours or until fork tender. Add water if necessary. Makes 6 servings. Serve 2 ribs with stuffing for each serving. Approximately 300 calories per serving.

SAUERBRATEN

No need to chop, chop, chop for the marinade. The blender does the work in seconds!

¾ cup wine vinegar
¼ cup wine (Rosé or Chianti)
1 onion, sliced
1 green pepper, coarsely chopped
1 large carrot, sliced
1 to 2 cups celery leaves
8 parsley sprigs
2 bay leaves
1 clove garlic
2 teaspoons marjoram
1 teaspoon peppercorns
1 teaspoon salt
1 teaspoon rosemary
1 teaspoon thyme
1 teaspoon basil
¼ teaspoon ginger
3 to 4 pounds boneless beef round
4 or 5 gingersnaps
1 cup dairy sour cream

LIQUEFY all ingredients except meat, gingersnaps and sour cream for 10 seconds. Place meat in glass baking dish or deep bowl and sprinkle lightly with salt and pepper. Pour liquefied ingredients over meat. Cover and refrigerate 48 hours, turning meat at least twice a day. Remove meat from marinade and drain well, reserving marinade. Brown meat well on all sides in Dutch oven. Pour marinade over; cover and simmer 3 to 4 hours or until meat is tender. Remove meat to hot platter and keep warm. Crumble gingersnaps into pan drippings. Blend in sour cream; cook and stir over low heat until smooth. Do not boil. Slice meat and spoon sauce over to serve. Makes 6 servings.

BEEF BURGUNDY

3 onions (3-inch) cut into eighths and sliced
1 cup (½-inch) carrot slices
8 sprigs parsley, no stems
⅓ cup flour
2½ teaspoons salt
½ teaspoon garlic salt
¼ teaspoon pepper
3 pounds boneless beef chuck, cut into 1½-inch cubes
¼ cup butter or margarine
⅓ cup cognac or tomato juice
4 slices bacon, cut into ½-inch pieces
½ teaspoon thyme
1 bay leaf
1 cup Burgundy or tomato juice
8 to 12 small cooked or canned onions
2 cans (4-ounce) sliced mushrooms, drained, or ½ pound fresh mushrooms, sliced and sautéed
6 to 8 servings, hot, buttered, seasoned, cooked noodles

Dry chop onions until coarsely chopped (see page 7 for directions). Dry chop carrots and parsley until coarsely chopped (see page 7 for directions). Reserve. Combine next 4 ingredients; mix. Dredge meat in flour mixture. Heat butter or margarine in large Dutch oven with heat proof handles. Add meat; brown well, turning pieces as needed to brown evenly. Sprinkle remaining flour mixture over meat; mix. Pour cognac, if used, over meat and ignite. If preferred, substitute tomato juice for cognac and omit flaming. Cook bacon pieces and blender chopped vegetables in frypan over low heat until bacon browns; stir in thyme. Pour over meat. Add bay leaf and pour Burgundy or tomato juice over all. Cover; cook in slow oven (325°F.) until meat is tender, about 2¼ hours. Add whole onions and mushrooms; bake vegetables until hot. Serve with noodles. Makes 6 to 8 servings.

SWISS-STYLE GOULASH ON BUTTERED NOODLES

3 (3-inch) onions, cut into eighths and sliced
1 can (8-ounce) tomato sauce
1 clove garlic, sliced
1 tablespoon sugar
2 teaspoons paprika
2 teaspoons Worcestershire sauce
2 teaspoons salt
¼ teaspoon pepper
3 tablespoons butter or margarine
2½ pounds boneless beef chuck, cut into 1½-inch cubes
1 teaspoon dill seed
1½ teaspoons caraway seed
½ pint (1 cup) dairy sour cream
6 to 8 servings hot, buttered, seasoned, cooked noodles

Dry chop onions until coarsely chopped (see page 7 for directions). Set aside. Combine next 7 ingredients in container. **STIR** until garlic is minced, about 3 to 5 seconds. Heat butter or margarine in large frypan. Add beef; brown well, turning pieces as needed to brown evenly. Add onions, tomato mixture, dill and caraway seed; mix and cover. Cook slowly until beef is fork tender, about 2½ hours. Stir sour cream into mixture just before serving. Serve atop hot noodles. Makes about 6 to 8 servings.

GERMAN MEAT BALLS

1 pound ground beef
¼ cup blender-made dry bread crumbs (page 8)
1 teaspoon salt
¼ teaspoon poultry seasoning
¼ cup milk
1 egg
6 parsley sprigs
¼ teaspoon peppercorns
1 (10½-ounce) can beef bouillon
1 (4-ounce) can mushrooms or ½ cup fresh
  mushrooms
1 medium onion, sliced
1 cup dairy sour cream
1 tablespoon flour
½ to 1 teaspoon caraway seed

Place beef, crumbs, salt and poultry seasoning in large bowl. **LIQUEFY** milk, egg, parsley and peppercorns 5 seconds. Pour over beef and mix thoroughly. Shape into 2 dozen meat balls about 1½ inches in diameter. Brown balls in small amount of hot fat, turning frequently to keep them round. **GRATE** bouillon, mushrooms and onion 5 seconds. Pour over meat balls and stir just enough to loosen pan drippings. Simmer 30 minutes. Combine sour cream, flour and caraway. Blend into pan juices and heat to boiling, stirring constantly. Lower heat and simmer 5 minutes. Makes 6 servings.

CHILI CON CARNE

1 can (1-pound 12-ounce) tomatoes
4 medium (2-inch) onions, quartered and sliced
1 clove garlic, sliced
2 teaspoons chili powder, or to taste
2 teaspoons salt
¼ teaspoon pepper
1 tablespoon shortening
1½ pounds ground beef
1 tablespoon flour
1 can (1-pound) kidney beans, drained

Combine tomatoes, onions, garlic, chili powder, salt and pepper in blender container. **MIX** until onions are finely chopped, about 10 to 15 seconds. Stop motor and push ingredients into blades with rubber spatula as needed. Heat shortening in Dutch oven over moderate heat. Add meat and brown. Leave meat in bite-size chunks. Sprinkle flour over meat; mix carefully. Add tomato mixture and beans. Bring to simmering stage. Cover; simmer gently until meat is cooked and flavors blended, about 30 minutes. Makes 6 servings.

VEAL SCALLOPINE

2 pounds veal cutlets
Salt, pepper and flour as needed
¼ cup butter or margarine
½ pound fresh mushrooms, sliced
1 cup dry white wine
1 large onion, sliced
1 tablespoon sugar
1 parsley sprig
¼ teaspoon rosemary
¼ teaspoon marjoram
¼ teaspoon peppercorns

Season veal with salt and pepper and dip in flour. Brown quickly in butter. Add mushrooms and set aside. **LIQUEFY** all remaining ingredients 5 seconds. Pour over meat in skillet. Cover and simmer 15 minutes or until meat is tender. Makes 6 servings.

SWEET-SOUR HAM BALLS

Shown in the photo at the right

2 cups cubed cooked ham
1 small onion, coarsely chopped
1 egg
¼ small green pepper, coarsely chopped
1 teaspoon dry mustard
¼ cup butter or margarine
1 (8-ounce) can sliced pineapple
¼ cup vinegar
2 tablespoons cornstarch
2 tablespoons brown sugar
1 teaspoon dry mustard
½ teaspoon salt
1½ cups water
¾ small green pepper, sliced

SHRED ½ cup cubed ham 10 seconds. Empty into a large bowl. Repeat with remaining ham. **SHRED** egg, onion, chopped green pepper and mustard 20 seconds. Add to ham and mix well. Form into 12 balls, using about 3 tablespoons ham mixture for each ball. Heat butter in large skillet; add ham balls and brown on all sides over medium heat, turning often to keep balls round. Drain pineapple slices, reserve slices and **BLEND** syrup with vinegar, cornstarch, brown sugar, dry mustard and salt for 10 seconds. Remove ham balls to heated platter. Add water to skillet and stir to mix with pan drippings. Add mixture from blender, pineapple slices and green pepper slices. Cook, stirring gently, until clear and thickened. Arrange pineapple slices on platter with ham balls, sauce and green pepper slices over. Makes 4 servings.

SWEDISH MEAT BALLS

¾ pound ground beef chuck
¼ pound ground lean pork
1 cup soft bread crumbs (see page 8 for directions)
¾ cup milk
1 egg
1½ teaspoons salt
¼ teaspoon nutmeg
⅛ teaspoon pepper
½ medium (2-inch) onion, thinly sliced
2 tablespoons shortening
3 tablespoons flour
½ teaspoon dry mustard
2 cups half and half (half milk, half cream)

Combine first 3 ingredients in mixing bowl. Combine ¼ cup milk, egg, 1 teaspoon salt, nutmeg, pepper and onion slices in container. **BLEND,** switching motor on and off until onions are coarsely chopped. Add to meat mixture; mix well. Shape into 24 balls, using a rounded tablespoon of meat mixture for each ball. (Mixture is soft. Wet hands as needed to make shaping easier). Brown balls in hot shortening in large skillet over moderate heat. Turn frequently to brown evenly. Remove meat balls from skillet. Blend flour, remaining ½ teaspoon salt and mustard in pan drippings. Stir in half and half and remaining ½ cup milk. Cook, stirring until thick and smooth. Return meat balls to gravy. Cover; cook until done, about 30 minutes. Turn balls and stir gravy occasionally. Makes 4 servings, 6 meat balls per serving.

MIDGET MEAT BALLS: Shape meat mixture into 40 small balls using a level tablespoon of meat mixture for each ball. Reduce cooking time about 15 minutes. Makes 40 small meat balls.

Sweet-Sour Ham Balls page 84

BLENDER BEEF HASH

See photo below

¼ cup butter or margarine
3 cups chopped pared raw potatoes
1 small onion, sliced
3 cups cubed cooked beef
¼ green pepper, cubed
1½ teaspoons salt
½ cup drippings from meat
Chili sauce and parsley for garnish

Melt butter in 9-inch pie plate. **STIR** 1 cup potatoes and onion 10 seconds. Turn into pie plate. Repeat with remaining potatoes and spread evenly in pie plate. **SHRED** meat, ½ cup at a time, adding green pepper along with last ½ cup of meat. Spread meat evenly over potatoes. Sprinkle with salt and pour drippings over. Cover tightly with foil and bake in hot oven (400°F.) 20 minutes. Uncover and bake 10 to 15 minutes longer or until slightly crisp on top and bottom. Cut wedges to serve and garnish with chili sauce and parsley. Makes 6 servings. To match photo: Bake hash for 20 minutes. Cut tops from 6 medium tomatoes; scoop out insides and fill with hash. Place on baking sheet and return to oven for 10 to 15 minutes.

PORK 'N SWEETS CASSEROLE

6 pork chops, ½-inch thick
4 medium sweet potatoes or yams, cooked, peeled and sliced
1 medium onion, sliced
½ green pepper, cubed
1 cup cider
1 teaspoon salt
1 teaspoon Worcestershire sauce

Brown chops on both sides in skillet; set aside. **SHRED** 3 or 4 slices sweet potato, 1 slice onion, several chunks of green pepper and ¼ cup cider 30 seconds, stopping motor to push ingredients to blades, if necessary. Turn into buttered 2-quart baking dish. (Choose a dish that will be large enough to arrange chops in single layer). **SHRED** remaining potatoes onion, green pepper and cider in amounts given above and add to baking dish. Repeat until all vegetables are ground. Sprinkle with salt and Worcestershire sauce and spread mixture evenly over bottom of pan. Arrange chops over potato mixture, pressing down slightly. Cover tightly and bake in moderate oven (375°F.) about 1½ hours or until chops are fork tender and potatoes are lightly browned on bottom. Remove cover during last 20 minutes of baking to give potatoes a crisp top, if you wish. Makes 6 servings.

Blender Beef Hash

SPANISH PORK TENDERLOIN

1 pound pork tenderloin patties
Salt, pepper and flour as needed
1 (4-ounce) can mushrooms
1 (6-ounce) can tomato paste
1 small onion, sliced
½ green pepper, sliced
½ teaspoon chili powder
1 clove garlic

Season pork with salt and pepper, dip in flour. Brown quickly on both sides in a small amount of hot fat. Drain mushrooms, reserving liquid. **SHRED** mushroom liquid, tomato paste, onion, green pepper, chili powder and garlic 20 seconds. Pour half into a 1½-quart casserole. Add pork patties and mushrooms, then remaining tomato mixture. Cover; bake in slow oven (325°F.) 40 minutes. Uncover and bake 20 minutes longer. Makes 4 servings.

INDIVIDUAL PORK PIES

¾ cup milk
1 egg
2 slices whole wheat bread, torn into several pieces
1 medium onion, sliced
½ teaspoon salt
¾ pound ground smoked ham
½ pound ground lean pork
½ pound ground lean beef

LIQUEFY milk, egg and 1 slice bread 50 seconds. Add remaining bread, onion and salt and **LIQUEFY** 60 seconds. Turn into large mixing bowl; add ham, pork and beef and mix well. Pack lightly into 8 or 9 (3-inch) muffin tins. Bake in moderate oven (350°F.) 1 hour. Makes 8 individual pies.

JAVA PORK KABOBS

2 pounds lean pork, cut in 1-inch cubes
1 orange, thin outer peel and fruit only (discard white portion of peel)
1 lemon, thin outer portion of peel and fruit only
1 small red onion, sliced
2 tablespoons brown sugar
1½ tablespoons soy sauce
1 tablespoon chili powder
3 cloves garlic
¾ teaspoon sugar

MINCE all ingredients, except pork, 10 seconds. Pour into large bowl along with pork and marinate in refrigerator at least 4 hours, stirring several times. String cubes on skewers, leaving small space between each cube. Broil 3 inches from hot coals or source of heat about 15 minutes, turning frequently to brown evenly. Makes 4 servings.

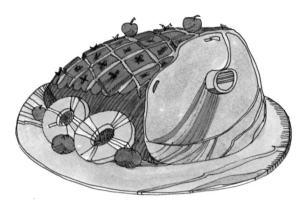

BAKED HAM

Place the ham on a rack in a shallow roasting pan. Insert the point of a meat thermometer into the center of the thickest part of the meat, not touching bone. Bake in slow oven (325°F.). For uncooked ham thermometer should read 160°; about 30 minutes per pound. For fully cooked ham thermometer should read 130°; about 20 minutes per pound. About 30 minutes before ham is cooked, remove the rind, trim off the excess fat and pour off fat from roasting pan. Score the fat covering on the ham in diamonds, insert whole cloves and glaze with Orange Sauce For Ham, page 168.

BAKED STUFFED SPARERIBS

Delicious stuffing, and a nice change from barbecued ribs

2 slabs spareribs (about 2 pounds)
10 slices bread
2 medium onions, coarsely chopped
2 small apples, cored and coarsely chopped
½ cup water
3 stalks celery, coarsely chopped
2 teaspoons salt
1 teaspoon sage
1 teaspoon dry mustard

Place ribs in shallow baking pan. Cover with foil and bake in moderate oven (350°F.) 1 hour. Tear 1 slice of bread into blender container and **CRUMB** 10 seconds, tearing second slice through opening in top while motor is running. Empty into large mixing bowl. Repeat with remaining slices of bread. **SHRED** all remaining ingredients 20 seconds. Add to bread and mix thoroughly. Remove ribs from oven; pour off all fat. Mound stuffing on 1 slab of ribs. Cover with second slab and press firmly over stuffing. Bake 1½ hours longer or until ribs are fork tender. Cut into 2 or 3 rib portions to serve. Makes 4 servings. If desired, spoon Glaze over ribs ½ hour before done.

GLAZE: LIQUEFY ¼ cup brown sugar, 2 tablespoons vinegar and ¼ teaspoon ground cloves 5 seconds.

HAM TIMBALES

2 slices bread, buttered
2 cups cubed cooked ham
¾ cup hot milk
¼ small onion, sliced
1 parsley sprig
4 eggs
2 tablespoons sherry
Dash pepper

Tear 1 slice bread into blender container and **CRUMB** 10 seconds, tearing second slice through opening in top while motor is running. Empty into large bowl. **SHRED** 1 cup ham, milk, onion and parsley 20 seconds. Add to crumbs. **SHRED** 2 eggs and ½ cup ham 10 seconds. Add to bowl. Repeat with remaining ingredients; add to bowl and mix thoroughly. Fill 6 buttered timbale molds or 6-ounce custard cups ⅔ full of ham mixture. Set in pan of hot water and bake in moderate oven (350°F.) 25 to 30 minutes. Cool a few minutes before unmolding onto heated platter. Serve with **MUSHROOM MUSTARD SAUCE:** heat 1 can frozen or condensed mushroom soup with 1 tablespoon dry mustard.

LASAGNE

1 pound ground beef
1 tablespoon shortening
1 can (1-pound 12-ounce) tomatoes
1 cup (½-inch) carrot slices
2 cloves garlic, sliced
1 cup (1-inch) celery slices
1 medium (2-inch) onion, quartered and sliced
2 teaspoons basil
2 teaspoons oregano
1½ teaspoons salt
1 teaspoon rosemary leaf
½ pound lasagne noodles, cooked and drained
1 pint creamed cottage cheese or 1 pound ricotta cheese, sliced
1 package (6-ounce) sliced Mozzarella cheese
½ cup blender-grated Parmesan cheese (see page 6)

Lightly brown meat in hot shortening in heavy frypan over moderate heat. **CHOP** tomatoes, carrots and garlic until coarsely chopped, 8 to 10 seconds. Add next 6 ingredients. **CHOP** vegetables very fine, about 5 seconds. Stop motor and push ingredients into blades with rubber spatula as needed. Pour over meat; mix. Cover; simmer to blend flavors about 45 minutes. Uncover; continue cooking until sauce thickens, about 15 minutes. Spread ⅓ of the sauce over bottom of shallow 2-quart casserole. Top with a layer of noodles, sauce and cheese using ½ of the noodles and cottage or ricotta and Mozzarella cheese and ⅓ of Parmesan cheese. Repeat layers. Top with remaining sauce and Parmesan cheese. Bake in moderate oven (350°F.) until hot and bubbly, 35 to 40 minutes. Cool 10 to 15 minutes before serving. Makes 6 to 8 servings.

ITALIAN SPAGHETTI SAUCE

You can see it in the photo at the right

1 pound ground beef
¼ pound ground lean pork
¼ cup olive oil
1½ cups coarsely chopped tomatoes or 1 (1-pound 13-ounce) can tomatoes
1 cup beef broth or bouillon cube and 1 cup hot water
1 (6-ounce) can tomato paste
½ cup dry red or white wine
½ cup dried or fresh mushrooms
1 medium onion, sliced
1 carrot, sliced
1 stalk celery, sliced
2 cloves garlic
2 bay leaves
2 whole cloves
1 teaspoon thyme
1 teaspoon basil
Hot cooked spaghetti
Parmesan or Romano cheese, blender-grated (page 6)

Cook beef and pork in olive oil in large skillet, stirring constantly until lightly browned and broken up. **MINCE** all remaining ingredients, except spaghetti and cheese, 20 seconds. Pour into skillet with meat. Simmer 1 hour, stirring often. Serve over spaghetti and top with grated cheese. Makes 4 to 6 servings.

JAMBALAYA

1 cup (1-inch) celery slices
1 small (1½-inch) onion, sliced
1 clove garlic, sliced
4 slices bacon, diced
2 tablespoons butter or margarine
½ cup (1-inch) green pepper squares
1 cup (½-inch) fully-cooked ham cubes
3 cups water
1 can (1-pound) tomatoes
1 cup uncooked rice
1½ teaspoons salt
¼ teaspoon leaf thyme
¼ teaspoon hot red pepper sauce
1 bay leaf
2 cans (4½-ounce) deveined shrimp, drained

PURÉE first 3 ingredients, ½ cup at a time, switching motor on and off until vegetables are coarsely chopped. Empty into bowl; repeat as needed. Sauté bacon in heavy frypan over moderate heat until ½ done. Add butter or margarine and chopped vegetables. Cook until vegetables are tender. **PURÉE** green pepper, switching motor on and off until very coarsely chopped; add to cooked vegetables. **CHOP** ham as suggested for vegetables until coarsely chopped. Add ham and next 7 ingredients to frypan; mix. Cover; cook slowly until rice is tender, about 25 minutes. Fold in shrimp; heat. Makes 6 servings.

MEXICAN ENCHILADAS

Corn pancakes are rolled around spicy filling, then topped with a flavorful sauce.

TORTILLAS:
¾ cup whole corn kernels
1¾ cups water
1 egg
¾ cup all-purpose flour
1 teaspoon salt
Olive oil

SHRED corn 45 seconds to 1 minute or until almost as fine as corn meal. Add all remaining ingredients and **GRIND** 15 seconds. Lightly grease a small skillet with olive oil. Pour in ¼ cup tortilla batter; spread evenly over bottom of pan and bake until bottom is brown and top is set. Bake remaining batter, stirring before pouring batter for each tortilla.

FILLING:
¾ pound ground beef
1 tablespoon olive oil
10 pitted ripe olives
6 green onions
1 teaspoon salt
1 clove garlic
¾ cup cubed sharp Cheddar cheese

Cook beef in oil just until lightly browned. Drain on paper towels and place in mixing bowl. **GRATE** olives, onions, salt and garlic 5 seconds, stopping motor once to push ingredients to blades. Set at **GRIND** and add cheese through opening in top while motor is running, about 10 seconds. Turn into bowl with meat and mix well. Place about ¼ cup filling on each tortilla; roll tortilla around filling tightly. Place filled enchilada, seam side down, in rectangular baking dish. Cover and refrigerate while making sauce.

SAUCE:
1 (1-pound) can tomatoes
1 (8-ounce) can tomato sauce
1 large onion, sliced
2 cloves garlic
2 or 3 canned green chilies
1 teaspoon sugar
½ tablespoon chili powder
1 cup cubed sharp Cheddar cheese

LIQUEFY all ingredients except cheese 10 seconds. Pour sauce over enchiladas. **PURÉE** cheese, ½ cup at a time and sprinkle over enchiladas. Bake in moderate oven (350°F.) 30 to 35 minutes. Makes 6 to 8 servings.

NOTE: Enchiladas and sauce may be made ahead, chilled and combined when ready to bake. Increase baking time to 1 hour.

Mexican Enchiladas

Crown Roast of Lamb

CROWN ROAST OF LAMB WITH APPLE RAISIN STUFFING

8 to 16-rib roast of lamb, tied for crown roast
Ground lamb, trimmed from roast
20 slices bread, buttered
4 apples, cored and cubed
2 eggs
1 cup coarsely chopped onion
1 cup coarsely chopped celery
½ cup water
6 parsley sprigs
2 tablespoons mint leaves
1½ teaspoons salt
1 clove garlic
1 cup seedless raisins, plumped
Cherry tomatoes, for garnish

Place roast on rack in shallow pan. Cover tips of ribs with aluminum foil. Roast in slow oven (325°F.) 1 hour. Meanwhile, prepare stuffing. Cook and stir ground lamb in skillet until lightly browned. Drain on paper towels and put in large bowl. Tear 1 slice of bread into blender container and **CRUMB**, tearing second slice of bread into container through opening in top while motor is running, about 10 seconds. Turn into bowl with meat. Repeat until all bread is crumbed. **GRATE** apples and 1 egg 20 seconds. Turn into bowl with crumbs. **SHRED** all remaining ingredients except raisins; add to crumbs along with raisins and mix well. Remove partially cooked roast from oven; pour off all fat. Mound stuffing in center of roast. Insert meat thermometer in center of stuffing. Return to oven and continue to roast until meat thermometer reads 180°. Carefully arrange roast on heated platter. Remove foil from bone tips and garnish with cherry tomatoes, paper frills or blanched mushroom caps. Carve between bones to serve. Plan on 2 rib portions with stuffing per serving.

91

STUFFED LAMB SHOULDER ROAST

1 (4- to 5-pound) lamb shoulder, boned
1 pound bulk pork sausage
3 slices bread
1 egg
1 medium onion, sliced
3 parsley sprigs
1 tablespoon mint leaves
1 carrot, cubed
⅛ teaspoon thyme
1 bay leaf
1 clove garlic, halved
1 cup hot water
1 bouillon cube

Cook sausage in Dutch oven just until pink color is gone and meat is broken up. Drain meat on paper towels and place in large bowl. Tear 1 slice bread into blender container and **CRUMB** 5 seconds. Add to sausage and repeat with remaining bread. **GRATE** egg, onion, parsley and mint leaves 10 seconds and add to sausage; mix thoroughly. Lightly pack stuffing into pocket of lamb roast; fasten open edges with poultry pins or wooden picks and string. Brown stuffed roast in sausage drippings in Dutch oven. Pour off any remaining fat and slip a rack under roast. Add carrot, thyme, bay leaf and garlic. Dissolve bouillon cube in water and pour over roast. Cover and bake in moderate oven (350°F.) 1½ hours. Remove roast, on rack, to warm platter. Skim all fat from pan juices. **LIQUEFY** vegetables and pan juices 5 seconds. Return roast on rack to Dutch oven. Pour liquefied ingredients over and bake 1½ hours longer. Remove picks and string. Serve with sauce. Makes 8 servings.

MARINATED LEG OF LAMB

1 (5-pound) leg of lamb
2 cups red wine
3 onions, sliced
1 carrot, sliced
¼ lemon (thin outer portion of peel and fruit only, discard white portion of peel)
1 tablespoon fresh mint leaves
2 teaspoons salt
2 teaspoons oregano
2 cloves garlic
3 parsley sprigs
¼ teaspoon whole cloves

LIQUEFY all ingredients, except lamb, 10 seconds. Place lamb in deep bowl and pour marinade over. Cover and refrigerate 24 hours, turning meat frequently. To roast, place meat on rack in shallow baking pan. Insert meat thermometer in center of the thickest part of flesh. (Tip of thermometer should not touch bone). Roast in slow oven (325°F.) until meat thermometer reads 165° to 170°. About ½ hour before roast is done, pour off all fat and pour marinade over meat. To serve, remove roast to warm platter. Heat marinade to boiling, stirring to mix with pan drippings. Serve marinade as sauce. Makes 8 to 10 servings.

LAMB KABOBS

1 medium onion, quartered
¼ cup parsley sprigs
1 clove garlic
½ teaspoon peppercorns
¼ cup salad oil
1 lemon, peeled
1 teaspoon salt
1 teaspoon marjoram
1 teaspoon thyme
2 pounds lean boneless lamb, cut in 1-inch cubes
Green pepper chunks, red pepper chunks, onion chunks

GRIND onion, parsley, garlic, peppercorns, oil, lemon, and spices 30 seconds. Place lamb in deep bowl; pour marinade over and marinate 2 or 3 hours at room temperature or refrigerate overnight. Lift lamb from marinade and string on skewers with green and red pepper chunks and onion chunks. Broil over hot coals until desired doneness. (Best when served medium rare). Makes 6 servings.

INDIAN LAMB SKEWERS

2 pounds lean boneless lamb, cut in 1½-inch cubes
2 large onions, sliced
1 (1-pound) can apricot halves
¼ cup brown sugar
3 tablespoons vinegar
2 tablespoons curry powder
1 teaspoon salt
½ garlic clove
Dash of cayenne

MINCE all ingredients, except lamb, 15 seconds. Pour into saucepan and bring to boiling. Place meat in large bowl and pour hot mixture over it. Mix well; cover and marinate in the refrigerator 24 hours. Thread meat on skewers, leaving a small space between pieces. Broil 3 or 4 inches from source of heat for 20 minutes or until desired doneness, basting with marinade while broiling. Turn meat often to brown evenly. Makes 4 servings. These kabobs are nice served with hot cooked rice, sautéed zucchini slices, a mixed green salad and blender-made ice cream or sherbet (page 76).

LAMB CURRY

2 pounds boneless lamb cubes
¼ cup flour
1½ teaspoons salt
2 tablespoons cooking oil or shortening
1 can (1-pound) tomatoes
1 clove garlic, sliced
1½ cups coarsely chopped apple
1 medium (2-inch) onion, sliced thin
1 tablespoon brown sugar
1 tablespoon curry powder
½ teaspoon dry mustard
¼ teaspoon ginger
Hot fluffly cooked rice

Dredge lamb cubes in flour and salt. Brown in hot oil or shortening in heavy frypan over moderate heat, turning meat as needed to brown on all sides. Sprinkle with any remaining flour mixture. **CHOP** tomatoes, garlic, apple and onion until finely chopped, about 10 seconds. Stop motor and push ingredients into blades with rubber spatula as needed; pour over meat mixture. Add remaining ingredients except rice; mix carefully. Cover; cook slowly until meat is tender, 1½ to 2 hours, stirring occasionally. Serve with fluffy rice. Makes 6 servings.

CHICKEN FRICASSEE

You and your blender can make this sauce match that of any chef!

3 large leeks or 6 large green onions
2 stalks celery
2 carrots
8 chicken legs and thighs
1 teaspoon salt
10 parsley sprigs
½ cup cognac
1 tablespoon flour
1 cup half and half (half milk, half cream)

Wash vegetables; cut in chunks and place in casserole that has a tight-fitting lid. Arrange chicken over vegetables and sprinkle with salt and parsley. Pour cognac over. Cover and bake in slow oven (325°F.) 1 hour and 15 minutes or until chicken is tender. Remove chicken to heated platter and keep warm. Pour all drippings and vegetables from casserole into blender container. Add flour and **MINCE** 10 seconds. Pour into skillet; cook and stir until thick. Gradually blend in half and half; cook and stir until piping hot, but do not boil. Pour over chicken to serve. Makes 4 to 6 servings.

CHICKEN CROQUETTES

4 to 5 slices bread
¾ cup milk or meat stock
1 large onion, sliced
¼ cup butter or margarine, softened
¼ cup flour
½ teaspoon salt
¼ teaspoon pepper
2 parsley sprigs
2½ cups cubed cooked chicken
1 egg, slightly beaten
2 tablespoons water
Blender-made dry bread crumbs as needed (page 8)

Tear one slice of bread into blender container and **CRUMB** 5 seconds. Empty into a 1-cup measure. Repeat until you have 1 cup of crumbs. **GRIND** milk, onion, butter, flour, salt, pepper and parsley 20 seconds. Pour into 2-quart saucepan and cook and stir over low heat until very thick. Set aside to cool. **GRATE** chicken, ½ cup at a time, and add to cream sauce. Mix chicken and cream sauce thoroughly and chill. Shape chilled mixture into 8 cones, balls or patties, using about ⅓ cup for each croquette. Chill several hours. About ½ hour before serving time, dip croquettes in mixture of egg and water, then in crumbs. Let dry ½ hour. Fry in deep hot fat (375°F.) Drain on paper towels. Serve with Spicy Tomato Sauce (page 168), peas or cut green beans in cream sauce or mushroom sauce made by heating canned mushroom soup. Makes 8 croquettes, 4 dinner-size or 8 luncheon-size servings.

CHICKEN NOODLE CASSEROLE

This quick and easy casserole has pretty layers. Great for pot luck and covered dish suppers.

8 ounces egg noodles
2 cups cubed cooked chicken
¼ cup butter or margarine, softened
1 (10½-ounce) can tomato soup
½ cup coarsely chopped celery
½ cup Rosé wine
½ green pepper, coarsely chopped
¼ cup coarsely chopped onion
1 teaspoon salt
3 parsley sprigs
1 slice bread, torn into several pieces
2 tablespoons cubed Cheddar cheese

Cook noodles in boiling salted water according to package directions. Drain well and arrange over bottom of buttered 1½-quart casserole. Scatter chicken over noodles and dot with butter. **LIQUEFY** soup, celery, wine, green pepper, onion, salt and parsley 10 seconds. Pour over chicken and noodles. **CRUMB** bread and cheese together 10 seconds. Sprinkle over chicken. Bake in moderate oven (350°F.) 30 minutes or until lightly browned and bubbly. Makes 6 to 8 servings.

CHICKEN CACCIATORE

1 frying chicken (3-pound), cut in serving pieces
¼ cup butter or margarine
1¼ teaspoons salt
1 can (1-pound) Italian-style tomatoes
1 medium onion (2-inch), quartered and sliced
½ cup (1-inch) green pepper squares
1 small clove garlic, sliced
1 teaspoon oregano
½ teaspoon basil
⅛ teaspoon pepper
2 tablespoons flour
2 tablespoons sherry, optional
1 can (4-ounce) sliced mushrooms, drained

Brown chicken pieces in heavy frypan in butter or margarine over moderate heat. Turn pieces as needed to brown evenly. Drain off excess fat. Sprinkle 1 teaspoon salt over chicken pieces. Combine next 9 ingredients and remaining ¼ teaspoon salt in container. **CHOP** until onion and green pepper are coarsely chopped, about 5 seconds. Pour over chicken. Sprinkle mushrooms over top. Bring to simmering stage. Cover; cook slowly until chicken is fork tender, about 50 to 60 minutes. Makes 4 servings.

ROAST ROCK CORNISH GAME HENS WITH CELERY STUFFING

These beautifully glazed little birds make an elegant entrée for your most important dinners. Serve with buttered asparagus, soufflé potatoes, bibb lettuce and curly endive salad. Finish off with Ginger Cream (page 70) and demitasse for dessert.

4 (1-pound) rock cornish game hens, fresh or frozen, thawed
2 stalks celery, coarsely chopped
1 small onion, sliced
1½ cups sliced mushrooms, fresh or canned
¼ cup butter or margarine
2 slices bread
Salt and pepper
⅓ cup melted butter or margarine
¼ cup bouillon or canned consommé
¼ cup corn syrup

GRATE celery and onion 20 seconds. Empty into skillet. Add mushrooms and the ¼ cup butter. Cook and stir over medium heat 5 minutes. Tear 1 slice of bread and **CRUMB** 10 seconds tearing second slice of bread through opening in top, while motor is running. Empty bread into skillet and mix with vegetables. Rinse hens with cold water and drain. Season hens inside and out with salt and pepper. Stuff lightly with celery mixture. Place breast up on a rack in baking pan. Brush with melted butter. Roast in moderate over (350°F.) 1½ hours. During last hour baste with combined bouillon and syrup. Makes 4 servings.

BOMBAY CHICKEN CURRY

Photo at right

1 frying chicken (3-pound), cut in serving pieces
¼ cup flour
1 teaspoon salt
⅛ teaspoon pepper
2 tablespoons butter or margarine
½ cup light raisins
1 cup water
1 medium onion (2-inch), quartered and sliced
1 clove garlic, sliced
¼ cup chutney, optional
1 chicken bouillon cube
2 teaspoons curry powder
¼ teaspoon ginger
2 medium-size apples, peeled, cored, and sliced
6 servings hot fluffy cooked rice
¼ cup toasted slivered almonds, optional

Dredge chicken pieces in mixture of flour, salt and pepper. Melt butter or margarine in heavy frypan over moderate heat; add chicken and brown well, turning pieces as needed to brown evenly. Sprinkle any remaining flour mixture over chicken; add raisins. Combine next 7 ingredients in blender container; **CHOP** until onion is finely chopped, about 5 seconds. Add apples; **CHOP** until coarsely chopped, about 5 seconds. Stop motor and push ingredients into blades with rubber spatula as needed. Pour over chicken. Cover; bring to simmering stage and cook slowly until chicken is fork tender, 50 to 60 minutes. Keep chicken warm in Electric Chafing Dish. Serve with rice; sprinkle with almonds, if desired. Makes 6 servings.

BARBECUED CHICKEN

¼ cup water
¼ cup vinegar
2 tablespoons chili sauce
1 (1-inch wide) strip of green pepper, sliced
3 green onions, sliced
1 teaspoon salt
1 teaspoon paprika
1 teaspoon Worcestershire sauce
½ teaspoon liquid sugar substitute
½ teaspoon chili powder
¼ teaspoon dry mustard
1 clove garlic
1 (2½-pound) frying chicken, cut up or 2 (1¼-pound) broilers, quartered

GRIND all ingredients, except chicken, 20 seconds. Arrange chicken in baking pan; pour sauce over. Bake in moderate oven (375°F.) about 1 hour or until fork tender. Makes 4 servings, approximately 125 calories per serving.

Bombay Chicken Curry

ROAST TURKEY WITH GIBLET STUFFING

See photo at right

1 (10- to 12-pound) turkey
½ cup celery leaves
1 teaspoon salt
5 parsley sprigs

GIBLET STUFFING:
20 slices bread, lightly buttered
3 stalks celery, coarsely chopped
2 medium onions, sliced
¼ cup butter or margarine
Cooked giblets, coarsely chopped
1½ teaspoons salt
10 parsley sprigs
¼ teaspoon sage
¼ teaspoon marjoram
¼ teaspoon rosemary
½ cup milk

GRAVY:
1¼ cups drippings from roasting turkey
½ cup flour
1 teaspoon salt
3 cups liquid from cooking giblets

If turkey is frozen, thaw it the day before roasting and remove giblets. Simmer in enough water to cover turkey neck and giblets, celery leaves, salt and parsley; until fork tender. Strain liquid and refrigerate. Remove meat from neck and **GRATE** coarsely along with giblets. Refrigerate for use in stuffing.

STUFFING: Tear 1 slice of bread into container and **CRUMB** 10 seconds adding another slice, through opening in top, while motor is running. Empty into a large bowl. Repeat for remainder of bread. **SHRED** 1 stalk of celery 10 seconds. Empty into a large skillet. Repeat with remainder of celery. **SHRED** ⅓ of onion 10 seconds. Repeat with remaining onion. Empty into skillet with celery. Add ¼ cup of butter to skillet and cook and stir over medium heat 5 minutes. Pour into bowl with bread crumbs. **GRATE** ½ cup of giblets and neck meat, salt and parsley 10 seconds. Empty into bowl with bread crumbs. Repeat with remainder of giblets. Add sage, marjoram, rosemary and milk to bread. Mix thoroughly. Add water depending on moistness desired in stuffing. Makes about 10 cups stuffing.

Rinse body and neck cavities of thawed turkey with cold water. Drain and salt lightly. Pack stuffing lightly into cavities. Fasten neck skin with a poultry pin. Fold wings akimbo. Fasten legs of turkey according to packer's directions. Place stuffed turkey on a rack in a shallow roasting pan, breast side up. Brush with melted butter. Cover lightly with a tent of aluminum foil. Roast in slow oven (325°F.) for 3 to 3½ hours. A meat thermometer, inserted in thickest part of the thigh, should register 185°.

GRAVY: Pour or skim fat from drippings in pan. **LIQUEFY** 1¼ cups of drippings, flour, salt and liquid from cooking giblets 5 seconds. Pour into a large saucepan. Cook and stir until gravy is thick and boiling. Season to taste. Makes about 16 servings.

HALIBUT CREOLE

½ green pepper, coarsely chopped
2 stalks celery, sliced
2 (2-inch) pieces lemon peel
¼ lemon, peeled
2 peppercorns
1 cup tomatoes, fresh or canned
1 green onion, sliced
2 teaspoons liquid sugar substitute
¼ teaspoon basil
¼ teaspoon oregano
½ pound halibut, fresh or frozen, thawed

GRATE green pepper, celery, lemon peel and fruit and peppercorns 10 seconds. Pour into saucepan. **GRATE** tomatoes, green onion, sugar substitute, basil and oregano 10 seconds. Add to saucepan and cook 5 minutes. Pour half into shallow baking dish. Arrange halibut over. Cover with remaining tomato sauce. Bake in slow oven (325°F.) 20 to 30 minutes or until fish flakes with a fork. Makes 2 servings, approximately 150 calories per serving.

BAKED STUFFED TROUT

1 (2 or 3-pound) trout, cleaned and boned, or 2 to 3 (12 to 16-ounce) trout, cleaned
Salt, lemon juice as needed
3 slices bread, buttered
¼ pound fresh mushrooms, sliced
1 (1 x 2-inch) strip lemon peel
½ stalk celery, sliced
3 parsley sprigs
1 teaspoon chopped chives
½ teaspoon salt
⅛ teaspoon pepper
Dash nutmeg
Lemon slices and parsley for garnish

Place fish on buttered rack or on buttered foil in a shallow baking pan. Season cavity or cavities with salt and lemon juice and fill with Stuffing. Fasten with skewers or wooden picks and string. Brush with melted butter. Bake in hot oven (400°F.) about 15 to 20 minutes per pound. Fish will flake easily with a fork when done.

STUFFING: Tear 1 slice of bread into blender container and **CRUMB** 10 seconds, tearing second slice into container through opening in top while motor is running. Turn into large bowl. **CRUMB** third slice of bread 10 seconds, adding mushrooms through opening in top while motor is running. Add to bread in bowl. **GRATE** all remaining ingredients, except trout and garnish ingredients, 10 seconds. Add to bowl and mix thoroughly. Makes 2 to 3 servings. Serve on heated platter garnished with lemon slices and watercress or parsley.

SHRIMP CURRY

1 fresh coconut
1 apple, cored and quartered
1 medium onion, sliced
½ cup milk
¼ cup flour
1 tablespoon curry powder
1 teaspoon salt
⅛ lemon (thin yellow portion of peel and fruit only, discard white portion of peel)
1 pound peeled and deveined shrimp, cooked

Puncture coconut and pour coconut milk into blender container. Remove shell and brown membrane from coconut meat and put ½ cup small pieces of coconut into blender container. **SHRED** with all remaining ingredients, except shrimp, 30 seconds. Pour into 2-quart saucepan; add shrimp. Cook and stir over medium heat until hot and thick, about 20 minutes. Lower heat if mixture starts to stick to bottom of pan. Serve over hot cooked rice with a variety of condiments. Makes 4 servings.

NOTE: 2 cups cooked cubed lamb or chicken may be substituted for shrimp.

If smooth texture is preferred, **GRATE** coconut meat 5 seconds, then soak in coconut milk 1 hour. Strain milk through cheesecloth, discard coconut and use milk as above.

DEVILED CRAB

3 hard-cooked eggs, quartered
1½ cups milk or half and half (half milk, half cream)
3 tablespoons flour
3 tablespoons butter or margarine
1 teaspoon salt
2 teaspoons prepared mustard
⅛ teaspoon pepper
1 teaspoon Worcestershire sauce
2 dashes hot red pepper sauce
¼ cup (1-inch) green pepper squares
½ medium (2-inch) onion, sliced and quartered
2 packages (6-ounce) frozen crabmeat, thawed
⅓ cup buttered bread crumbs (directions page 8)

Add eggs to container. Turn speed to **BLEND** and switch motor on and off as needed to coarsely chop eggs. Turn eggs into bowl; save. Combine all ingredients except eggs, crabmeat and crumbs in container. **BLEND** until green pepper and onion are coarsely chopped, about 5 seconds. Pour into saucepan. Cook over medium heat until thickened, stirring constantly. Fold in crabmeat and eggs. Spoon into 4 to 6 buttered individual baking dishes or shells. Sprinkle with bread crumbs. Bake in moderate oven (350°F.) until bubbly hot and lightly browned, 20 to 25 minutes. Makes 4 to 6 servings.

TASTY TUNA TURNOVERS

PASTRY:
6 tablespoons shortening
1¼ cups sifted all-purpose flour
1½ teaspoons salt
4 to 5 tablespoons water

STIR shortening, flour and salt 10 seconds. Scrape down sides of blender container and push ingredients to blades. **STIR** 15 seconds longer. Turn into mixing bowl or onto large piece of waxed paper. Make a hole in center of flour mixture; put 3 tablespoons of water in hole. Push flour into a ball over water. Repeat with remaining water. Let ball of pastry rest 15 minutes. Roll pastry out on lightly floured surface to 8 x 16-inch rectangle. Cut into 8 squares 4 x 4-inches each. Arrange squares on buttered baking sheet.

FILLING:
1 (10½-ounce) can cream of mushroom soup
1 (7-ounce) can tuna, drained and flaked
¼ small onion, sliced
¼ stalk celery, sliced
2 parsley sprigs
½ teaspoon oregano
¼ teaspoon tarragon

GRIND half the can of soup and all remaining ingredients 20 seconds. Place about ¼ cup tuna mixture in center of each pastry square. Moisten edges with water and fold pastry over to form triangle. Seal edges with tines of fork. Bake in hot oven (400°F.) 20 minutes. Serve with curry sauce made by heating remaining ½ can of soup with ⅓ cup milk and 1 teaspoon curry powder. Makes 8 turnovers.

BAKED MACARONI AND CHEESE

Rich, flavorful and ready in no time at all!

2 slices white bread
1½ cups hot milk
½ cup cubed Cheddar cheese
2 tablespoons butter or margarine
¼ teaspoon salt
3 eggs
1 (2-ounce) jar pimiento
¼ green pepper, sliced
¼ small onion, sliced
8 ounces macaroni, cooked and drained

Tear 1 slice of bread into blender container and **CRUMB** 10 seconds, tearing second slice into container through opening in top while motor is running. Empty into a large bowl. **LIQUEFY** hot milk, cheese, butter and salt 20 seconds, adding eggs through opening in top while motor is running. If necessary, STOP BLENDER, use rubber spatula to keep mixture around processing blades. Cover and continue to process at **LIQUEFY**. Add pimiento, green pepper and onion and **GRATE** 5 seconds. Combine with bread crumbs and macaroni and mix lightly. Spoon into buttered 9 x 5 x 3-inch loaf pan and bake in moderate oven (350°F.) 1 hour or until firm and brown. Cool in pan 10 minutes. Turn out onto warm platter. Slice and serve with Spicy Tomato Sauce (page 168). Makes 8 servings.

NOTE: you may bake macaroni and cheese in 9 x 13 x 2-inch pan for 45 minutes and then cut squares to serve.

GOLDEN SOUFFLÉ

2 eggs, separated
1 green onion, sliced
¼ teaspoon salt
¼ teaspoon Worcestershire sauce
½ cup hot milk
2 tablespoons butter or margarine, softened
2 slices rye bread, torn into small pieces
½ cup cubed sharp Cheddar cheese

Beat egg whites with rotary or electric beater until stiff. **STIR** egg yolks, green onion, salt and Worcestershire sauce 10 seconds. Stir milk and butter together. Set on **GRIND** and add milk, butter, bread and cheese to egg yolk mixture through opening in top while motor is running, about 30 seconds or until smooth. STOP MOTOR, scrape down sides of blender container and push ingredients to center with rubber spatula, if necessary. **GRIND** 5 seconds longer. Pour cheese mixture over egg whites and gently fold in until blended. Pour into buttered 1-quart casserole. Bake in moderate oven (350°F.) 25 to 30 minutes. Serve immediately. Makes 4 servings. Garnish with parsley sprigs.

CHEESE AND EGG PUFFS

SAUCE:
¼ cup butter or margarine
1 (15-ounce) can tomato sauce
1 medium onion, sliced
½ green pepper, coarsely chopped
2 teaspoons flour
2 teaspoons sugar
2 (4-ounce) cans sliced mushrooms, drained

PUFFS:
¾ cup sifted all-purpose flour
1½ teaspoons baking powder
½ teaspoon salt
½ teaspoon onion salt
¾ cup cubed Cheddar cheese
6 eggs

SAUCE: Heat butter in saucepan. **PURÉE** tomato sauce, onion, green pepper, flour and sugar 15 seconds. Add to saucepan along with mushrooms. Cook and stir over low heat until thick. Simmer 2 minutes.

PUFFS: Sift together flour, baking powder, salt and onion salt. **PURÉE** cheese 10 seconds and mix with flour. **GRIND** eggs 60 seconds. STOP MOTOR, scrape down sides of blender container with rubber spatula; **GRIND** 60 seconds longer. Add to flour and cheese and fold in only until blended. Drop ¼ cup batter onto hot buttered griddle for each puff and bake both sides. Top with sauce. Makes 4 to 6 servings.

EGG FOO YUNG

Almost as easy as opening a package!

6 eggs
¼ cup water chestnuts, coarsely chopped
½ green pepper, sliced
1 stalk celery, sliced
¼ cup fresh mushrooms or 1 (4-ounce) can mushrooms, drained
¼ cup bamboo shoots
1 teaspoon salt
6 peppercorns
¾ cup cubed cooked chicken or 1 (5-ounce) jar cooked chicken, cubed
¼ cup butter, margarine or shortening

GRATE 2 eggs and water chestnuts 10 seconds; pour into a large bowl. **GRATE** remaining eggs and all remaining ingredients except butter 15 seconds. Add to bowl and mix well. Heat butter in large skillet. Pour in ¼ cup egg mixture for each patty. Fry over medium heat, turning once, until nicely browned. Makes 8 patties. Serve with Fugi Sauce.

FUGI SAUCE: LIQUEFY ¾ cup water, 1 tablespoon cornstarch, 1 tablespoon sugar, 1 tablespoon vinegar and 1 teaspoon dry mustard 2 seconds. Turn into saucepan and cook and stir about 5 minutes, until clear and thick.

CHEESE RAREBIT

1 cup milk, scalded
1 pound Cheddar cheese, in ½-inch cubes
1 thin (⅛-inch) onion slice, (1½-inch diameter), quartered
2 tablespoons flour
1½ teaspoons Worcestershire sauce
½ teaspoons dry mustard
Dash cayenne

Pour hot milk into container; turn speed to **GRATE** and add cheese cubes through top opening, one at a time, blending until smooth. Add remaining ingredients; **GRATE** until smooth, about 5 seconds. Stop motor; push ingredients into blades with rubber spatula as needed. Cook in heavy saucepan over low heat, stirring constantly, until thickened. Makes about 2½ cups sauce.

MEXICAN RAREBIT: Increase onion to 2 slices and add ½ teaspoon chili powder to cheese mixture before blending. Fold 1 medium tomato, diced, and ½ cup diced green pepper into hot rarebit; heat. Makes about 3¼ cups sauce.

RANCH-STYLE OMELET

½ cup Cheddar cheese cubes (½-inch)
6 eggs
⅓ cup milk or half and half (half milk, half cream)
½ teaspoon salt
⅛ teaspoon white pepper
2 (⅛-inch) onion slices (2-inches diameter), quartered
¼ cup (1-inch) green pepper squares
2 tablespoons butter or margarine

CRUMB cheese, switching motor on and off until chopped moderately fine, about 10 seconds; pour into bowl. Stop motor and push ingredients into blades with rubber spatula as needed. **BLEND** next 6 ingredients until onion and green pepper are coarsely chopped, 8 to 10 seconds. Stop motor as needed and push ingredients into blades. Melt butter or margarine in large frypan over low heat; add egg mixture to pan. Run spatula around edge of omelet during cooking and lift omelet slightly while cooking to let uncooked egg flow underneath. When omelet is soft cooked on top, sprinkle grated cheese over surface. Crease omelet in center; fold in half. Serve plain or with favorite tomato sauce. Makes 3 to 4 servings.

SCRAMBLED EGGS

Cook slowly and carefully for a light, lovely texture

6 eggs
⅓ cup milk or half and half (half milk, half cream)
½ teaspoon salt
¼ teaspoon white pepper
2 tablespoons butter or margarine

WHIP eggs, milk, salt and pepper 5 seconds. Heat butter in skillet or top of double boiler until hot but not sizzling. Pour in eggs and cook over medium heat or boiling water. As eggs begin to set, stir cooked portion away from sides and bottom of pan and push to center. Continue to stir until mixed and soft, but not runny. Remove from heat and serve immediately. Makes 4 servings.

VARIATIONS

Follow above recipe and change as follows:

CHEESE SCRAMBLED EGGS: GRATE ½ cup cubed sharp Cheddar cheese and sprinkle over eggs as they cook.

CURRY SCRAMBLED EGGS: Add ¾ teaspoon curry powder to eggs before whipping.

HAM SCRAMBLED EGGS: CHOP 1 cup cubed cooked ham, ½ cup at a time, 10 seconds and add to skillet along with butter. Add eggs and cook as above.

ONION SCRAMBLED EGGS: CHOP 3 sliced green onions 10 seconds and add to skillet along with butter and margarine. Add eggs and cook as above.

SPICY-SAUCED DEVILED EGGS

6 hard-cooked eggs
2 tablespoons Blender Mayonnaise (page 154)
2 teaspoons lemon juice
1 teaspoon dry mustard
1 teaspoon Worcestershire sauce
½ thin slice onion
½ gherkin pickle
Spicy Tomato Sauce (page 168)

Peel eggs and halve lengthwise. Remove yolks and **PURÉE** with all remaining ingredients except egg whites 10 seconds. Spoon yolk mixture into egg whites. Pour Spicy Tomato Sauce into a heatproof serving dish and arrange eggs in sauce. Cover and heat over low heat until eggs are hot and sauce is bubbly. Makes 4 to 6 servings.

QUICHE LORRAINE

CRUST:
1 cup flour
½ teaspoon onion salt
⅛ teaspoon basil
4 tablespoons shortening
2 to 3 tablespoons cold water

FILLING:
8 ounces Swiss Cheese, cubed
6 slices bacon, crisp-cooked
2 cups half and half (half milk, half cream)
4 eggs
1 tablespoon cornstarch
½ teaspoon salt
¼ teaspoon freshly ground nutmeg
Dash cayenne pepper
2 tablespoons grated Parmesan cheese

GRIND flour, onion salt, basil and shortening 10 seconds. STOP MOTOR, scrape down sides of container with rubber spatula and push to center. **GRIND** 5 seconds longer. Turn mixture out onto waxed paper or plastic wrap. Make a hole in the center and pour in 1 tablespoon water. Put hands under paper and push flour into a ball around water. Repeat with remaining water. Wrap ball of dough in paper and let rest 15 minutes. Roll pastry out on lightly floured surface. Fit into a 9-inch pie pan and flute the edge.

PURÉE cheese, ½ cup at a time, 10 seconds. Empty into prepared pie crust. Repeat with remaining cheese. **CRUMB** bacon 10 seconds. Empty into pie crust with cheese. Spread and mix cheese and bacon evenly in crust. **WHIP** half and half, eggs, cornstarch, salt, nutmeg and cayenne 10 seconds. Pour over cheese-bacon mixture. Sprinkle Parmesan cheese over top. Bake in moderate oven (375°F.) 40 minutes. Let stand 10 minutes before serving.

Quiche Lorraine

FRITTERS & DOUGHNUTS

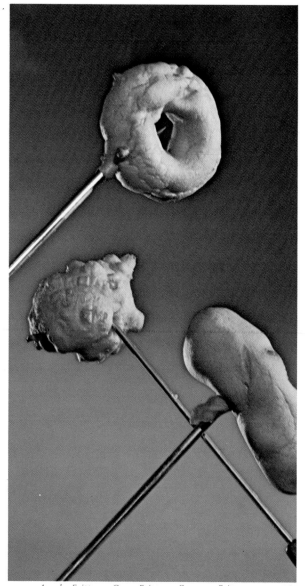

Fritters and doughnuts, all puffy and golden, are wonderfully good eating!

Fruit fritters make great desserts served hot and crispy, dusted with confectioners' sugar or topped with a fruity sauce. Vegetable fritters also add interest to any meal. Doughnuts are fun foods for folks of all ages and, like fritters, they're fun to make the blender way.

Try the recipes that follow. They all make tender scrumptious treats.

Apple Fritters, Corn Fritters, Banana Fritters page 103

FRITTER BATTER
FOR SEAFOOD AND VEGETABLES

1½ cups sifted flour
1 tablespoon sugar
1½ teapoons baking powder
½ teaspoon salt
¼ teaspoon paprika
2 eggs
¾ cup milk
1 tablespoon cooking oil

Sift first 5 ingredients. **CREAM** remaining ingredients in blender container until well mixed, 3 to 5 seconds. Add dry ingredients; **STIR** just until smooth, 5 to 8 seconds. Stop motor and push ingredients into blades with rubber spatula as needed. Makes about 1½ cups batter.

CORN FRITTERS: Prepare Fritter Batter For Seafood and Vegetables (recipe above), increasing flour to 1¾ cups. Stir in 1 can (12-ounce) kernel corn, well drained, or 1 cup cooked corn into batter. Drop tablespoonfuls of mixture, a few at a time, into deep hot oil (375°F.). Brown, turning once, about 4 minutes. Drain on paper toweling. Serve hot with syrup, a fruit sauce, gravy or confectioners' sugar. Makes about 4 servings.

CORN AND BACON FRITTERS: Prepare Corn Fritters (recipe above) and fold ⅓ to ½ cup crisp-cooked bacon bits into batter just before frying. Serve with syrup or applesauce.

FRIED SHRIMP: Dip large, cooked, cleaned and deveined shrimp into Fritter Batter for Seafood and Vegetables (recipe above). Drain and fry, a few at a time, in deep hot fat (375°F.) until golden brown, about 4 minutes, turning once. Drain on paper toweling. Serve hot with favorite seafood sauce (pages 169 and 170 for recipes). Makes batter for about 2 pounds large size shrimp.

FRITTER BATTER FOR FRUITS: Follow recipe for Fritter Batter For Seafood and Vegetables (recipe at left) and change as follows. Increase sugar to 3 tablespoons, substitute melted butter or margarine for oil and add ½ teaspoon vanilla. Makes about 1½ cups batter.

APPLE FRITTERS: Prepare Fritter Batter for Fruits (recipe above). Peel and core 4 to 5 medium-size apples; cut crosswise into ½-inch slices. Lightly dust apple slices with flour. Dip into batter; drain. Fry a few rings at a time in deep hot oil (375°F.) until a golden brown on both sides, about 4 minutes, turning once. Drain on paper toweling. If desired, serve with a fruit sauce or sprinkle with confectioners' or cinnamon sugar. Makes about 4 servings.

BANANA FRITTERS: Prepare Fritter Batter for Fruits (recipe above). Cut 6 small-size bananas in half lengthwise and crosswise. Dip pieces into lemon juice or rum; drain and prepare as for Apple Fritters (recipe above). Serve with favorite lemon, rum or chocolate sauce (pages 171 and 172) or sprinkle with confectioners' or cinnamon sugar. Makes about 6 servings.

PINEAPPLE FRITTERS: Prepare Fritter Batter for Fruits (above). Drain 10 to 12 small slices canned pineapple on paper toweling. Cut pineapple slices in half, if desired. Dip into batter; drain and fry in deep hot oil (375°F.) until a golden brown, about 4 minutes, turning once. Drain on paper toweling. Serve hot, sprinkled with confectioners' sugar or with Orange Sauce (page 172).

SPICY DOUGHNUTS

4 cups sifted flour
4 teaspoons baking powder
1 cup sugar
1 teaspoon salt
¾ teaspoon cinnamon
½ teaspoon nutmeg
3 eggs
⅔ cup milk
¼ cup room temperature butter or margarine
1½ teaspoons vanilla
Cooking oil for frying

Combine flour, baking powder, ½ cup sugar, salt and spices; sift into mixing bowl. Combine eggs, milk, remaining ½ cup sugar, butter or margarine and vanilla in container. **BLEND** until smooth, 50 to 60 seconds. Stop motor; push ingredients into blades with rubber spatula as needed. Add liquids to dry ingredients stirring until dry ingredients are moistened. Turn onto lightly floured board. Roll ½-inch thick; cut with floured 2½-inch doughnut cutter. Fry in deep hot oil (375°F.) until doughnuts are done and brown, about 3 minutes, turning doughnuts once. Fry doughnut holes 2 minutes. Drain doughnuts and holes on paper toweling. Dust with cinnamon sugar, if desired, or frost with Chocolate Butter Cream Frosting (page 52) and sprinkle with blender-chopped pecans (chopping directions page 7). Makes about 2½ dozen doughnuts.

ORANGE POTATO DOUGHNUTS

4½ cups sifted flour
4½ teaspoons baking powder
1¼ teaspoons salt
1 teaspoon nutmeg or mace
1¼ cups sugar
3 eggs
1 square (1-inch) orange rind, cut into strips
1 cup instant mashed potatoes (page 193)
¼ cup room temperature butter or margarine
1½ teaspoons vanilla
1½ cups milk
Cooking oil for frying

Combine first 4 ingredients and ½ cup sugar; sift into bowl. Combine eggs and orange rind in container; **MINCE** until orange rind is finely chopped, 10 to 12 seconds. Add potatoes, butter or margarine, vanilla, remaining sugar and milk. **BLEND** until smooth, 40 to 50 seconds. Stop motor; push ingredients into blades with rubber spatula as needed. Make a well in center of dry ingredients; add liquids, stirring during addition. Mix just until dry ingredients are moistened. Turn dough onto lightly floured board. Roll ½ inch thick; cut with floured 2½-inch doughnut cutter. Fry in deep hot oil (375°F.) until doughnuts are done and brown, about 3 minutes, turning doughnuts once. Fry doughnut holes until done and brown, about 2 minutes. Drain doughnuts and holes on paper toweling. Serve plain or dust with granulated or confectioners' sugar while warm. Makes about 2½ dozen doughnuts.

BANANA NUT DOUGHNUTS

2½ cups sifted flour
2 teaspoons baking powder
½ teaspoon soda
1 teaspoon salt
¾ teaspoon nutmeg
¼ teaspoon cinnamon
⅔ cup pecan halves
2 eggs
¼ cup sour milk or buttermilk
½ cup sugar
2 tablespoons soft shortening
1 teaspoon vanilla
1 cup sliced (¼-inch) banana (about 1 large banana)

Combine first 6 ingredients; sift into mixing bowl. **CHOP** pecans, ⅓ cup at a time, switching motor on and off until coarsely chopped. Pour into dry ingredients; repeat. Stir nuts into dry ingredients. **BLEND** eggs and next 4 ingredients in container until smooth, about 10 seconds. Add ½ of the banana slices. **BLEND** until smooth, about 5 seconds. Add remaining banana slices. **BLEND** until smooth, about 5 seconds. Turn into flour mixture; stir just until dry ingredients are moistened. Cover; refrigerate 2 to 2½ hours. Roll, ¼ of the dough at a time, ½-inch thick on lightly floured board. Cut with floured 2½-inch doughnut cutter and fry in deep hot fat (365°F.) until done and brown, about 3 minutes, turning once. Fry doughnut holes until done and brown, about 2 minutes. Drain on paper toweling. Makes about 1½ dozen doughnuts and holes.

APPLE DOUGHNUTS: Follow above recipe and substitute 1½ cups raw peeled apple slices, halved for banana slices. Add ½ of the apple pieces at a time. **BLEND** until coarsely chopped, about 8 seconds. Makes about 1½ dozen doughnuts and holes.

CHILDREN'S DELIGHTS

It's fun to entertain the young! Make the next party
for tots or teens a special affair, serve them one or
more of the gay, festive, easy-made desserts that
follow.

SNOW CONES AND SLUSH CUPS

Let the kids watch while you fix snow cones or slush cups but it's best to have an adult do the fixing

4 cups crushed ice
2 cups cold water
½ cup fruit-flavored syrup*

GRIND ice and water about 1 minute. STOP MOTOR. Push ice to blades with rubber spatula. Turn into sieve or colander and let drain briefly, then pile ice in 4 paper cups or cones. Drizzle about 2 tablespoons syrup over each cone and serve at once. Makes 4 large snow cones.

*Use bottled table and pancake syrups (raspberry, blueberry, boysenberry, etc.) available at your supermarket, or flavor light corn syrup with extracts or flavorings to taste and food coloring as desired. (Examples: peppermint extract and red food coloring; orange extract and orange food coloring; banana extract and yellow food coloring; lemon extract and yellow food coloring; spearmint extract and green food coloring.)

PEANUTTY CARAMEL APPLES

2 cups salted peanuts
1 pound vanilla or chocolate caramels (about 56)
2 tablespoons hot water
¼ teaspoon salt
4 to 5 medium-size eating apples, washed and dried
4 to 5 heavy meat skewers

CHOP peanuts, ½ cup at a time, switching motor on and off until coarsely chopped, about 6 to 8 times. Pour into pie plate or shallow dish. Repeat until all nuts are chopped. Combine caramels, water and salt in top of double boiler over simmering water. Heat, stirring often, until caramels are melted and sauce smooth. Plunge a skewer ½ way into stem end of each apple. Twirl apple in caramel mixture until skin is coated. Drain; roll in chopped peanuts. Place on waxed paper on cookie sheet. Chill until firm. Makes 4 to 5 caramel apples, depending upon size of apples.

CHOCOLATE MARSHMALLOW BITES: *See photo page 109.* Melt 1 cup semi-sweet chocolate bits and 1 tablespoon vegetable shortening in top of double boiler over simmering water. Twirl large marshmallows in chocolate and roll in blender-chopped nuts or candy. Makes enough chocolate mixture to coat 25 to 30 large marshmallows.

Snow Cones and Slush Cups

COOL CAT CONES

Fill ice cream cones or cups with alternate layers of vanilla ice cream and Fudge Sauce (recipe page 171). Sprinkle tops with blender-chopped nuts (chopping directions page 7). Store in freezer until serving time. Plunge a tiny lollypop or candy stick in center of cone before serving, if desired.

TRICKY DOUGHNUT TREATS

Push large wooden meat skewer or craftstick into center of one side and ½ way through large plain commercial or Banana Nut Doughnuts (recipe page 104). Frost top of doughnuts with Chocolate Butter Cream or Butterscotch Frosting (recipes page 52) or Confectioners' Sugar or Peanut Butter Frosting (recipes page 53). Sprinkle with blender-chopped nuts (see directions for chopping page 7) or decorate with ornamental or blender-chopped candy (chopping directions page 6). Chill until frosting sets.

PRETTY PARTY CAKES

Prepare favorite cake mix (recipe page 41). Bake in paper baking cups in muffin cups. Cool, frost and decorate in one of the following ways.

ZOO PARADE BIRTHDAY CAKES: Remove paper baking cups from cake; turn top side down. Frost with Chocolate Butter Cream Frosting (recipe page 52). Press animal crackers around sides of cake. Top cake with blender-chopped peppermint stick candy (chopping directions page 6). Plunge a tiny birthday candle in center of cake.

PATRIOTIC CAKES: Remove paper baking cups from cake; turn top side down. Frost with Confectioners' Sugar Frosting (recipe page 53). Sprinkle sides of cake with blender-chopped strawberry or raspberry stick candy (chopping directions page 6). Plunge a blue candle or tiny flag in center of cake.

ICE CREAM TEPEES

Fill pointed paper drinking cups with favorite flavored ice cream. Freeze until hard. Peel paper from 1 cone at a time; roll in blender-chopped nuts or blender-chopped brittle or stick candy (chopping directions page 6 and 7). Break thin pretzel sticks in half and push 3 pieces into point of ice cream to make ice cream resemble a tepee. See photo page 109.

A. Zoo Parade Birthday Cakes;
B. Patriotic Cakes; C. Tricky Doughnuts;
D. Peanutty Caramel Apples page 106

CANDY ICE CREAM PADDLE DIPS

1 pint brick ice cream
4 craftsticks or small wooden tongue depressors
1½ to 2 cups blender-chopped peppermint, orange, lemon, lime or licorice stick candy, peanut brittle or chocolate coated toffee bars (chopping directions page 6)

Cut a pint brick of ice cream into 4 crosswise slices or in half lengthwise and crosswise. Push ½ of the length of craftstick into center of one end of each ice cream piece. Place on freezer chilled cookie sheet; return to freezer to harden. Just before serving time coat ice cream on stick with blender-chopped candy desired. See following directions for making 5 great Candy Ice Cream Paddle Dips. Makes 4 paddle dips.

MINTY PADDLE DIPS: Coat ice cream on stick with blender-chopped peppermint stick candy. Delicious on chocolate, peppermint stick or vanilla ice cream.

SPOOKY PADDLE DIPS: Press candy corn eyes and nose into one side of ice cream on stick; coat with blender-chopped licorice stick candy. Best on vanilla or New York ice cream.

JEWEL PADDLE DIPS: Coat opposite sides of ice cream on stick with a different color blender-chopped stick candy. Use orange stick candy on 2 sides, lime on 2 sides; strawberry or raspberry on 2 sides, lime on 2; lemon candy on 2 sides, licorice on 2, etc.

NUTTY CANDY PADDLE DIPS: Coat ice cream on stick with blender-chopped peanut brittle or toffee. Wonderful on butter brickle, butter pecan, almond crunch, maple, chocolate or vanilla ice cream.

ORANGE PADDLE DIPS: Coat ice cream on a stick with blender-chopped orange stick candy. Great on cherry, chocolate or vanilla ice cream.

CRAZY CUTOUTS

Line a 13 x 9 x 2-inch baking pan, carefully, both ways with double-thick strips of aluminum foil. Leave a 1-inch overhang on all sides to make removal of ice cream from pan easy. Sprinkle a layer of blender-chopped vanilla or chocolate wafer crumbs over bottom of pan (crumbing directions page 8). Spread an even layer of slightly softened ice cream of desired flavor over crumbs. Sprinkle another layer of blender-chopped crumbs over top. Freeze hard. Lift ice cream from pan with aid of foil ends. Loosen ice cream from foil with long spatula. Quickly cut ice cream into desired fancy shapes, using large cookie cutters. Place cutouts on freezer chilled cookie sheet. Return to freezer to harden. (Pack trimmed-off ends into plastic container; freeze for eating). At serving time plunge a small candle or figure (santa on a pick, animal cracker, candy doll, etc.) in center of cutout. Serve with Fudge Sauce (recipe page 171).

FIRECRACKERS

Cut vanilla ice cream into sticks 3 inches long and 1½ inches wide and thick. Place cut ice cream pieces on waxed-paper covered, freezer chilled cookie sheet; freeze until hard. Make a hole in small end of each ice cream piece with wooden skewer. Insert ½ of a tiny candle in hole so it can be lit when served. Freeze. Blender-chop strawberry, raspberry or other bright red stick candy (chopping directions page 6). Befrore serving time, quickly roll long sides of each ice cream stick in blender-chopped candy; return to freezer to harden. Light candle before serving.

ICE CREAM FLOWER POTS

Scoop favorite flavored light colored ice cream into small paper drinking cups. Store in freezer. Just before serving time sprinkle tops generously with blender-chopped green (lime) stick candy (chopping directions page 6). Push a small lollypop and 2 small gum drop leaves, on wooden picks, into center of ice cream. Store in freezer until serving time.

PEANUT BALLS

Scoop favorite ice cream into balls with large ice cream scoop. Roll balls in blender-chopped peanuts (chopping directions page 7). Store in freezer until serving time. Serve with Fudge Sauce (recipe page 171).

ROCKY ROAD BALLS: Prepare as directed for Peanut Balls above; substitute blender-chopped peanut brittle (chopping directions page 6) for peanuts.

ICY PADDLE STICKS

1½ cups ice cubes and cold water to fill blender container to 3 cup level
1 package (1-ounce) beverage powder, any flavor
½ cup sugar
1 cup light corn syrup

Combine ingredients in blender container in order listed. **CRUSH** until sugar dissolves and ice is crushed. Pour into paddle pop molds, ice cube freezing trays, cone shaped paper cups or aluminum foil corn stick pans. Freeze until partially solid. Push wooden craftsticks or small wooden tongue depressors into center of one end so handle will stay in during eating. Freeze hard. Makes 4 cups, 10 to 12 sticks.

FRUIT ICE STICKS

Combine 1 can (6-ounce) frozen lemonade or limeade, ½ cup corn syrup and water called for in mixing directions on can label in blender container. **BLEND** until mixed, 2 to 4 seconds. Pour into molds; freeze as directed in recipe for Icy Paddle Sticks above. Makes 2½ cups, about 6 to 8 servings.

Cool Cat Cones page 107

Peanut Balls page 108

Ice Cream Flower Pots page 108

Ice Cream Tepees page 107

Icy Paddle Sticks page 108

Spooky Paddle Dips page 108

Firecracker page 108

Choc. Marshmallow Bites page 106

Orange Paddle Dips page 108

OUTDOOR COOKING

When days are warm and bright outdoor eating is a way of life in most homes. Everyone loves a barbecue. It's informal and the food tastes better than ever right off the grill.

A juicy fork-tender broiled steak is probably the most popular meat cooked on the grill. But, you'll like the fine and fancy burgers, chuck steaks, spareribs, barbecued pork loin, broiled lobster tails, and the like, prepared as directed in the recipes on the following pages. All foods are made-easy with the help of the blender, all are winners for flavor.

PATIO BURGERS

2 pounds ground beef chuck, round or hamburger
1½ cups soft bread crumbs (crumbing directions
    page 8)
2 eggs
½ cup catsup
¼ cup milk
1 teaspoon Worcestershire sauce
2 teaspoons salt
¼ teaspoon pepper
1 medium-size onion, quartered and sliced

Combine meat and crumbs in mixing bowl. Combine remaining ingredients in blender container in order listed. **BEAT** switching motor on and off until onion is chopped moderately fine, 8 to 10 times. Add to meat and crumbs; mix well. Shape into 8 4-inch patties. Broil to desired doneness on rack 4 to 5 inches above a bed of low burning charcoal, 8 to 10 minutes, turning once. While broiling brush with favorite basting sauce (recipes page 168), or a tangy Butter (recipes page 39). Serve with barbecue sauce desired (recipes page 168). Serve as an entrée or on buns. Makes 8 large patties.

FINE 'N FANCY BURGERS

Follow above recipe for Patio Burgers and change as suggested below:

BURGERS ITALIANO: Decrease salt to 1 teaspoon and add 1 teaspoon garlic salt and 1 teaspoon oregano to egg mixture before blending. Brush patties during broiling with Garlic or Onion Butter (recipes page 39). A few minutes before end of broiling time top each patty with a tomato slice, 1 teaspoon sliced green onions and a Mozzarella cheese slice. Allow cheese to soften. Top with a small sweet red pepper pickle. Serve as an entrée or in a bun. Makes 8 large patties.

FRENCHY BURGERS: Mix 1 can (4-ounce) sliced mushrooms, drained, into meat mixture before shaping into patties. Crumble 1 (4-ounce) package Roquefort or blue cheese; save. Brush patties while broiling with Herb Butter (recipe page 39). Top broiled patties with a dollop of sour cream, crumbled cheese and a bacon curl. Serve as an entrée. Makes 8 large patties.

BURGERS MEXICANA: Sprinkle hot Patio Burgers with chili powder just after turning. Top each broiled burger with a thin slice of Spanish onion and tomato, a dollop of sour cream and 2 or 3 thin avocado wedges. Serve as an entrée. Makes 8 large patties.

PEANUT BURGERS: Reduce salt to 1¾ teaspoons. **CHOP** ⅔ cup salted peanuts in blender container, ⅓ cup at a time, switching motor on and off until nuts are coarsely chopped, 5 to 6 times. Add to meat mixture before shaping patties. Spread hot burgers with creamy-style peanut butter; garnish with a dill pickle slice or fan. Serve as an entrée or on whole wheat or sesame seed buns. Makes 8 large patties.

CHEESY-BACON BURGERS: During last 3 or 4 minutes of broiling top each Patio Burger with 1 or 2 slices of process American cheese. Allow cheese to soften; top with a few 1-inch crisp bacon pieces. Serve as an entrée or in buns. Makes 8 large patties.

HONOLULU BURGERS: Decrease salt to 1 teaspoon and add ¾ teaspoon ginger to Patio Burger meat mixture; substitute ¼ cup soy sauce for ¼ cup of the catsup. Brush during broiling with Curry Butter (recipe page 39). Top each broiled burger with a grilled pineapple slice, 2 thin wedges of avocado and a few chopped toasted Macadamia nuts. Serve as an entrée. Makes 8 large patties.

CHARCOAL BROILED
SIRLOIN STEAK

Photo at right.

1 large (1½ to 2-inch) sirloin steak, about 5 pounds
¼ cup red wine vinegar
1 tablespoon Worcestershire sauce
1 teaspoon horseradish
1 (5-inch) green onion, cut in 1-inch lengths
1 small clove garlic, quartered
½ teaspoon salt
½ teaspoon whole black pepper
¼ teaspoon of basil and thyme
½ cup butter or margarine

Trim excess fat from edge of steak; slash fat edge, not meat, 1 to 2 inches apart to keep steak flat during broiling. Combine remaining ingredients, except butter or margarine, in blender container; **BLEND** until onion and pepper are finely chopped, 10 to 12 seconds. Pour into saucepan. Add butter or margarine; heat. Place steak on greased grill or in greased hinged wire grill. Broil 3 to 4 inches above a bed of hot charcoal. Broil first side until browned, about ½ of time. Turn and broil second side. Allow 35 to 40 minutes to broil a 2-inch steak, 25 to 30 minutes for a 1½-inch steak. To test steak for doneness make a slash in center of steak away from bone; examine color. Continue broiling if desired. Brush steak often during broiling with sauce. To serve, cut in thin slices, diagonally. Dip slices in remaining hot sauce. Allow ¾ to 1 pound of raw steak for each adult, ½ pound for each child.

BARBECUED CHUCK STEAK

1 (2-inch) slice beef chuck, blade or round bone
Meat tenderizer
Garlic, Onion or Herb Butter (recipes page 39)
Southwestern Barbecue Sauce or Steak Sauce (recipes page 168)

Score fat edges of steak, do not cut into meat. Sprinkle tenderizer over both sides of steak using amounts and method suggested by manufacturer on meat tenderizer label. Cover; let stand at room temperature 30 minutes. Broil on greased grill or in well-greased hinged rack about 4 inches above a bed of hot charcoal until well browned on first side, 20 to 30 minutes. Turn; broil second side, 25 to 30 minutes. Brush steak often, during broiling, with Garlic, Onion or Herb Butter. To test steak for degree of doneness make a slash in center of steak away from bone and examine color. Continue broiling if undercooked. To serve slice thin, on the diagonal, and serve with barbecue or steak sauce. Allow ¾ to 1 pound raw steak per adult, ½ pound per child.

SMALL CHUCK STEAK
WITH ITALIAN BUTTER

Prepare chuck steak, cut 1-inch thick, with unseasoned meat tenderizer used as directed by manufacturer on package label. Broil steak on well greased grill or hinged wire grill about 3 inches above hot coals until brown on first side, 8 to 10 minutes. Turn; brown and cook second side, about 5 minutes. Brush with Garlic Butter (recipe page 39) during broiling. Before serving spread with additional Garlic Butter.

CHEESE TOPPED CUBE STEAKS

Select 6-ounce cube steaks (½-inch). Brush steaks with Garlic Dressing (recipe page 151) or a commercial Italian pouring dressing. Broil steaks quickly on a well-greased wire grill, 2 to 3 inches above hot coals until brown on first side. Turn; sprinkle with oregano, dill weed or fines herbes blend and salt. Top each steak with a slice of Mozzarella or process American cheese and tomato. Continue cooking until under side of steak has browned. Serve on buttered crusty rolls.

GRILLED FLANK
STEAK TARRAGON

2 flank steaks (1 to 1½-pounds each)
1 cup salad oil
1 large onion, sliced
¼ cup tarragon vinegar
½ cup Burgundy wine
¼ lemon (thin yellow portion of peel and fruit only)
1 teaspoon dry mustard
1 teaspoon salt
3 cloves garlic
1 bay leaf
6 peppercorns

GRATE all ingredients, except steaks, 20 seconds. Score both sides of steaks in 1-inch diamonds, cutting about ⅛-inch deep. Place steaks in a flat dish. Pour marinade over steaks. Cover and refrigerate several hours, turning steaks several times. Lift steaks from marinade and broil 3 inches from hot coals about 5 to 10 minutes on each side. Baste with marinade occasionally. To serve, cut in thin diagonal slices. Makes 4 to 5 servings.

Charcoal Broiled Sirloin Steak

113

BROILED PORK CHOPS, CARIBBEAN STYLE

½ cup lemon or orange juice
⅓ cup strained honey
2 tablespoons sugar
2 tablespoons soy sauce
¼ teaspoon cloves
½ teaspoon salt
2 drops hot red pepper sauce
1 thin (¼-inch) slice lemon or orange, quartered
1 thin (⅛-inch) slice onion, quartered
2 tablespoons rum, optional
6 1-inch fresh or smoked pork chops
3 slices fresh pineapple, cut in large chunks
3 large oranges, peeled and cut into chunks
½ medium-size peeled and seeded cantaloupe or honeydew melon, cut in 6 slices and slices cut in half, crosswise

Combine all but last 5 ingredients in blender container. **BLEND** until onion and lemon or orange rind is very finely chopped, 10 to 15 seconds. Pour into saucepan; bring to boil; simmer 5 minutes. Cool. Stir rum into sauce, if desired. Arrange chops in large shallow baking dish; cover with sauce. Cover and refrigerate 45 minutes to 2 hours, turning chops once. Drain chops; save sauce. Arrange chops on well-greased grill or hinged wire rack. Broil 4 to 5 inches above a bed of low burning charcoal. Brown well on first side, about 15 minutes. Turn; brown and finish cooking on second side, about 15 minutes. Brush chops with sauce often during broiling. Thread fruit pieces on single or double pronged kabob skewers. Brush with sauce. Place on edge of grill to heat, but not brown, during last 5 minutes chops are broiling. Serve fruit with chops. Makes 6 servings.

SOUTHWESTERN SPARERIBS

5 pounds meaty spareribs, about 4 inches wide
1 teaspoon salt
1 recipe Southwestern Barbecue Sauce (recipe page 168)

Lace ribs accordian fashion on spit rod; lock securely in place with spit forks or prongs. Sprinkle salt evenly over ribs. Arrange hot charcoals at back of firebox. Place a foil drip pan in front of charcoal and under spit to catch drippings. Attach spit rod; start motor. Let ribs rotate until brown and meat is fully-cooked, 1¼ to 1½ hours. To test ribs for doneness make a slash between ribs and examine color of meat. Meat is done if there is no pink color and meat pulls back from the bones. Brush ribs with barbecue sauce often during last 20 minutes of barbecueing. Serve ribs with remaining sauce. Makes about 4 servings.

SWEET-SOUR SPARERIBS: Prepare as directed for Southwestern Spareribs, above, substituting Tangy Pineapple Barbecue Sauce (recipe page 168) or Sweet Sour Pineapple Sauce (recipe page 167) for Southwestern Barbecue Sauce. Makes about 4 servings.

GRILLED SWEET-SOUR SPARERIBS

½ cup frozen pineapple juice concentrate, thawed
⅓ cup brown sugar, firmly packed
½ cup wine vinegar
¼ small green pepper, sliced
1 slice onion
1 teaspoon soy sauce
1 teaspoon salt
3 to 4 pounds loin-back ribs

GRATE all ingredients except spareribs 10 seconds. Empty sauce into small bowl. Cut ribs in serving portions if using a spit basket, leave in one piece if using grill. Place ribs on grill or in basket over slow coals about 4 inches from coals. Cook about 45 minutes or until meat pulls back from bones, turning ribs frequently. Baste with sauce during last 10 minutes of cooking. Makes 3 to 4 servings.

ORANGE GLAZED BARBECUED PORK LOIN

4 to 6-pound center cut or boned and tied pork loin roast
½ cup water
½ cup catsup
⅓ cup orange marmalade
¼ cup soy sauce
1 small clove garlic, quartered
½ teaspoon salt
1 thin (⅛-inch) slice onion, quartered
2 tablespoons vinegar

Thread one spit fork on spit rod, points away from handle. Run spit rod through loin, end to end, making certain loin is perfectly balanced on rod so it will rotate smoothly. Put second spit fork onto spit rod, prongs toward meat. Center and balance roast. Push prongs into roast firmly; attach spit rod to motor. Start motor and roast over low burning charcoal until meat is tender and reaches an internal temperature of 170°F. (2½ to 2¾ hours). Prepare basting sauce while roast is barbecuing. Combine remaining ingredients in blender container; **BLEND** until onion and garlic are finely chopped, 8 to 10 seconds. Turn into saucepan; bring to a boil and simmer 10 minutes. Baste roast often with sauce during last 30 minutes of roasting. Serve with remaining sauce. Makes 10 to 15 servings.

BARBECUED PORK LOIN: Follow recipe for Orange Glazed Barbecue Pork Loin above. Substitute Southwestern Barbecue Sauce (recipe page 168) for the sweet sauce suggested in the recipe. Makes 10 to 15 servings.

Sweet-Sour Spareribs

BARBECUED HERB CHICKEN

2 (2½-pound) broiler-fryers, quartered
1 can (8-ounce) tomato sauce
¼ cup cider or wine vinegar
3 tablespoons salad oil
1 teaspoon salt
¼ teaspoon each of basil, thyme and savory, optional
1 thin (⅛-inch) slice onion, quartered
2 squares (1-inch) green pepper
¼ teaspoon whole black peppers

Wash chicken pieces; dry. Arrange pieces in single layer in shallow baking dish. Combine remaining ingredients in blender container in order listed. **BLEND** until vegetables and pepper are finely chopped, 10 to 15 seconds. Pour over chicken pieces. Cover; refrigerate 1 hour, turning chicken pieces twice. Drain chicken; arrange skin side up on greased grill or in greased hinged rack. Broil 4½ to 5 inches above a bed of low burning charcoal. Brush chicken pieces with marinade often, turning pieces every 10 minutes or so to brown and cook evenly. Cook until chicken is fork tender, 50 to 60 minutes. Heat remaining marinade and serve with chicken. Makes 8 servings.

BARBECUED FISH STEAKS

2 pounds halibut, swordfish or salmon steaks, ¾ to 1-inch thick
1 can (8-ounce) tomato sauce
¼ cup catsup
2 tablespoons lemon juice
3 tablespoons cooking oil
2 teaspoons Worcestershire sauce
2 teaspoons sugar
⅛ teaspoon salt
⅛ teaspoon pepper
1 small clove garlic, quartered
½ small (1¼-inch) onion, sliced
4 sprigs parsley, no stems

Cut fish into serving portions. Arrange fish in single layer in large shallow baking dish. Combine remaining ingredients in blender container. **BLEND** until onion and garlic are finely chopped, 8 to 10 seconds. Pour into saucepan; bring to boil and simmer gently 5 minutes. Cool; pour over fish. Cover; refrigerate 45 minutes to 1 hour, turning pieces 2 or 3 times. Drain fish; save marinade for basting. Place fish in well-greased hinged wire grill. Broil 4 inches above a bed of low burning charcoal 8 to 10 minutes on first side. Turn; broil second side 8 to 10 minutes or until fish flakes easily. Brush fish often during broiling with marinade. Serve with Tartar Sauce or Coral Fish Sauce (recipes on page 170). Makes 6 servings.

BROILED LOBSTER TAILS

4 (6 to 8-ounce) defrosted frozen lobster tails
Lemon Parsley Butter (recipe page 39)

Cut off undershells of lobster tails with kitchen scissors. Cut 4 (12-inch) squares of heavy duty aluminum foil. Center a lobster tail on each square. Brush meat with Lemon Parsley Butter. Wrap foil up around lobster tail; fold and crimp edges together. Place packages, shell side down, on grill 5 inches above a bed of burning charcoal. Heat about 25 minutes. Remove foil from tails and place, shell side up, on grill to lightly brown meat. Brush with Lemon Parsley Butter before serving. Makes 4 servings.

CHUTNEY GRILLED LAMB CHOPS

8 (1 to 1¼-inch) lamb shoulder or rib chops
⅔ cup chutney
⅓ cup salad oil
¼ cup orange juice
¼ cup honey or orange marmalade
½ teaspoon salt
½ teaspoon curry powder
1 thin (⅛-inch) slice unpeeled lemon, quartered

Trim excess fat from chops. Combine remaining ingredients in blender container in order listed. **BLEND** until chutney and lemon rind are finely chopped, 10 to 15 seconds. Pour into saucepan; bring to boil and simmer gently 6 to 8 minutes to blend flavors. Arrange chops on greased grill about 5 inches above burning charcoal. Broil about 10 minutes per side or until chops are browned on both sides and cooked to doneness desired. Brush occasionally with sauce while broiling. Serve with remaining sauce. Makes 8 servings.

HERBED LAMB CHOPS

Trim excess fat from 6 (1 to 1½-inch) shoulder or rib lamb chops. Broil as directed in recipe above for Chutney Grilled Lamb Chops. Use Herb Butter (recipe page 39) for basting chops instead of chutney sauce. Spread additional Herb Butter over chops just before serving. Makes 6 servings.

ORANGE NUT BREAD

1 loaf (1-pound) unsliced white or raisin bread
Double recipe Orange Marmalade Butter (recipe page 38)
⅓ cup blender-chopped almonds or pecans (chopping directions page 7)

Cut loaf of bread in half lengthwise, not quite through crust, starting on top of loaf. Start at top crust and cut in 1½-inch slices crosswise, not quite through bottom crust. Spread all cut bread surfaces with Orange Marmalade Butter and sprinkle lightly with nuts. Wrap loaf in double thickness of aluminum foil, closing top and ends tightly. Place to one side of grill while food is cooking and allow to heat to center of loaf. Serve hot. Separate each cut section into a serving portion with forks. Makes about 12 to 16 servings.

HOT GARLIC BREAD

Split a loaf of French or Vienna bread in half lengthwise. Spread cut surfaces with Garlic Butter (recipe page 39) and put together sandwich fashion. Wrap securely in a double thickness of heavy duty foil. Heat as directed for Orange Nut Bread (recipe above).

ITALIAN CHEESE BREAD

Split a loaf of French or Vienna bread in half lengthwise. Spread cut surfaces with Italian Butter (recipe page 39). Sprinkle with blender-chopped Parmesan cheese (chopping directions page 6). Wrap and heat as directed for Orange Nut Bread (recipe above.)

HOT GRILLED TOMATOES

4 large ripe tomatoes, washed and stemmed
Onion Butter (recipe page 39)
¼ cup blender-chopped Parmesan cheese (chopping directions page 6)
¼ cup blender bread crumbs (directions page 8)

Cut tomatoes in half. Place cut side up on 8 double thick squares of aluminum foil. Center tomatoes on foil squares. Top each tomato with 1 tablespoon Onion Butter. Mix cheese and crumbs; spoon onto tops of tomatoes. Fold foil over tomatoes; crimp edges together securely. Place packages, cut side up, on grill 4 to 5 inches above coals. Allow tomatoes to heat through, 8 to 12 minutes. Makes 8 servings.

CORN ON THE COB

Remove husks and silk from ears of corn. Spread ears generously with Herb Butter (recipe on page 39). Center each ear of corn in a square of double thickness heavy duty foil. Wrap ears in foil, crimping edges together securely; twist ends tightly. Place on grill to heat, 15 to 18 minutes turning ears often.

Corn On The Cob

PIES & PASTRIES

If there is a favorite American dessert it is probably pie. Fruit pies, cream pies, custard and pumpkin pies, ice cream and chiffon pies all have their backers.

"Easy as pie" is an old expression modern cooks find difficult to understand when they try many an old pie recipe. But, made the modern way with the help of the electric blender it takes just a wee bit of practice to turn out delicious picture-pretty pies.

Recipes follow for modern made pies, pastries and crusts galore. All make luscious pies that will delight the family. Count on the electric blender to make the preparation of fine crusts and fillings "easy as pie".

Butter Pecan Crust

BUTTER PECAN CRUST

See photo at left.

⅓ cup pecan halves
1⅓ cups sifted flour
¼ cup (packed) brown sugar
¼ teaspoon salt
½ cup butter or margarine, sliced

Pour pecan halves into blender container; **CHOP**, switching motor on and off until finely chopped. Combine all ingredients in mixing bowl. Mix with pastry blender until butter or margarine is well blended into dry ingredients. Turn mixture into 9-inch pie plate and press evenly over bottom and sides of plate, shaping crust into a standing rim around edge. Bake in slow oven (325°F.) until done, 20 to 25 minutes. Cool thoroughly before filling. Makes 1 9-inch pie crust.

ALMOND CRUST: Follow above recipe for Butter Pecan Crust and substitute blanched almonds for pecans. Use granulated instead of brown sugar. Makes 1 9-inch pie crust.

BLENDER PASTRY

5 tablespoons shortening
1 cup all-purpose flour
1 teaspoon salt
2 to 3 tablespoons cold water

GRIND shortening, flour and salt 10 seconds. Push ingredients to center of blender container with rubber spatula and **GRIND** 5 seconds longer. Empty mixture into a mound on waxed paper or plastic wrap. Make a hole in center of mound and pour in 1 tablespoon water. Put hands under paper and push flour into a ball around water. Repeat with remaining water. Wrap pastry in paper and let rest 15 minutes. Roll out to desired shape on lightly floured surface. Makes enough pastry for 1 9-inch pastry shell.

VARIATIONS

Follow above recipe and change as follows:

CHEESE PASTRY: GRATE ⅓ cup chilled cubed sharp Cheddar cheese until finely chopped, about 10 seconds. Stir into flour mixture before adding water. Makes 1 9-inch crust.

COCONUT PASTRY: GRATE ¼ cup cubed fresh coconut, switching motor on and off until finely chopped, 5 to 10 seconds. Stop motor and push coconut into blades with rubber spatula as needed. Combine with flour mixture before adding water. Makes 1 9-inch crust.

NUT PASTRY: CHOP ¼ cup nuts, switching motor on and off until finely chopped. Add to flour mixture before adding water. Makes 1 9-inch crust.

SEED PASTRY: Sprinkle 2 tablespoons poppy or sesame seeds over flour mixture before adding water. Makes 1 9-inch crust.

WHOLE WHEAT PASTRY

½ cup whole grains of wheat
½ cup sifted all-purpose flour
¾ teaspoon salt
¼ cup salad oil
2 tablespoons cold skim milk

SHRED ¼ cup wheat 60 seconds. Add to flour and repeat with remaining wheat. Sift wheat, flour and salt together. **STIR** oil and milk 10 seconds. Add flour mixture and **STIR** 10 seconds. Empty onto piece of waxed paper or plastic wrap. Put hands under paper and push ingredients together until all dry ingredients are moistened. Roll between waxed paper to fit an 8 or 9-inch pie plate or pan. Peel off top paper. If pastry tears, mend without moistening. Place, paper side up, in pie plate. Peel off paper. Ease and fit into pan. Flute edge. Prick with fork and refrigerate 15 to 20 minutes. Bake in hot oven (400°F.) 10 to 15 minutes. Cool thoroughly before filling. ⅛ of pastry shell (no filling) is approximately 150 calories.

GRAHAM CRACKER CRUMB CRUST

18 graham crackers, quartered*
3 tablespoons brown or granulated sugar
⅓ cup butter or margarine, melted
¼ teaspoon salt

GRIND 4 to 6 graham cracker pieces at a time until finely crumbed, 10 to 15 seconds. Pour into measuring cup. Repeat until all crackers are crumbed making about 1⅓ cups crumbs. Combine all ingredients in bowl; mix until well blended using pastry blender. Press evenly over bottom and sides of 9-inch pie plate. Bake in moderate oven (350°F.) 5 minutes. Chill well before filling. Makes 1 9-inch crust.

*Or use 1⅓ cups blender-chopped crumbs. For crumbing directions see page 8.

CHERRY JUBILEE PIE

1 (1-pound) can cherry pie filling
1 (9-inch) unbaked pastry shell (page 119)
1½ (8-ounce) packages cream cheese, cubed
2 eggs
½ cup sugar
1 teaspoon vanilla
1 cup dairy sour cream

Pour pie filling into pastry shell and bake in hot oven (425°F.) 15 minutes. **GRIND** cream cheese, eggs, sugar and vanilla 30 seconds. STOP MOTOR, scrape down sides of container with rubber spatula and **GRIND** 30 seconds longer or until smooth. Pour over hot cherry pie and spread evenly. Bake at 350° 30 minutes. Cool on rack. Spread sour cream over top and sprinkle with nutmeg. Chill. Makes 6 to 8 servings.

SLIM-JIM CHERRY PIE

2 (1-pound) cans water pack red tart cherries
3 tablespoons cornstarch
2 tablespoons liquid sugar substitute
½ teaspoon almond extract
1 (9-inch) baked whole wheat pastry shell (page 119)

Drain cherries and pour juice into blender container. Add cornstarch and sugar substitute and **STIR** 20 seconds. Pour into saucepan and cook and stir over medium heat until thick, about 5 minutes. Cool to room temperature. Add drained cherries and flavoring. Pour into pie shell. Makes 6 servings, approximately 202 calories per serving.

DUTCH APPLE PIE

4 cups pared, sliced apples
1 (9-inch) unbaked Sesame Seed pastry shell (page 119)
1 cup sugar
1 cup half and half (half milk, half cream)
1 egg
¼ cup flour
2 teaspoons cinnamon
½ cup nuts
1 tablespoon butter or margarine
1 teaspoon vanilla
½ cup cubed sharp Cheddar cheese

Arrange apples in pastry shell. **WHIP** sugar, half and half, egg, flour and cinnamon 30 seconds. Add nuts, butter, and vanilla and **GRATE** 5 seconds. Pour over apples. Bake in moderate oven (350°F.) 45 to 50 minutes or until apples are tender. **PURÉE** cheese 10 seconds. Sprinkle over hot pie and let cool slightly before serving. Makes 6 servings.

Cherry Jubilee Pie

VARIATIONS

Follow recipe for Graham Cracker Crumb Crust (page 119) and change as follows:

CHOCOLATE WAFER CRUST: Substitute 18 to 20 crisp thin (2½ inch) chocolate wafers for graham crackers and use granulated sugar. Makes 1 9-inch crust.

GINGERSNAP CRUST: Substitute 24 gingersnaps, broken in half, for graham crackers and use granulated sugar. Makes 1 9-inch crust.

VANILLA OR BROWN EDGE WAFER CRUST: Substitute 35 wafers, broken in half, for graham crackers and use granulated sugar. Makes 1 9-inch crust.

NUTTY CRUMB CRUST: Reduce graham crackers to 12, butter or margarine to ¼ cup, and add ½ cup pecan or walnut halves or peanuts, chopped. Prepare crackers as directed above. **CHOP** nuts, ¼ cup at a time, switching motor on and off until finely chopped. Pour into mixing bowl. Makes 1 9-inch crust.

SPICY CRUMB CRUST: Add ¾ teaspoon cinnamon and ¼ teaspoon nutmeg to crumbs before mixing. Use brown or granulated sugar. Makes 1 9-inch crust.

WHEAT GERM CRUMB CRUST: Follow recipe for Nutty Crumb Crust (recipe above) and substitute ½ cup wheat germ for chopped nuts. Makes 1 9-inch crust.

CEREAL FLAKE CRUMB CRUST

6 cups (about) corn or whole wheat flakes
½ cup sugar
½ cup butter or margarine, melted

BLEND ½ cup cereal flakes at a time, switching motor on and off until finely chopped, 8 to 10 seconds. Pour into 2-cup measuring cup. Repeat as needed to make 1½ cups crumbs. Pour into mixing bowl. Add remaining ingredients; mix well using a pastry blender. Pour into 9-inch pie plate; press in even layer over bottom and sides of pie plate. Bake in moderate oven (350°F.) 5 minutes. Cool. Makes 1 9-inch crust.

8-INCH CRUMB CRUST

GRAHAM CRACKER CRUMB CRUST: Follow Graham Cracker Crumb Crust (9-inch) recipe (page 119). Reduce graham crackers to 14, butter or margarine to ¼ cup and sugar to 2 tablespoons.

CHOCOLATE WAFER CRUST: Follow Chocolate Wafer (9-inch) recipe to left. Reduce chocolate wafers to 14, butter or margarine to ¼ cup and sugar to 2 tablespoons.

GINGERSNAP CRUST: Follow Gingersnap Crust recipe (9-inch) to left. Reduce cookies to 18, butter or margarine to ¼ cup and sugar to 2 tablespoons.

VANILLA OR BROWN EDGE WAFER CRUST: Follow Vanilla or Brown Edge Wafer Crust (9-inch) recipe to left. Reduce wafers to 24, butter or margarine to ¼ cup and sugar to 2 tablespoons.

CEREAL FLAKE CRUMB CRUST: Follow Cereal Flake Crumb Crust (9-inch) recipe above. Reduce flakes to 4½ cups, butter or margarine to ¼ cup and sugar to 2 tablespoons.

CHOCOLATE
SUNDAE PIE

⅔ cup pecan halves
1 9-inch Chocolate Wafer Crust (recipe page 121)
⅔ cup undiluted evaporated milk
¼ teaspoon salt
1¼ cups semi-sweet chocolate bits
1¼ cups miniature marshmallows
1 teaspoon vanilla
2 pints vanilla or New York ice cream

CHOP pecans, ⅓ cup at a time, switching motor on and off until coarsely chopped; save. Chill Chocolate Wafer Crust in freezer. Combine milk and salt in saucepan; scald. Pour chocolate bits into blender container. Add marshmallows and vanilla. Pour hot milk into blender container; **BLEND** until thick and smooth, 60 to 70 seconds. Stop motor; scrape down sides and push ingredients into blades with rubber spatula as needed. Cool to room temperature. Spoon ½ of ice cream over bottom of crust; cover with ½ of chocolate sauce and ½ of chopped nuts; repeat layers. Freeze until firm, 4 to 6 hours or overnight. Let stand at room temperature 5 minutes before cutting. Makes 8 servings.

VARIATIONS

Follow recipe for Chocolate Sundae Pie above; change as follows:

CHERRY PECAN ICE CREAM PIE: Use a Graham Cracker Crumb Crust (recipe page 119) instead of Chocolate Wafer one. Substitute cherry for vanilla or New York ice cream. Makes 1 9-inch pie.

FROZEN NEOPOLITAN PIE: Use a Vanilla or Brown Edge Wafer Crust (recipe page 121) instead of Chocolate Wafer one. Substitute strawberry for vanilla or New York ice cream. Makes 1 9-inch pie.

PEACHY PECAN PIE: Use a chilled Butter Pecan Crust (page 119) instead of Chocolate Wafer one. Substitute peach for vanilla or New York ice cream. Makes 1 9-inch pie.

BUTTERSCOTCH PECAN
ICE CREAM PIE

1 baked 9-inch Butter Pecan Crust (recipe page 119), chilled in freezer
2 pints maple, coffee or butter pecan ice cream
Butterscotch Sauce (recipe page 170)

Spoon ice cream into crust; return to freezer to harden. Let stand at room temperature 5 minutes before cutting. Serve with Butterscotch Sauce. Makes 8 servings.

CHOCOLATE
PEPPERMINT PIE

1 9-inch Chocolate Wafer Crust (recipe page 121)
1 quart peppermint stick ice cream*
½ cup blender-chopped peppermint stick candy (chopping directions page 6)

Chill crust in freezer before filling. Spoon ice cream into crust and return to freezer to harden. Just before serving sprinkle chopped candy over pie. Let stand at room temperature 5 minutes before cutting. Makes 6 servings.

*If no peppermint stick ice cream is available fold ⅓ cup of blender-chopped peppermint stick candy or 1 teaspoon peppermint extract into slightly softened vanilla ice cream. Refreeze ice cream if necessary before filling pie.

VALENTINE PARTY PIES

For other holidays — Washington's Birthday or Christmas — bake pastry in tart shell or over tree molds

5 tablespoons shortening
1 cup all-purpose flour
1 teaspoon salt
1 to 2 tablespoons maraschino cherry juice
¼ cup drained maraschino cherries
1½ pints vanilla ice cream
¼ cup heavy cream, whipped
4 stemmed maraschino cherries

GRIND shortening, flour and salt 10 seconds. If necessary, STOP BLENDER, use rubber spatula to keep mixture around processing blades. Cover and continue to process at **GRIND** 5 seconds longer. Empty mixture into a mound on waxed paper or plastic wrap. **GRATE** maraschino cherries and add to flour mixture. Make a hole in center of mound and pour in 1 tablespoon cherry juice. Put hands under paper and push flour into a ball around juice. Repeat with remaining juice, making certain that chopped cherries are evenly distributed throughout pastry. Wrap pastry in paper and let rest 15 minutes. Roll ¼ of pastry into circle on lightly floured surface. Fit over outside of an individual heart-shaped mold. Trim edges. Prick with fork and place on baking sheet. Repeat with remaining pastry, making 4 heart shells. Bake in very hot oven (450°F.) 10 minutes. Cool pastry on molds. Carefully remove shells and place, hollow side up on dessert plates. Carefully spoon ice cream into shells. Garnish with whipped cream and cherries. Makes 4 servings.

Pecan Pumpkin Pie, Butterscotch Pecan Pie page 125, Cheese Fruit Tarts page 129

BLACK BOTTOM PIES

35 gingersnaps or 1 (1-pound) package gingersnaps
¾ cup butter or margarine, melted
2 cups milk, scalded
4 egg yolks
½ cup sugar
1½ tablespoons cornstarch
2 (1-ounce) squares unsweetened chocolate
1 teaspoon vanilla
1 envelope unflavored gelatin
½ cup cold water
2 tablespoons cognac
4 egg whites
½ cup sugar
1 cup heavy cream, whipped
Shaved chocolate for garnish

Break 3 gingersnaps into blender container and **CRUMB** 10 seconds, adding 2 more gingersnaps through opening in top while motor is running. Empty into measuring cup. Repeat until you have 2 cups crumbs. Add butter and mix well. Press over bottoms and up sides of 2 (7 or 8-inch) buttered pie plates or pans. Bake in slow oven (325°F). 10 minutes. Cool. **GRIND** milk, egg yolks, sugar and cornstarch 20 seconds. Pour into saucepan and cook and stir over medium heat until mixture coats a metal spoon, about 5 minutes. Pour 1½ cups hot custard mixture into blender container. Cut each piece chocolate into 6 pieces and add to container along with vanilla. **GRIND** 30 seconds. If necessary, STOP BLENDER, use rubber spatula to keep mixture around processing blades. Cover and continue to process at **GRIND** 30 seconds longer, if necessary, to mix chocolate completely. Pour ¾ cup chocolate mixture into each crust and chill. Rinse blender container **BLEND** remaining custard, gelatin and water 30 seconds. Add cognac and **BLEND** 20 seconds longer. Beat egg whites with rotary or electric beater until foamy. Gradually add ½ cup sugar and beat until stiff. Pour custard over egg whites and fold until smooth. Pour over chocolate layer in pastry shells and chill. Spread whipped cream over tops and sprinkle with shaved chocolate. Makes 2 (7 or 8-inch) pies, 10 to 12 servings.

DATE CREAM PIE

2 cups dairy sour cream
½ cup sugar
¼ cup cornstarch
1 teaspoon salt
2 eggs
1 cup pitted dates
¼ cup pecans
⅛ lemon (thin yellow portion of peel and fruit only)
1 (9-inch) baked Blender Pastry shell (page 119)

GRIND 1 cup sour cream, sugar, cornstarch and salt 10 seconds. Pour into saucepan and cook and stir over low heat until slightly thickened. **GRATE** remaining sour cream, eggs, dates, pecans, lemon peel and

fruit 20 seconds. Add to sour cream mixture in saucepan and blend. Cook and stir over low heat until thick, about 3 minutes. Turn into pastry shell and chill. Makes 6 servings.

RHUBARB CREAM PIE

Springtime flavor from the blender

1½ cups boiling water
1 cup sugar
3 tablespoons cornstarch
½ teaspoon salt
3 egg yolks
Peel of 1 medium orange
2 cups pink rhubarb, cut in 1-inch pieces
1 tablespoon butter or margarine
1 (9-inch) unbaked pastry shell (flute edge high)
3 egg whites
⅓ cup sugar
⅛ teaspoon cream of tartar

BEAT water, sugar, cornstarch and salt 10 seconds. Empty into saucepan and cook and stir over medium heat until mixture comes to a boil, about 5 minutes. Remove from heat. **PURÉE** egg yolks and orange peel 20 seconds. If necessary, STOP BLENDER, use rubber spatula to keep mixture around processing blades. Cover and continue to process at **PURÉE** 10 seconds. Add hot cornstarch mixture and **PURÉE** 20 seconds, adding rhubarb and butter through opening in top while motor is running. Pour into pastry shell. Bake in moderate oven (375°F.) 30 to 45 minutes or until custard is set. Beat egg whites and cream of tartar with rotary or electric beater until foamy. Add ⅓ cup sugar and continue beating until stiff. Spread meringue over hot pie, carefully sealing to edges. Return to oven and bake 20 to 30 minutes or until meringue is golden. Cool. Makes 6 servings.

COTTAGE CHEESE APRICOT PIE

A rich fruited custard pie

1 cup dried apricots or pitted prunes
½ cup cream-style cottage cheese
2 eggs
¾ cup sugar
½ teaspoon salt
½ cup milk
½ cup half and half (half milk, half cream)
1 (9-inch) baked pastry shell (page 119)

GRATE apricots 15 seconds and spread over bottom of pastry shell. **BEAT** cottage cheese, eggs, sugar and salt 20 seconds. Add milk and half and half and **GRIND** 10 seconds. Pour over apricots. Bake in very hot oven (450°F.) 10 minutes. Lower heat to 325° and bake 1 hour or until knife inserted in center comes out clean. 6 servings.

PUMPKIN PIE

1⅔ cups undiluted evaporated milk
1⅔ cups canned pumpkin
½ cup granulated sugar
½ cup (packed) brown sugar, broken up
2 eggs
1 tablespoon pumpkin pie spice (or 1¼ teaspoons cinnamon, ½ teaspoon each of nutmeg, allspice and ginger and ¼ teaspoon cloves)
½ teaspoon salt
1 9-inch unbaked Blender Pastry crust (recipe page 119)

Combine first 7 ingredients in blender container in order listed. **PURÉE** until mixture is smooth, 40 to 50 seconds. Stop motor; scrape down inside of container and push ingredients into blades with rubber spatula as necessary. Pour into crust. Bake in hot oven (425°F.) 15 minutes; lower heat to moderate (350°F.) and bake until done, about 45 minutes. Filling is baked when silver knife blade comes out clean when inserted in center of pie. Cool. Serve plain or with whipped cream or dessert topping. Makes 1 9-inch pie.

PECAN PUMPKIN PIE

Photo page 123

Follow recipe for Pumpkin Pie above. Fold ½ cup blender-chopped pecans (see chopping directions page 7) into pumpkin mixture before pouring into crust. Combine 2 tablespoons butter or margarine, ¼ cup brown or maple sugar and ½ cup blender chopped pecans; mix well with pastry blender. Sprinkle over pie 10 minutes before end of baking time. Serve plain or with dollops of whipped cream or dessert topping. Makes 1 9-inch pie.

SOUTHERN PECAN PIE

1½ cups pecan halves
3 eggs
1 cup dark corn syrup
2 tablespoons room temperature butter or margarine
1 teaspoon vanilla
¼ teaspoon salt
1 (9-inch) unbaked Blender Pastry crust (recipe page 119)

CHOP 1 cup pecans, ½ cup at a time, in container switching motor on and off until chopped moderately fine, about 10 seconds. Pour into mixing bowl. Combine eggs, syrup, butter or margarine, vanilla and salt in container. **BLEND** until smooth, 20 to 30 seconds. Add to chopped pecans; mix. Pour into unbaked crust. Sprinkle pecan halves over top. Bake in hot oven (400°F.) 10 minutes. Reduce oven heat to moderate (350°F.) and finish baking, 35 to 40 minutes. If done, filling will be firm when pie is gently shaken. Cool on wire rack. Serve plain or with whipped or sour cream or dessert topping. Makes 1 9-inch pie.

CRUNCHY PEANUT PIE

Follow recipe for Southern Pecan Pie at left and make the following changes. Substitute salted peanuts for pecans. Reduce nuts to 1 cup. Chop peanuts as directed for pecans. Fold ½ cup chopped peanuts into syrup mixture and sprinkle remaining nuts over pie before baking. Makes 1 9-inch pie.

DOUBLE CHOCOLATE BANANA PIE

Prepare Chocolate Wafer Crust (recipe page 121); chill. Prepare favorite chocolate pudding and pie filling as directed on package label. Pour ⅓ of filling into pie crust; cover with a layer of thinly sliced bananas. Add ½ of remaining filling; cover with a second layer of bananas. Pour remaining filling over bananas; chill until firm. Serve plain or with dollops of whipped cream or dessert topping. Makes 1 9-inch pie.

CREAMY CHERRY BANANA PIE

Follow recipe for Double Chocolate Banana Pie and change as follows: Use a 9-inch baked and chilled Butter Pecan Crust (recipe page 119) or Wheat Germ Crumb Crust (recipe page 121). Substitute vanilla for chocolate pudding and pie filling and fold in ¼ cup quartered maraschino cherries before filling pie. Makes 1 9-inch pie.

BUTTERSCOTCH PECAN PIE

Prepare favorite butterscotch pudding and pie filling as directed on package label. Pour into baked chilled Butter Pecan Crust or Graham Cracker Crumb Crust (recipes page 119); sprinkle ½ cup blender-chopped pecans (see chopping directions page 7) over top. Chill until firm. Serve plain or with dollops of whipped cream or dessert topping. Makes 1 9-inch pie.

STRAWBERRY, RASPBERRY OR PEACH PIE

Prepare Almond Crust (recipe page 119); chill. Prepare 1 package favorite vanilla pudding and pie filling as directed on package label; pour into chilled crust. Chill until filling is set. Just before serving top with sliced sweetened fresh strawberries or peaches, or red raspberries. Serve plain or top with dollops of whipped cream or dessert topping. Makes 1 9-inch pie.

PEPPERMINT CHIFFON PIE

⅓ cup nuts
⅔ cup (about ⅓ pound) broken peppermint stick
   candy
1 envelope unflavored gelatin
¼ cup cold water
1½ cups milk
3 egg yolks
2 tablespoons sugar
3 egg whites
⅛ teaspoon salt
2 tablespoons sugar
1 (9-inch) baked Chocolate Wafer Crust (page 121)

GRATE nuts 5 seconds. Empty into bowl. **LIQUEFY** ½
cup of candy 10 seconds. Empty into measuring cup
and repeat until you have ⅔ cup crushed candy.
Sprinkle gelatin over cold water. **STIR** milk, egg yolks
and 2 tablespoons sugar 10 seconds. Pour into saucepan; add candy. Cook and stir over low heat until
mixture coats metal spoon, about 10 minutes. Add
gelatin and stir until blended. Cool. Beat egg whites
and salt with rotary or electric beater until soft peaks
form. Gradually add 2 tablespoons sugar and beat
until stiff. Fold egg whites into gelatin mixture. Turn
into cooky crust. Sprinkle nuts over top. Chill until
firm. Makes 6 servings.

APRICOT CHIFFON PIE

*Try this flavorful apricot filling in a Gingersnap Crust or
Cornflake Crumb Crust, page 121 or Whole Wheat Pastry,
page 119. The addition of the cracked ice helps the filling
to set up extra fast.*

2 eggs, separated
2 tablespoons sugar
2 envelopes unflavored gelatin
½ cup dried apricots
½ cup orange-juice concentrate or apricot nectar
½ cup hot milk
¼ cup sugar
1 cup heavy cream
1 heaping cup crushed ice
1 (9-inch) baked Blender Pastry shell (page 119)

Beat egg whites with electric or rotary beater until
soft peaks form. Gradually add the 2 tablespoons
sugar and continue beating until stiff. **GRIND** gelatin,
apricots, orange-juice concentrate or apricot nectar
and hot milk 40 seconds. Add sugar and egg yolks
and **GRIND** 15 seconds. Add cream and **SHRED** 40
seconds, gradually adding ice through opening in
top while motor is running. Fold apricot mixture into
beaten egg whites until smooth. Pile in pastry shell,
garnish with grated orange rind, if desired; chill until
firm, at least 4 hours. Makes 6 servings.

Peppermint Chiffon Pie   *Apricot Chiffon Pie*

NESSELRODE CHIFFON PIE

¼ cup maraschino cherries, very well drained
¼ cup walnuts
¼ cup semi-sweet chocolate pieces
1 envelope unflavored gelatin
¼ cup cold milk
3 egg yolks
⅓ cup sugar
⅛ teaspoon salt
¾ cup milk, scalded
3 egg whites
⅓ cup sugar
3 tablespoons sherry or rum
½ cup heavy cream, whipped (see page 9)
1 (9-inch) baked Blender Pastry shell (page 119)
Shaved chocolate and whole maraschino cherries for garnish

GRATE cherries 5 seconds. Empty into bowl. **GRATE** walnuts and chocolate pieces 5 seconds; add to cherries. **STIR** gelatin and cold milk 10 seconds. Add egg yolks, ½ cup sugar and salt and **STIR** 60 seconds, adding hot milk through opening in top while motor is running. Pour into bowl and chill until mixture mounds when spooned. Beat egg whites with rotary or electric beater until foamy. Gradually add ⅓ cup sugar and continue beating to stiff peaks. Add sherry to gelatin mixture and pour over egg whites. Add cherries, nuts, chocolate and whipped cream and fold all together until smooth. Pile into pastry shell. Chill until firm. Garnish with shaved chocolate and cherries. Makes 6 servings.

CHOCOLATE CHIFFON PIE

1 cup evaporated milk, chilled icy-cold
1 envelope unflavored gelatin
¾ cup sugar
⅛ teaspoon salt
1 egg yolk
¾ cup milk
3 (1-ounce) squares unsweetened chocolate, cut in 4 pieces each
1 teaspoon vanilla or mint flavoring
1 (9-inch) baked Blender Pastry shell (page 119)

WHIP evaporated milk 60 seconds or until stiff, being careful not to overbeat. Empty into a bowl and chill while preparing filling. **BEAT** all remaining ingredients, except vanilla and pastry shell, 20 seconds. Empty into sauce pan and cook and stir over medium heat just until mixture begins to steam *Do not boil.* Return to container and **BLEND** 40 seconds or until smooth. Pour into bowl and chill until mixture mounds when spooned. Fold in whipped milk and vanilla. Turn into baked pastry shell and chill until firm. Garnish with whipped cream, if you wish. Makes 6 servings.

Chocolate Chiffon Pie

HEAVENLY CHOCOLATE PIE

1 cup heavy cream
1 cup milk, scalded
½ pound marshmallows
2 (1-ounce) squares unsweetened chocolate, cut up
1 teaspoon vanilla
½ teaspoon salt
½ cup walnuts
1 (9-inch) baked Blender Pastry shell (page 119)
¼ cup shredded coconut

WHIP cream 40 to 50 seconds. Empty into a bowl and chill. BEAT milk, marshmallows, chocolate, vanilla and salt 60 seconds. Chill in container until mixture mounds when spooned. Add walnuts, GRATE 10 seconds. Pour over whipped cream; fold together. Turn into pastry shell; top with coconut. Chill firm. Makes 6 servings.

LEMON CHIFFON PIE

4 egg yolks
½ cup sugar
1 envelope unflavored gelatin
½ lemon (thin yellow portion of peel and fruit only)
¼ cup water
⅛ teaspoon salt
4 egg whites
½ cup sugar
1 (9-inch) baked pastry shell or crumb crust (pages 119 and 121)

GRIND egg yolks, ½ cup sugar, gelatin, lemon, water and salt 40 seconds. Pour into saucepan and cook and stir over low heat until slightly thickened. Chill until beginning to set. Beat egg whites with rotary or electric beater until foamy. Gradually add ½ cup sugar and beat to stiff peaks. Pour egg yolk mixture over egg whites and fold until smooth. Turn into pastry shell and chill until firm. Makes 6 servings.

APRICOT SOUFFLÉ PIE

1 cup dried apricots
¼ cup water
3 eggs
1¼ cups sugar
1 cup dairy sour cream
1½ teaspoons vanilla
1 (9-inch) baked Blender Pastry shell (page 119)

Soak apricots in water about 1 hour. BEAT eggs 10 seconds. GRIND 30 seconds, adding sugar through opening in top while motor is running. Add apricots and water and SHRED 10 seconds. Add sour cream and vanilla; WHIP 10 seconds. Pour into pastry shell or crumb crust and bake in moderate oven (375°F.) 45 minutes or until filling is firm in center. Makes 6 servings.

CHOCOLATE ANGEL PIE

ANGEL PIE SHELL:
3 egg whites
⅛ teaspoon salt
⅛ teaspoon cream of tartar
¾ cup sugar
⅔ cup blanched almonds
1 teaspoon almond extract

FILLING:
¼ pound sweet chocolate
3 tablespoons hot strong coffee
1 tablespoon cognac
1 cup heavy cream, whipped (see page 9)

ANGEL PIE SHELL: Beat egg whites, salt and cream of tartar with rotary or electric beater until foamy. Gradually add sugar and continue to beat until stiff. GRATE almonds 10 seconds. Add to egg whites along with almond extract. Fold together until nuts are evenly distributed. Spread over bottom and up sides of buttered 9-inch pie plate and bake in moderate oven (350°F.) 45 minutes or until firm and lightly browned. Cool completely.

FILLING: Break chocolate into small pieces into blender container. Add coffee and PURÉE 30 seconds or until smooth. Add cognac and BLEND 5 seconds longer. Pour over whipped cream and fold together until blended. Pour into cooled pie shell. Chill at least 3 hours. Makes 6 to 8 servings.

LEMON ANGEL PIE

You can fill the delicate Angel Pie Shell with fresh or frozen fruit, prepared whipped dessert mix or prepared pudding or pie filling

Angel Pie Shell (above)
4 egg yolks
½ cup sugar
Thin yellow portion of peel of 1 lemon
½ lemon, peeled
1 cup heavy cream, whipped (see page 9)
3 tablespoons sugar
1 teaspoon vanilla

Prepare Angel Pie Shell as in Chocolate Angel Pie, above. GRIND egg yolks, sugar, lemon peel and fruit 30 seconds. STOP MOTOR, scrape down sides of container with rubber spatula. BLEND 20 seconds. Pour into saucepan and cook and stir over low heat until thick. Cool, stirring occasionally. Add sugar and vanilla to whipped cream and spread half the cream over bottom of cooled Angel Pie Shell. Top with lemon filling and then with remaining cream, allowing lemon filling to show around edges and center. Chill 2 or 3 hours. Makes 6 to 8 servings.

CRANBERRY RELISH PIE

Double recipe for Blender Pastry (page 119)
2½ cups raw cranberries
4 small apples, cored and sliced
1 medium orange (thin orange portion of peel and fruit)
½ cup nuts
1½ cups sugar
2 tablespoons flour
½ teaspoon cinnamon
¼ teaspoon salt
¼ teaspoon nutmeg
2 teaspoons butter or margarine

Roll out half the pastry and use to line 9-inch pie plate or pan. **SHRED** ½ cup cranberries 10 seconds. Empty into large bowl. Repeat with remaining cranberries. **SHRED** apples, ½ cup at a time and add to cranberries. **SHRED** orange and peel 10 seconds and add to cranberries. **GRATE** nuts 5 seconds. Add to cranberries along with all remaining ingredients except pastry and butter. Turn into pastry shell and dot with butter. Roll out remaining pastry and place over pie. Seal edges and flute, slashing top crust in Christmas tree or other pattern. Bake in hot oven (425°F.) 45 to 50 minutes. Makes 6 servings. Serve with Hard Sauce (page 172).

MINCEMEAT PIE

Double recipe Blender Pastry (page 119)
1 cup nuts
1 quart Old-Fashioned Mincemeat (page 137)

Roll out half the pastry and fit into a deep 9-inch pie plate or pan. Roll out remaining pastry and cut ¼ to ½-inch wide strips. **GRATE** nuts 10 to 15 seconds, stir into mincemeat. Fill pastry-lined pan with mincemeat. Arrange pastry strips over filling to form crisscross lattice. Seal ends of pastry strips to bottom crust by pressing against rim of pan with tines of fork. Trim off any pastry hanging over edge of pan. Bake in hot oven (425°F.) 40 to 50 minutes. Serve warm with Hard Sauce (page 172). Makes 6 servings.

CHEESE FRUIT TARTS

8 3-inch baked tart shells, chilled (see Blender Pastry page 119)
¼ cup lemon juice
¾-inch square lemon rind (no white) cut in strips
2 eggs
⅓ cup sugar
⅛ teaspoon salt
1 package (3-ounce) room temperature cream cheese, cubed
1¼ cups well-drained fresh sliced strawberries, peaches or bananas, raspberries or blueberries
Whipped cream or dessert topping, if desired

Combine lemon juice and rind in container; **LIQUEFY** until rind is minced, 15 to 20 seconds. Add eggs, sugar and salt; **BLEND** until well mixed, 5 to 10 seconds. Pour into heavy saucepan. Cook over very low heat until thickened, stirring constantly. Cool slightly; pour into container. Add cheese; **BEAT** until smooth, 50 to 60 seconds. Stop motor and push ingredients into blades with rubber spatula, as needed. Spoon mixture into tart shells; chill. Just before serving spoon desired fruit over cheese mixture. Serve plain or top with dollops of whipped cream or dessert topping. Makes 8 tarts.

PRESERVE TARTS: Follow recipe for Cheese Fruit Tarts above and substitute 1 jar (12-ounce) favorite thick preserves (strawberry, cherry, peach, apricot or raspberry) for fresh fruit called for. Makes 8 tarts.

BANBURY TARTS

Blender Pastry for 9-inch pie (page 119)
2 or 3 single saltine crackers
½ cup raisins
½ lemon (thin yellow portion of peel and fruit only)
¼ cup walnuts
1 egg yolk
½ cup sugar
1 tablespoon butter or margarine

Roll pastry to 8 x 8-inch rectangle. Cut in 4 (4-inch) squares. Break crackers into blender container and **CRUMB** 20 seconds. Measure 1½ tablespoons crumbs and empty into bowl. **SHRED** raisins, lemon and walnuts 10 seconds. Add egg yolk, sugar and butter; **SHRED** 10 seconds longer. Add to crackers; mix. Spread over half of each pastry square. Moisten edges, fold in triangles and seal. Prick tops. Bake on baking sheet in hot oven (450°F.) 12 to 15 minutes. Makes 4 tarts.

PRESERVES & RELISHES

Few young homemakers know how much fun and how easy it is to make their own delicious jams, preserves, and relishes. Easy-as-pie, too, because the modern electric blender takes all of the hard work out of preparing these old fashioned goodies.

Sparkling delicious preserves and jams can be made in small or large batches most any time of the year and with the use of pectin they're doubly easy to make and practically failure-proof.

Try the following recipes for some of the best-liked jams, preserves, relishes, etc. All are delicious; all make great gifts, too.

2 packages (10- or 12-ounce) frozen sliced and sweetened strawberries, partially defrosted and cut in 1-inch cubes
3 cups sugar
1 package (2½-ounce) powdered fruit pectin
1 cup cold water

CHOP strawberries, about 1 cup at a time, in blender container until berries are finely chopped, 20 to 25 seconds. Pour into mixing bowl. Add sugar, stir well. Let stand at room temperature 20 to 25 minutes, stirring often. Combine powdered pectin and water in saucepan; mix. Bring to a boil over high heat; boil rapidly 1 minute, stirring constantly. Remove from heat. Add strawberry mixture; stir constantly 5 minutes. Pour into ½-pint freezer containers. Cover. Let stand at room temperature 1 hour then refrigerate until mixture jells, about 24 hours. Seal; label, date and freeze. Makes about 4 ½-pints.

FROZEN FRESH STRAWBERRY JAM: Follow recipe for Frozen Strawberry Jam above and make the following changes. Substitute 2 cups blender-chopped fresh strawberries for frozen strawberries called for in recipe and increase sugar to 4 cups. Makes about 4 ½-pints.

OLD FASHIONED APPLE BUTTER

¾ cup water, cider or apple juice
¼ cup lemon juice
4 pounds tart apples, peeled, cored and cut into eighths
1 teaspoon cinnamon
½ teaspoon allspice
½ teaspoon cloves
¼ teaspoon nutmeg
3 cups sugar

CRUMB ¼ cup water, cider or apple juice, lemon juice and ½ cup of apple pieces in blender container until smooth, about 8 to 10 seconds. With motor running, add remaining apple pieces through top opening until container is ⅔ full. Stop motor; add spices; push ingredients into blades with rubber spatula, as necessary. **CRUMB** until well mixed, about 5 seconds. Empty into large heavy saucepan or Dutch oven. Repeat process with remaining liquid and apples. Add sugar to saucepan; mix well. Cook over very low heat, stirring often, until consistency of thick applesauce, 40 to 45 minutes. Pour into hot sterilized ½-pint jars; cover at once with hot paraffin. Makes about 6 ½-pints.

FROZEN FRESH RED RASPBERRY JAM

8 cups fresh red raspberries, washed
2¼ pounds (6½-cups) sugar
1 package (2½-ounce) powdered fruit pectin
1 cup cold water

CHOP raspberries, 1 cup at a time, in blender container until very fine, 20 to 25 seconds. Stop motor; push ingredients into blades with rubber spatula as needed (3 cups finely chopped raspberries). Pour into mixing bowl; stir in sugar. Combine pectin and water in Dutch oven or large saucepan; mix well. Bring to a rapid boil over moderate heat, stirring constantly. Boil rapidly 1 minute, stirring constantly. Remove from heat; add berry-sugar mixture. Stir 5 minutes or until sugar is dissolved and mixture begins to thicken. Ladle into ½-pint freezer containers; cover. Let stand at room temperature 1 hour then refrigerate until mixture jells, about 24 hours. Seal; label, date and freeze. Makes about 8 ½-pints.

FROZEN BLACKBERRY, BLUEBERRY OR BOYSENBERRY JAM: Follow above recipe for Frozen Fresh Red Raspberry Jam above and substitute fresh blueberries, blackberries or boysenberries for red raspberries. Makes about 8 ½-pints.

CRANBERRY-ORANGE MARMALADE

2 medium-size (2½-inch) oranges
1 medium-size lemon
1 cup water
1 pound cranberries, washed and stemmed
⅛ teaspoon baking soda
6¾ cups sugar
½ bottle (6-ounce) liquid pectin

Wash, quarter, slice and seed oranges and lemon. Combine orange and lemon pieces and water in blender container. **PURÉE** until orange and lemon rind is finely chopped, 60 to 70 seconds. Pour into large Dutch oven or heavy saucepan. Add cranberries and soda; mix well. Bring to a boil. Cover; simmer gently 20 minutes, stirring occasionally. Add sugar; mix. Bring to a full rolling boil; boil hard 1 minute, stirring constantly. Remove from heat; stir in pectin immediately. Skim off foam. Cool 5 minutes; skim off foam; pour into hot sterilized ½-pint jars or glasses. Makes 8 to 10 ½-pints.

132

A. Frozen Fresh Red Raspberry Jam page 131; B. Short-Cut Strawberry Preserves; C. Fresh Peach Jam; D. Golden Orange Marmalade; E. Spiced Blueberry Jam page 133

SHORT-CUT STRAWBERRY PRESERVES

2 packages (10- to 12-ounce) frozen strawberries, partially defrosted and cubed
1 tablespoon lemon or lime juice
2½ cups sugar
½ bottle (6-ounce) liquid fruit pectin

GRATE 1½ packages of berries, ½ package at a time, switching motor on and off until berries are coarsely chopped. Pour into heavy 4½ to 5-quart saucepan or Dutch oven. Add remaining unchopped berries, lemon or lime juice and sugar. Bring to a full rolling boil; boil 3 minutes, stirring constantly. Remove from heat; stir in pectin. Skim off any foam from surface. Let stand 5 minutes; skim again and pour into small (½-pint) sterilized jars. Cover with paraffin. Label and date. Makes about 4½ cups.

SHORT-CUT RASPBERRY PRESERVES: Follow recipe for Strawberry Preserves above and substitute frozen raspberries for strawberries. Makes about 4½ cups.

SHORT-CUT PEACH PRESERVES: Follow recipe for Strawberry Preserves above and change as follows. Substitute 3 packages (10- to 12-ounce) frozen sliced peaches for strawberries, increase sugar to 4½ cups, lemon juice to ¼ cup and liquid fruit pectin to 1 bottle. Makes about 8 ½-pints.

FRESH PEACH JAM

2 pounds (about) ripe peaches*
1 square (1-inch) lemon rind (no white), cut into strips
3¾ cups sugar
2 tablespoons fresh lemon juice
¼ teaspoon each cloves, cinnamon and allspice
½ bottle (6-ounce) liquid fruit pectin

Peel, pit and slice peaches. BLEND 1 cup sliced peaches at a time in blender container until finely chopped, about 20 seconds. Stop motor and push ingredients into blades with rubber spatula as needed. Pour into measuring cup. Process lemon rind with first cup of peaches. *Repeat process as needed to obtain 4 cups chopped fruit. Pour into Dutch oven or large saucepan. Stir in sugar, lemon juice and spices. Bring to boiling point quickly. Boil hard 1 minute, stirring constantly. Remove from heat; stir in fruit pectin at once. Skim foam from surface, if necessary; pour into hot sterilized ½-pint jars or glasses. Cover at once with hot paraffin. Label and date. Makes about 5 ½-pints.

PEACH AND PEAR JAM: Follow recipe for Fresh Peach Jam (recipe above); substitute peeled, cored, sliced bartlett pears for ½ of the peaches. Omit spices. Makes about 5 ½-pints.

PLUM JAM: Follow recipe for Fresh Peach Jam (recipe at left); substitute washed, unpeeled, halved, pitted fresh Italian plums for peaches, increasing plums to 2½ pounds or 4½ cups chopped plums. Makes about 6 ½-pints.

SPICED BLUEBERRY JAM

2 quarts fresh blueberries, washed
2 pounds (4 cups) sugar
¾ teaspoon each of cinnamon and allspice
1 bottle (6-ounce) liquid fruit pectin

CHOP blueberries, 1 cup at a time, in blender container until finely chopped, 8 to 10 seconds. Stop motor as needed and push ingredients into blades with rubber spatula. Pour into Dutch oven or large saucepan. Stir in sugar and spices. Bring to a boil quickly, stirring often. Boil hard 2 minutes, stirring constantly. Remove from heat; stir in pectin. Let stand 5 minutes; skim off any foam present. Pour into hot sterilized ½-pint jars or glasses. Seal or paraffin at once. Label and date. Makes about 5 ½-pints.

GOLDEN ORANGE MARMALADE

3 medium oranges, washed
1 medium lemon, washed
Cold water
1½ cups hot water
⅛ teaspoon baking soda
5 cups sugar
½ bottle (6-ounce) liquid fruit pectin

Trim rind (orange or yellow only) from oranges and lemon. Trim excess white from rind. Cut ¾ cup very thin slivers of rind (1/16-inch wide and as long as possible). Turn into saucepan. Cover with cold water; simmer gently 5 minutes. Pour water off rind slivers; repeat process 2 more times. Save rind. While slivers are simmering cut remaining rind into 1-inch squares; cut squares into strips and put into blender container. Add 1 cup cold water. CHOP until rind is very finely chopped, 40 to 60 seconds. Empty into sieve; drain off and discard liquid. Turn into Dutch oven or large saucepan. Add hot water and soda; simmer gently 20 minutes. Trim all white from oranges and lemon; cut each fruit into eighths. CHOP 1 cup fruit at a time, switching motor on and off until coarsely chopped. Add to Dutch oven at end of 20 minutes cooking time. Stir in sugar and reserved orange slivers; mix. Bring to a boil quickly; boil rapidly 1 minute, stirring constantly. Remove from heat; stir in fruit pectin at once. Skim foam from surface, if necessary. Let stand 5 minutes; stir and pour into hot sterilized ½-pint jars. Cover at once with hot paraffin. Label and date. Makes about 5 ½-pints.

CHERRY RAISIN CONSERVE

1 cup pecan or walnut halves
½ cup lemon juice
2 1-inch squares lemon rind (no white), cut into thin
   strips
1 cup seedless light or dark raisins
2½ pounds pitted red sweet or sour or sweet Bing
   cherries
3½ pounds (7 cups) sugar
1 bottle (6-ounce) liquid fruit pectin

CHOP nuts, ½ cup at a time, switching motor on and off until coarsely chopped. Pour into bowl. Add ¼ cup lemon juice and rind to blender container; **SHRED** until rind is finely chopped, 8 to 10 seconds. Add ½ of raisins; **CHOP,** switching motor on and off, until raisins are coarsely chopped, 15 to 20 seconds. Pour into Dutch oven or large saucepan. Repeat processing using remaining ¼ cup lemon juice and ½ cup raisins. **CHOP** cherries, 1 cup at a time, until finely chopped, 35 to 40 seconds. Stop motor and push ingredients into blades with rubber spatula as needed. Add to raisins. Add sugar; mix well. Bring mixture to a boil, stirring often. Add nuts. Boil hard 2 minutes, stirring constantly. Remove from heat; stir in pectin. Stir; cool 5 minutes and skim off foam. Stir; pour into hot sterilized ½-pint jars. Paraffin at once. Label and date. Makes about 10 ½-pints.

ORANGE CRANBERRY RELISH

1 medium-size orange (2½ to 3-inch), washed
2 cups (½-pound) fresh cranberries, washed and
   stemmed
1 cup sugar

Trim 4 1-inch squares (no white) of peel from orange; cut into thin strips. Finish peeling orange and discard peeling. Quarter orange, slice and remove seeds. Combine orange peel, pieces and ½ cup sugar in blender container. **PURÉE** until orange rind is finely chopped, 40 to 60 seconds; pour into bowl. Add 1 cup cranberries and ¼ cup sugar at a time to container; **BLEND** until cranberries are coarsely chopped, 30 to 35 seconds. Stop motor and push ingredients into blades with rubber spatula as needed. Store in covered refrigerator dish. Refrigerate several hours or overnight before serving. Makes about 1 pint.

CRANBERRY PECAN RELISH: CHOP ½ cup pecans in blender container, switching motor on and off until coarsely chopped. Prepare Orange Cranberry Relish (recipe above); fold in nuts before chilling. Makes about 1 pint.

SPICED ORANGE CRANBERRY RELISH: Prepare Orange Cranberry Relish (recipe above); add ¼ teaspoon each of cloves and allspice to sugar before adding to fruit. Makes about 1 pint.

SPICY FRESH PLUM RELISH

1 cup pecan or walnut halves
16 fresh Italian blue plums
1 medium-size (3-inch) orange
1 medium-size (3-inch) apple
1¾ cups sugar
¼ teaspoon cinnamon
⅛ to ¼ teaspoon cloves

CHOP nuts, ½ cup at a time, switching motor on and off until coarsely chopped, 15 to 20 seconds. Empty into mixing bowl. Wash plums, cut in half; remove pits. Wash orange, quarter, slice and remove seeds. Peel and core apple; cut into 1-inch chunks. **CHOP** all plum and apple pieces, ½ cup at a time, until finely chopped, 50 to 60 seconds. Stop motor; push ingredients into blades with rubber spatula as needed. Add to nuts. **CHOP** orange pieces, ½ cup at a time, until very finely chopped, 60 to 80 seconds. Stop motor; push ingredients into blades with rubber spatula, as needed. Add to nuts. Add sugar and spices; mix well. Pack in covered refrigerator container. Chill in refrigerator 8 to 12 hours before serving. Delicious with meats and poultry. Makes about 3 cups.

SWEET PICKLE RELISH

8 medium apples, peeled, cored and cut into eighths
8 medium tomatoes, peeled and cut into wedges
8 medium (2½-inch) onions, peeled, quartered and
   sliced
8 green peppers, cleaned and cut into 1-inch squares
4 cups sugar
3 cups cider vinegar
3 tablespoons salt

CHOP apples, tomatoes, onions and peppers, ½ cup at a time, switching motor on and off, until food is coarsely chopped, about 20 seconds. Stop motor; push ingredients into blades with rubber spatula as needed. Empty into a large heavy Dutch oven. Repeat until all fruit and vegetables are processed. Add remaining ingredients; mix. Bring to a boil, stirring constantly. Simmer gently, about 30 minutes, stirring often. Pack in hot sterilized ½-pint jars. Seal tightly, label and date. Makes about 10 ½-pints.

Sweet Pickle Relish, Orange Cranberry Relish page 134   *Speedy Corn Relish, Horseradish Beet Relish page 136*

Garden Relish

GARDEN RELISH

1 cup tarragon vinegar
1 cup sugar
2 teaspoons salt
½ teaspoon celery seed
½ teaspoon mustard seed
2 cups sliced cabbage
1 large sweet red pepper, seeded and cubed
1 large green pepper, seeded and cubed
1 onion, sliced
2 carrots, sliced

BLEND vinegar, sugar and seasonings 10 seconds. Add all remaining ingredients and **GRATE** 10 seconds. Turn into glass or plastic refrigerator container and chill 24 hours. Pour off excess liquid before serving. Makes about 3½ cups relish.

FRESH CUCUMBER RELISH

1 carrot, sliced
½ onion, sliced
2 large cucumbers, cubed
¼ cup vinegar
2 teaspoons salt
¾ teaspoon dill seed

GRATE carrot and onion, turn into glass or plastic refrigerator dish. **GRATE** cucumber with vinegar and seasoning; pour into refrigerator dish and mix. Chill thoroughly. Makes about 2 cups.

SPEEDY CORN RELISH

⅓ cup prepared French Dressing (page 151)
1 tablespoon vinegar
¼ cup coarsely chopped green pepper
1 stalk celery, sliced
1 slice onion
2 tablespoons coarsely chopped pimiento
½ teaspoon salt
1 (1-pound) can whole kernel corn, drained

GRATE all ingredients, except corn, 15 seconds. Pour over corn and toss to mix. Turn into pint jar or refrigerator container and refrigerate several days so that flavors can blend. Makes about 1 pint.

HORSERADISH BEET RELISH

2 tablespoons vinegar
¼ cup horseradish
1 thin (⅛-inch) slice onion, quartered
2 tablespoons sugar
1 teaspoon salt
⅛ teaspoon pepper
2 cups drained sliced cooked beets

Combine ingredients in container in order listed. **GRATE** until beets are finely chopped, about 10 seconds. Stop motor; push ingredients into blades with rubber spatula, as necessary. Pack into covered storage container and chill. May be stored in refrigerator 2 or 3 days. Serve with beef or pork roast, corned beef, ham, tongue or cold cuts. Makes about 1½ cups.

CHILI SAUCE

12 large red, ripe tomatoes, peeled and cut in wedges
4 hot or sweet red peppers, cleaned and cut into 1-inch squares
4 large green peppers, cleaned and cut into 1-inch squares
4 large onions, cleaned, quartered and sliced
1½ cups granulated or light brown sugar (packed)
4 teaspoons salt
2¼ cups cider vinegar
1½ teaspoons cinnamon
1½ teaspoons allspice
1½ teaspoons cloves

CHOP tomatoes, 1 cup at a time, in blender container, switching motor on and off until tomatoes are very fine, about 40 seconds. Pour into large Dutch oven or heavy saucepan. Repeat until all tomatoes are processed. **CHOP** both peppers and onions, ½ cup at a time, switching motor on and off until peppers and onions are very finely chopped, about 40 seconds. Add to tomatoes. Repeat until all vegetables are processed. Add remaining ingredients; mix. Bring to boiling point, stirring constantly. Turn heat to low; simmer gently until ½ of original volume, about 2 hours. Stir frequently to prevent sticking. Cool 5 to 10 minutes; pour into hot sterilized ½-pint jars. Seal tightly, label and date. Makes about 10 ½-pints.

PEPPER RELISH

2 cups cider vinegar
6 green peppers, cleaned and cut in 1-inch squares
6 sweet red peppers, cleaned and cut in 1-inch squares
6 small (2-inch) onions, quartered and sliced
1 cup sugar
2 tablespoons salt

Combine ⅓ cup vinegar and green pepper squares in blender container. **GRATE** until finely chopped, 40 to 50 seconds. Stop motor as needed and push ingredients into blades with rubber spatula. Pour into heavy saucepan. Repeat process, using ⅓ cup vinegar and red peppers. Repeat process with ⅓ cup vinegar and onions until onions are finely chopped, 70 to 80 seconds. Stop motor as needed and push ingredients into blades with rubber spatula. Add sugar, salt and remaining vinegar; mix and bring to a boil. Simmer gently 25 to 30 minutes until flavors are well blended, stirring occasionally. Cool 5 minutes. Spoon into hot sterilized ½-pint jars. Seal tightly; label and date. Makes about 8 ½-pints.

CATSUP

4 pounds tomatoes (about 16 small to medium-size)
1 sweet red pepper
1 green pepper
2 medium-size (2½-inch) onions
1½ cups cider vinegar
1½ cups sugar
4 teaspoons salt
1½ teaspoons dry mustard
¾ teaspoon each of allspice, cloves and cinnamon
⅛ teaspoon cayenne or ¼ teaspoon white pepper

Wash, peel and cut each tomato into 8 wedges. Clean peppers; cut into 1-inch squares. Peel, quarter and slice onions. Mix vegetables. Fill blender container ½ full of mixed vegetables; **CHOP** until finely chopped, about 25 to 30 seconds. Stop motor as needed and push ingredients into blades with rubber spatula. Turn speed to **LIQUEFY** and process 10 seconds. Pour into Dutch oven or roaster pan with heat-proof handles. Repeat as needed to process all vegetables. Stir in remaining ingredients. Cook in slow oven (325°F.) or over low heat until mixture is ½ original volume. Stir often. Pour catsup into hot sterilized ½-pint jars or bottles. Seal immediately; label and date. Makes about 5 ½-pints.

TOMATO-APPLE CATSUP: Prepare Catsup (recipe above); stir 1 cup thick applesauce (recipe page 78) into catsup a few minutes before end of cooking time. Makes about 6 ½-pints.

OLD-FASHIONED MINCEMEAT

2 pounds lean beef, coarsely ground
½ pound suet
1 cup beef bouillon or 1 bouillon cube and 1 cup water
4 pounds tart apples, cored and sliced
½ pound currants
1 pound raisins
1½ pounds brown sugar
1 quart apple cider
1 lemon, peeled and quartered
1 tablespoon cinnamon
2 teaspoons nutmeg
2 teaspoons ground cloves
1 teaspoon salt

Place beef in heavy 4 to 6-quart saucepan or pot. **PURÉE** half the suet and ½ cup bouillon 10 seconds. Add to meat. Repeat with remaining suet and bouillon. **GRATE** 1 cup apples 10 seconds and add to meat. Repeat with remaining apples. **GRATE** ½ cup currants 10 seconds. Add to meat. Repeat with remaining currants and raisins. **GRIND** ½ pound brown sugar, 1 cup cider, lemon and spices 20 seconds, stopping motor to push ingredients to blades, if necessary. Add to meat along with remaining cider and sugar. Simmer uncovered 1 hour, stirring frequently. Makes 4 quarts filling, enough for 4 pies. Mincemeat can be refrigerated several days. Freeze mincemeat to store for longer period.

SALADS

Salad time is anytime. Beautiful tempting salads, brimming with vitamins, are served with a lavish hand in American homes for salad fixings are readily available in most markets the year round.

The electric blender simplifies salad preparations. It chops vegetables, fruits, meats, poultry, eggs, etc. in seconds and blends gelatin and cheese mixtures for tasty molded and frozen salads perfectly in seconds.

The following recipes include thrifty salads to complement a hearty dinner, quick and easy main dish salads for supper or luncheon, shimmering ones that tempt, salads for dessert and many more than can add interest and variety to family meals.

AVOCADO MOLD

A creamy salad with beautiful pale-green color

1 (3-ounce) package lime or lemon-flavored gelatin
1 cup hot water
1 lime or lemon (thin colored portion of peel and fruit only)
1 large ripe avocado, peeled, seeded and cut in chunks
1 (3-ounce) package cream cheese, cubed
¼ teaspoon salt

GRIND gelatin and hot water for 40 seconds. Add remaining ingredients and GRIND 1 minute longer, or until smooth. Turn into 1-quart mold or 8-inch square pan and chill until firm. Makes 6 servings. Serve with tomato slices, cherry tomatoes, strawberries or other fruit.

SEABREEZE SALAD

2 (3-ounce) packages lime-flavored gelatin
1½ cups hot water
1 cup evaporated milk
1 (3-ounce) package cream cheese, cubed
4 ice cubes
2 tablespoons lemon juice
1 (8¾-ounce) can crushed pineapple
½ cup pecans
⅛ teaspoon salt

GRIND gelatin and water for 40 seconds. Add milk, cream cheese, ice cubes and lemon juice and GRIND 20 seconds. Add pineapple, pecans and salt and GRIND 5 seconds. Turn into 2-quart mold and chill until firm. Makes 10 to 12 servings.

FROSTY PINEAPPLE MOLD

An extra-cool and refreshing salad

1 (13½-ounce) can crushed pineapple
1 (3-ounce) package lime-flavored gelatin
1 (1-inch) piece orange peel
1 medium orange, peeled
½ medium cucumber, sliced
1 stalk celery, sliced
⅛ teaspoon salt
Cucumber slices for garnish

Drain pineapple well, reserving syrup. Heat syrup and GRIND with gelatin 40 seconds. Add all remaining ingredients except cucumber slices for garnish and GRIND 5 seconds longer. Turn into 1-quart mold and chill firm. Makes 6 servings.

DOUBLE APPLE SALAD

Younger members of the family will want you to add the peanuts

1 envelope unflavored gelatin
1 cup hot apple juice
⅓ cup sugar
¼ cup lemon juice
2 apples, cored and quartered
½ cup roasted peanuts (optional)
½ teaspoon ginger

GRIND gelatin and apple juice 40 seconds. Add all remaining ingredients and GRIND 10 seconds. Turn into 1-quart mold and chill until firm. Makes 6 servings.

GOLDEN SALAD FREEZE

A great make-ahead salad

1 (8-ounce) can apricot halves
1 (3-ounce) package orange, peach or lemon-flavored gelatin
1 (1-pound 13-ounce) can fruit cocktail
1 cup heavy cream
2 (3-ounce) packages cream cheese, cubed
½ lemon (thin yellow portion of peel and fruit only)
¼ cup mayonnaise
1 cup tiny marshmallows
½ cup halved maraschino cherries

Drain apricots, reserving syrup. Add water to syrup to make 1 cup and heat. GRIND hot syrup and gelatin 40 seconds. Add apricots. Drain fruit cocktail, reserving syrup and add syrup to blender container along with cream, cheese, lemon and mayonnaise; GRIND 20 seconds. Add fruit cocktail, marshmallows and cherries and turn into decorative molds, loaf pans or 2 1-quart plastic milk containers and freeze firm. Unmold and let stand at room temperature about 5 minutes before cutting. Makes 8 to 10 servings.

CRANBERRY-WALDORF SALAD

2 cups cranberry juice cocktail or cranberry-apple drink
1 (3-ounce) package lemon-flavored gelatin
2 medium apples, cored and quartered
3 stalks celery, sliced
¼ cup nuts

Heat 1 cup cranberry juice and GRIND with gelatin for 40 seconds. Add all remaining ingredients and GRATE 5 seconds. Turn into a 1-quart or 6 individual molds and chill until firm. Makes 6 servings.

TWO-GRAPEFRUIT SALAD

Fresh fruit flavor you can have any time of the year

1 envelope unflavored gelatin
½ cup hot water
1 (1-pound) can grapefruit sections
1 (6-ounce) can grape juice concentrate
¼ cup sugar
⅛ teaspoon salt

GRIND gelatin and hot water 40 seconds. Drain grapefruit, reserving juice and add juice to blender container along with concentrate, sugar and salt. **GRIND** 20 seconds. Add grapefruit sections and turn into 4 or 6 individual molds or a 1-quart mold and chill until firm. Makes 6 servings.

PERFECTION SALAD

An old-fashioned favorite quickly made in your blender. No chopping by hand!

1 envelope unflavored gelatin
1 tablespoon sugar
½ teaspoon salt
1 cup hot water
4 ice cubes
⅓ cup lemon juice
4 stalks celery, sliced
½ cup sliced green cabbage
1 pimiento

GRIND gelatin, sugar, salt and hot water 40 seconds. Add ice cubes and lemon juice and **GRIND** 20 seconds. Add celery, cabbage, and pimiento and **GRATE** 3 to 5 seconds. Turn into 1-quart mold and chill until firm. Makes 6 to 8 servings.

PETER RABBIT RING

You get lots of fresh vegetable flavor in this tasty, nutritious salad

1 (3-ounce) package lemon-flavored gelatin
1 cup hot water
1½ cups cream-style cottage cheese
1 cup sliced carrots
1 cup sliced celery
¼ cup watercress or parsley sprigs
1 tablespoon lemon juice
½ teaspoon salt

GRIND gelatin and hot water 40 seconds. Add remaining ingredients and **GRATE** 15 seconds. Stop motor and push ingredients down, if necessary; **GRATE** 5 seconds longer. Turn into 2-quart ring or other mold and chill until firm. Makes 10 to 12 servings.

FROZEN FRUIT CREAM

Joan Oster Favorites

1 can (1-pound 14-ounce) peach slices, drained, cut in half
1 can (1-pound 4-ounce) pineapple chunks, drained
1 can (11-ounce) mandarin orange sections, drained
1 cup miniature marshmallows
26 maraschino cherries, halved
⅔ cup pecan halves
1 package (8-ounce) room temperature cream cheese, cubed
½ cup Blender Mayonnaise (recipe page 154)
3 tablespoons milk or cream
⅓ cup confectioners' sugar
2 slices preserved ginger, cut in strips, optional
2 cups whipped cream or dessert topping
Red food color, optional

Combine first 6 ingredients in mixing bowl. Combine next 5 ingredients in blender container; **CHOP** 8 to 10 seconds. Stop motor and push ingredients into blades with rubber spatula. **CHOP** until smooth, 8 to 10 seconds. Stop motor and push ingredients into blades as needed. Pour over fruits. Add whipped cream or dessert topping and mix carefully. Fold in red color to tint mixture a pale pink color, if desired. Spoon into an aluminum foil lined 9 x 5 x 3-inch loaf pan. Freeze. To serve, unmold and serve plain or arrange on salad greens and decorate with whipped cream and maraschino cherries as desired. Makes 10 to 12 servings.

MOLDED TOMATO SALAD

See photo at right

2 packages (3-ounce) lemon-flavored gelatin
1 cup hot tomato juice
2 thin (⅛-inch) slices unpeeled lemon, quartered
1 thin (⅛-inch) slice onion
1 cup cold tomato juice
½ medium cucumber, peeled, cut in half and sliced
1 small tomato, washed, diced, and stem end removed
⅓ cup vinegar
½ teaspoon salt

PURÉE gelatin and hot tomato juice until gelatin is dissolved, about 10 seconds. Add lemon pieces and onion; **CHOP** 10 seconds, or until both lemon and onion are finely chopped. Add remaining ingredients. **BLEND** 30 seconds, or until vegetables are finely chopped. Chill until mixture starts to thicken. Pour into 4½-cup oiled mold. Chill until firm. Unmold on salad greens. Garnish with vegetables, relishes, tuna or salmon chunks, if desired. Makes 4½ cups, about 6 servings.

Crabmeat Salad in Avocado Shells page 148; Molded Tomato Salad page 140; Caesar Salad page 144

COOL-AS-A-CUCUMBER MOLD

A perfect salad for a sultry summer day

2 envelopes unflavored gelatin
½ cup hot water
3 cups cream-style cottage cheese
1 medium cucumber, sliced
½ cup Blender Mayonnaise (page 154)
1 (3-ounce) package cream cheese, cubed
2 slices onion
3 stalks celery, sliced
¼ cup walnuts

GRIND gelatin and hot water 40 seconds. Add all remaining ingredients and **GRIND** 20 seconds longer, stopping motor to push ingredients to blades, if necessary. Turn into 1½-quart mold and chill until firm. Makes 8 servings.

CREAMY TOMATO MOLDS

Serve these molds along with cold cuts, chicken or shrimp salad

1 (3-ounce) package lemon-flavored gelatin
⅔ cup hot tomato juice
⅔ cup cold tomato juice
⅔ cup cream-style cottage cheese
⅓ cup Blender Mayonnaise (page 154)
¼ green pepper, cubed
1 stalk celery, sliced
1 tablespoon lemon juice
½ teaspoon salt

GRIND gelatin and hot tomato juice 40 seconds. Add all remaining ingredients and **GRIND** 15 seconds longer. Turn into 4 or 6 individual molds or an 8-inch square pan and chill firm. Makes 4 to 6 servings. Serve with mayonnaise if desired.

CREAMY VEGETABLE MOLD

1 envelope unflavored gelatin
1 cup hot milk
1 (3-ounce) package cream cheese, cubed
1½ tablespoons lemon juice
1 teaspoon Dutch or Dijon mustard
½ teaspoon salt
2 cups sliced red or green cabbage
1 stalk celery, sliced
6 parsley sprigs

GRIND gelatin and milk for 40 seconds. Add cream cheese, lemon juice, mustard and salt and **GRIND** 10 seconds. Add vegetables and **GRATE** for 5 seconds or just until coarsely chopped. Turn into 6 individual molds, 1-quart mold or 8-inch square pan and chill until firm. Makes 6 servings.

TUNA-TOMATO ASPIC

Chill this pretty red salad in a fish-shaped mold

2 envelopes unflavored gelatin
1 tablespoon sugar
½ teaspoon salt
Dash hot pepper sauce
1 cup hot water
8 or 9 ice cubes
2 (8-ounce) cans tomato sauce
2 (7-ounce) cans tuna

GRIND gelatin, sugar, salt, hot pepper sauce and hot water 40 seconds. Add ice cubes and **GRIND** 30 seconds longer. Add tomato sauce and **GRIND** 10 seconds. Drain and flake tuna. Add to gelatin mixture, then turn into 1½-quart mold and chill until firm. Makes 8 servings.

CREAMY SALMON RING MOLD

½ unpeeled cucumber, sliced
½ cup cold water
2 envelopes (2 tablespoons) unflavored gelatin
1½ cups boiling water
1 thin slice unpeeled lemon, quartered
½ inch slice peeled lemon, halved
3 ice cubes (or ½ cup ice water)
1 teaspoon seasoned salt
½ teaspoon salt
4 drops hot red pepper sauce
1 cup Blender Mayonnaise (recipe page 154)
2 cans (1-pound) salmon, drained, boned and broken into chunks

GRIND cucumber in ½ cup cold water 5 seconds. Pour into bowl. **PURÉE** next 4 ingredients 10 seconds, or until gelatin is dissolved. Add ice cubes, seasonings and mayonnaise. **PURÉE** 10 seconds, or until smooth. Chill until syrupy. Add to cucumber mixture. Fold in ½ of the salmon pieces. Pour into oiled 6½ cup ring mold. Chill until firm. Unmold on salad greens. Fill center with greens and remaining salmon chunks. Makes about 6 cups, 6 to 8 servings.

SCANDINAVIAN CUCUMBERS

A summer time favorite!

¾ cup dairy sour cream
2 tablespoons tarragon vinegar
2 tablespoons sugar
6 parsley sprigs
1 slice onion
½ teaspoon dill seed
2 medium cucumbers, sliced

GRIND sour cream, vinegar, sugar, parsley, onion and dill seed 10 seconds. Pour over cucumbers. Chill thoroughly. Makes 6 servings.

CEYLON CHICKEN SALAD

¼ green pepper, cubed
2 stalks celery, sliced
2 tablespoons almonds
2 cups cubed, cooked chicken
¼ cup Blender Mayonnaise (page 154)
¼ cup drained pineapple tidbits
¼ cup seeded red or green grapes
1 teaspoon salt
1 teaspoon lemon juice
Lettuce cups

GRATE green pepper, celery and almonds 5 to 10 seconds. Add to all remaining ingredients in a mixing bowl and toss to mix thoroughly. Chill. Serve in lettuce cups. Makes 3 or 4 servings.

Scandinavian Cucumbers

CUCUMBER SLICES
IN SOUR CREAM OR YOGURT

½ cup French Dressing (recipe page 151)
½ cup dairy sour cream or yogurt
1 sliver garlic
3 sprigs mint (no stems), optional
1 teaspoon sugar
½ teaspoon salt
2 (5-inch) green onions, in 1-inch lengths
4 cups thin, peeled cucumber slices

BLEND first seven ingredients until vegetables are finely chopped, about 10 seconds. Pour over cucumber slices; mix carefully. Chill 1 to 2 hours. Makes about 3¾ cups, 6 to 8 servings.

HAM MOUSSE

1 cup tomato juice
2 envelopes unflavored gelatin
1 (1 x ½-inch) strip lemon peel
1 teaspoon sugar
½ tablespoon chopped chives
½ bay leaf
¼ teaspoon salt
½ cup cubed cooked ham
1 teaspoon paprika
1 cup heavy cream
1 cup crushed ice

Heat tomato juice, gelatin, lemon peel, sugar, chives, bay leaf and salt to boiling, stirring constantly. Cool slightly. **SHRED** ham, paprika and tomato juice mixture 10 seconds. Push mixture to center of container with rubber spatula. **SHRED** 30 seconds, adding cream and ice through opening in top while motor is running. Pour into oiled 1-quart mold; chill firm. Unmold. Makes 4 to 6 servings.

VEGETABLE BASKET SALAD

2 (1-pound) cans mixed vegetables
½ cup French Dressing (page 151)
2 envelopes unflavored gelatin
½ cup hot water
1½ cups cream-style cottage cheese
1¼ cups Blender Mayonnaise (page 154)
¾ cup heavy cream
2 tablespoons parsley sprigs
1 whole pimiento
1 slice onion
1 tablespoon lemon juice
½ teaspoon salt
½ teaspoon Worcestershire sauce

Drain vegetables; pour French Dressing over and chill while preparing rest of salad. **GRIND** gelatin and hot water 40 seconds. Add all remaining ingredients and **GRIND** 15 seconds longer. Turn into 5-cup ring mold and chill until firm. Unmold onto serving plate and fill center with marinated vegetables. Makes 8 servings.

GREEN GODDESS
SALAD

¾ cup Blender Mayonnaise (page 154)
¼ cup cooked, peeled and deveined shrimp
¼ cup dairy sour cream
1 hard-cooked egg, quartered
2 tablespoons lemon juice
2 tablespoons parsley sprigs
3 green onions, sliced
1 (4-ounce) can anchovies, drained
1 teaspoon Worcestershire sauce
1 clove garlic
½ teaspoon dry mustard
3 quarts assorted crisp salad greens
2 cups cooked, peeled and deveined shrimp

GRIND mayonnaise, the ¼ cup shrimp, sour cream, egg, lemon juice, parsley, onions, anchovies, Worcestershire sauce, garlic, and dry mustard 20 seconds. Pour dressing over greens and shrimp in large salad bowl and toss to coat greens. Makes 10 to 12 servings.

CAESAR SALAD

See photo page 141

1 clove garlic, sliced
½ cup salad oil
1 cup small bread cubes
1 thin (⅛-inch) slice unpeeled lemon, quartered
1½ teaspoons Worcestershire sauce
¾ teaspoon salt
¼ teaspoon pepper
1 egg
8 cups torn Boston and head lettuce or salad greens
¼ cup shredded Parmesan cheese (page 6)
6 to 8 anchovy fillets

GRATE garlic and oil until garlic is finely chopped, about 15 seconds. Heat 2 tablespoons of the oil mixture in frypan. Add bread cubes; brown lightly over moderate heat, stirring constantly. Drain cubes on paper toweling. Add lemon, Worcestershire sauce, salt and pepper to remaining oil in container. **GRATE** until lemon is finely chopped, about 30 seconds. Chill. Break egg over salad greens; toss to coat greens well. Add dressing, cheese and bread cubes; toss. Top with anchovy fillets. Makes about 7½ cups, 8 servings.

Cabbage Patch Slaw

CABBAGE PATCH SLAW

Choose cabbage with the curly outer leaves left on and reserve these leaves for a cabbage "bowl"

4 cups sliced cabbage
2 medium carrots, sliced
½ green pepper, cubed
1 slice onion
4 parsley sprigs
3 tablespoons vinegar
3 tablespoons sugar
2 tablespoons salad oil
1 teaspoon salt
½ teaspoon dill or celery seed
⅛ teaspoon dry mustard

Fill blender container with cabbage, carrots, green pepper, onion and parsley. Add water to cover. **GRATE** 3 to 5 seconds or just until ingredients at top reach the blades. Drain in sieve. Repeat with remaining cabbage, if necessary. Place in large mixing bowl. **BLEND** all remaining ingredients 5 seconds. Combine cabbage and dressing and mix well. Chill before serving. Makes 8 servings.

COLESLAW WITH SOUR CREAM DRESSING

4 cups sliced cabbage
2 carrots, peeled and sliced
½ green pepper, sliced
Cold water
1 cup dairy sour cream
¼ cup wine vinegar
4 (5-inch) green onions, in 1-inch lengths
2 tablespoons sugar
1 teaspoon salt
½ teaspoon celery seed

Fill container loosely, ⅔ full, with mixture of first 3 vegetables. Add cold water to cover vegetables. **MINCE** just until vegetables at top travel down to blades, about 5 seconds. Empty into sieve; drain vegetables very well. Refill container; repeat process. Chill vegetables. **CRUMB** remaining ingredients until onion is coarsely chopped, about 6 seconds. Drain vegetables well and add dressing; mix. Serve at once. Makes about 3 cups, 4 to 6 servings.

SUNNY CARROT SALAD

3 cups sliced carrots
¾ cup drained pineapple chunks
½ cup seedless raisins
⅓ cup mayonnaise
½ teaspoon salt
¼ teaspoon nutmeg

Place carrots in blender container; add water to cover and **GRATE** 2 to 3 seconds, or just until carrots on top reach the blades. Drain in sieve. Add remaining ingredients and toss thoroughly to mix. Makes 6 servings.

FRUITED COLESLAW

Prepare recipe for Coleslaw with Sour Cream Dressing (page 145), omit onions. Fold ½ cup each of well-drained crushed pineapple, seedless green grape halves and ¼ cup seedless raisins into mixture. Serve immediately. Makes about 4 cups, 5 to 6 servings.

CRANBERRY MARSHMALLOW SALAD

¼ pound (1-cup) washed, stemmed, raw cranberries
¼ cup sugar
2 cups miniature marshmallows
½ cup pecan halves
⅓ cup diced unpeeled apples
1 cup whipped cream or dessert topping

Pour cranberries, ⅓ cup at a time, into blender container. Set speed at **BLEND** and switch motor on and off until cranberries are coarsely chopped, 4 to 6 seconds. Empty into bowl. Stir sugar and marshmallows into berries. Cover and refrigerate overnight. Add pecan halves to blender container; **BLEND** switching motor on and off until coarsely chopped; add to cranberries. Chop apple as directed for nuts; add to cranberries. Fold in whipped cream; chill. Makes 4 to 6 servings.

RED AND GREEN SLAW

3 cups sliced green cabbage
1 cup sliced red cabbage
½ cup Blender Mayonnaise (page 154)
¼ cup dairy sour cream
¾ teaspoon dill seed
¾ teaspoon salt
⅛ teaspoon paprika
⅛ teaspoon pepper

Fill blender container with cabbage; add water to cover. **CHOP** 3 to 5 seconds, or just until ingredients at top reach blades. Repeat with remaining cabbage, if necessary. Drain in sieve. **MIX** all remaining ingredients 10 seconds; pour over cabbage and toss to mix. Chill. Makes 6 to 8 servings.

AMBROSIA

This salad can double as a dessert. Try serving it as an accompaniment to roast duckling

10 pitted dates
½ cup coconut
1 (1-inch) strip orange peel
1 (1-inch square) piece candied ginger
3 oranges, peeled and sliced
1 or 2 bananas, peeled and sliced
1 cup halved, seeded red or green grapes

GRATE dates, coconut, orange peel and ginger 10 seconds. Mix with orange and banana slices and red or green grapes, chill thoroughly. Makes 4 to 6 servings. Serve on crisp salad greens, in sherbet glasses or in sauce dishes.

SALMON COLESLAW

4 cups sliced cabbage
1 (1-pound) can salmon
½ cup Blender Mayonnaise (page 154)
¼ cup drained capers

Fill blender container with cabbage; add water to cover. **GRATE** 3 to 5 seconds, or just until cabbage at top reaches blades. Drain in sieve. Repeat with remaining cabbage, if necessary. Drain and flake salmon, add to cabbage along with mayonnaise and capers and toss thoroughly to mix. Chill before serving. Makes 6 servings.

SAUSAGE VEGETABLE SALAD

½ cup salad oil
¼ cup vinegar
1¼ teaspoons salt
½ teaspoon paprika
¼ teaspoon dry mustard
¼ teaspoon pepper
1 small clove garlic, sliced
1 package (9-ounce) frozen, cross-cut green beans,
  cooked, drained and chilled
1 cup sliced raw cauliflower
½ cup sliced green onion
1 package (10-ounce) frozen peas, cooked, drained
  and chilled
1 cup (½-inch) bias-sliced celery
2 cups coarsely shredded lettuce
4 smoked sausage links, cut into ½-inch bias slices

Combine first 7 ingredients in blender container.
BEAT until garlic is finely chopped, 3 to 5 seconds.
Pour over green beans, cauliflower and onion; toss.
Cover and marinate in refrigerator 1 hour. Just before
serving add remaining ingredients to beans; toss
lightly and serve. Makes 4 to 6 servings.

STUFFED PEAR OR PEACH SALAD

¼ cup Blender Mayonnaise (page 154)
1 package (8-ounce) room temperature, cream cheese,
  cubed
8 maraschino cherries
½ thin slice unpeeled lemon, quartered
2 tablespoons milk
8 large canned pear or peach halves
Salad greens
½ cup blender chopped nuts (see page 7 for chopping
  directions)

MINCE first 5 ingredients until smooth, about 50 seconds. Stop motor as needed and push ingredients
into blades. Arrange pear or peach halves, cavity
side up, on salad greens. Spoon cheese sauce over
fruit; sprinkle with chopped nuts. Makes 8 servings.

SALMAGUNDI SALAD

2 packages (6 or 7-ounce) sliced, summer sausage,
  salami or bologna, cut in eighths
4 hard-cooked eggs, quartered
¾ cup Blender Mayonnaise (recipe page 154)
2 (5-inch) green onions, cut in ½-inch lengths
⅓ cup catsup or chili sauce
1 teaspoon salt
1 package (7-ounce) elbow macaroni, seasoned,
  cooked, cooled and drained
1½ cups bias-sliced (½-inch) celery
1 cup diced (½-inch) Cheddar cheese

BLEND sausage pieces in container ½ cup at a time,
switching motor on and off until coarsely chopped,
8 to 10 seconds. Empty into salad bowl. **BLEND** ½
of eggs at a time switching motor on and off until
coarsely chopped. Add eggs to sausage. Combine
next 4 ingredients in container; **BLEND** until onion
is coarsely chopped. Add to sausage; mix and add
macaroni, celery and cheese; mix carefully. Cover
and chill. Makes 8 servings.

SOUR CREAM POTATO SALAD

5 cups chilled sliced cooked potatoes
1 cup diced (½-inch) peeled cucumber
½ cup sliced radishes
4 hard-cooked eggs, quartered
½ cup Blender Mayonnaise (recipe page 154)
2 tablespoons vinegar
1 tablespoon prepared mustard
3 thin (⅛-inch) onion slices, quartered
1½ teaspoons salt
⅛ teaspoon pepper
1 cup (½-pint) dairy sour cream
½ teaspoon celery seed

Combine first 3 ingredients in bowl. **BLEND** ½ of the
eggs at a time, switching motor on and off until very
coarsely chopped. Pour onto potato mixture. Combine next 6 ingredients; **BLEND** until onion is finely
chopped. Pour onto potato mixture. Mix sour cream
and celery seed; add to potatoes. Mix carefully.
Makes 6 to 8 servings.

CRABMEAT SALAD IN AVOCADO SHELLS

See photo page 141

½ cup Blender Mayonnaise (recipe page 154)
1 (⅛-inch) slice unpeeled lime or lemon, quartered
1 tablespoon drained capers
1 thin (⅛-inch) slice small onion, quartered
3 or 4 sprigs parsley, no stems
1 package (10-ounce) frozen peas, cooked, chilled and drained
1 package (6 or 7-ounce) defrosted, frozen crabmeat, broken into chunks
½ cup diced celery
Washed lettuce leaves
2 ripe avocados, peeled, seeded and halved
1 tablespoon lime or lemon juice

Combine first 5 ingredients in blender container; **CREAM** until well mixed and smooth. Chill. Combine mayonnaise mixture and next 3 ingredients; mix carefully. Arrange lettuce leaves on 4 salad plates. Place an avocado half on each salad plate; drizzle lime or lemon juice over avocado halves; fill cavities with salad mixture. Makes 4 salads.

CHICKEN, TURKEY OR HAM SALAD

2 cups diced cooked chicken, turkey or ham
¾ cup (½-inch) bias-sliced celery
¾ cup Blender Mayonnaise (recipe page 154)
3 medium sweet pickles, in 1-inch slices or 8 medium stuffed olives, quartered
½ teaspoon salt

Combine first 2 ingredients in mixing bowl. **BLEND** next 3 ingredients until pickles or olives are coarsely chopped, switching motor on and off as needed. Add to poultry or ham; mix. Serve as salad or sandwich spread. Makes about 3 cups.

TUNA-MAC SALAD

¼ cup Blender Mayonnaise (page 154)
1 tablespoon lemon juice
½ green pepper, cubed
2 stalks celery, sliced
3 green onions, sliced
¼ cup sliced sweet pickle
1½ teaspoons salt
1 (7-ounce) can tuna, drained and flaked
4 cups chilled cooked macaroni
Hard-cooked egg slices and cherry tomatoes for garnish

GRIND mayonnaise, lemon juice, green pepper, celery, onions, pickle and salt 5 to 10 seconds. Add to tuna and macaroni and toss well to mix. Garnish with hard-cooked egg slices and cherry tomatoes. Makes 4 to 6 servings.

HOT POTATO SALAD

Perfect for a patio or barbecue supper

6 medium potatoes
4 slices bacon, diced
⅓ cup cider vinegar
2 slices onion
2 stalks celery, sliced
6 parsley sprigs
1 to 2 tablespoons sugar
1½ teaspoons salt
¼ teaspoon marjoram or basil

Cook potatoes in boiling salted water until tender. Drain; peel and keep warm. Cook bacon in skillet until crisp. **GRATE** vinegar, onion, celery, parsley and seasonings 2 to 3 seconds. Add to bacon and fat in skillet and heat to boiling. Cube or slice potatoes into large bowl and pour bacon mixture over. Toss lightly to mix. Serve hot. Makes 6 servings.

SALMON SALAD WITH LOUIS DRESSING

1 cup Blender Mayonnaise (recipe page 154)
¼ cup chili sauce or catsup
1 (5-inch) green onion, cut in 1-inch lengths
1 thin (⅛-inch) slice unpeeled lemon, quartered
3 or 4 sprigs parsley, no stems
1 tablespoon drained capers
½ cup whipped cream
1 can (1-pound) salmon, drained, boned and broken into bite-size chunks
2 ripe tomatoes, cut into wedges
4 hard-cooked eggs, sliced
½ cup pitted black olives, sliced
Crisp salad greens

Combine first 6 ingredients in blender container; **CREAM** until smooth, 3 to 5 seconds. Turn into bowl; fold in whipped cream and chill. Arrange salmon, tomato wedges, egg slices and olive slices attractively on a bed of salad greens. Serve with dressing. Makes 6 servings.

SALAD DRESSINGS

It takes a fine dressing to make a distinctive salad and fine dressings galore are inexpensive and fun to make when a blender is handy. Fresh home-made dressings are superior in flavor to the commercial ready-made dressings with their preservatives and artificial coloring.

No trick to make perfect satin-smooth mayonnaise, salad dressings or dozens of pouring dressings. Just use the easy-to-follow, blender-made recipes that follow. Served on a beautiful salad they'll make your salads conversation pieces.

FRENCH DRESSING

1 cup salad oil
⅓ cup cider or red wine vinegar
1 slice (⅛-inch) onion, quartered
¼ cup sugar
1 teaspoon dry mustard
½ teaspoon paprika
½ teaspoon salt
¼ teaspoon Worcestershire sauce
Dash hot red pepper sauce

CRUMB ingredients until smooth, 10 to 15 seconds. Makes about 1⅓ cups.

VARIATIONS

Follow above recipe for French Dressing and add the ingredients suggested below before blending.

AVOCADO DRESSING: Peel, seed and cube 1 avocado; add to container before blending. Makes about 1⅔ cups.

CAPER DRESSING: Add 1 tablespoon drained capers and 1 small sprig parsley (no stems) before blending. Makes about 1⅓ cups.

CHIFFONADE DRESSING: Add ¼ pimiento, 1 sliced hard-cooked egg, 4 sprigs parsley (no stems) and 2 green onions, in 1-inch lengths to container before blending. Makes about 1¾ cups.

CURRY DRESSING: Add 2 tablespoons honey or orange marmalade, 1 tablespoon chutney and 1 teaspoon curry powder to container before blending. Makes about 1½ cups.

GARLIC DRESSING: Add 1 or 2 garlic cloves, sliced, to container before blending. Makes about 1⅓ cups.

GINGER DRESSING: Add 1 or 2 pieces preserved ginger cut in strips, and 1 tablespoon preserved ginger syrup to container before blending. Makes about 1⅔ cups.

ITALIAN CHEESE DRESSING: Add 1 sliver garlic, ¼ teaspoon coarse black pepper and 1 teaspoon Worcestershire sauce to container before blending. Pour into bowl; stir in ½ cup blender-grated Parmesan cheese (chopping directions page 6). Makes about 1¾ cups.

LORENZO DRESSING: Add ¼ cup watercress leaves, 3 tablespoons chili sauce and 2 green onions (cut in 1-inch lengths) to container before blending. Makes about 1½ cups.

PARSLEY FRENCH DRESSING: Add ¼ cup parsley sprigs (no stems) and ¼ cup chili sauce to container before blending. Makes about 1½ cups.

BLUE CHEESE DRESSING

Shown in the tall slender bottle at the left. Serve over assorted greens, fruits or sliced tomatoes

¾ cup salad oil
¼ to ⅓-cup red or white-wine vinegar
1 (3 or 4-ounce) package Blue or Roquefort cheese, cubed
3 green onions, sliced
¼ teaspoon salt
¼ teaspoon paprika
⅛ teaspoon dry mustard
⅛ teaspoon pepper

GRIND all ingredients 10 seconds in blender container of wide-mouth canning and freezing jar. Makes about 1⅓ cups.

ROQUEFORT CREAM DRESSING

The nicest thing you can do to a salad!

1 (8-ounce) package cream cheese, cubed
1 (3 or 4-ounce) package Roquefort or Blue cheese, cubed
½ cup milk
1 tablespoon lemon juice
1 teaspoon salt
½ clove garlic (optional)
½ teaspoon tarragon or basil
¼ teaspoon pepper

GRIND all ingredients 30 to 40 seconds or until smooth, stopping motor once to push ingredients to blades, if necessary. Makes about 2 cups dressing.

FROZEN ROQUEFORT DRESSING

Cut small cubes of this dressing to scatter over fruit salads or melon wedges

½ cup heavy cream
¼ cup Blender Mayonnaise (page 154)
1 (3-ounce) package cream cheese, cubed
1 (3 or 4-ounce) package Roquefort or Blue cheese, cubed
1 (1-inch) piece lemon peel
1 whole lemon, peeled
2 stalks celery, sliced
¼ teaspoon salt

GRIND all ingredients 40 seconds. Pour into 8-inch square pan and freeze firm. Cut in cubes. Makes 6 servings.

ROQUEFORT DRESSING

⅔ cup half and half (half milk, half cream)
½ cup crumbled Roquefort cheese
1 teaspoon dry mustard
½ teaspoon salt
⅛ teaspoon pepper
2 teaspoons paprika
1-inch square lemon rind, cut into slivers
⅔ cup salad oil
2 tablespoons vinegar

CRUMB first 7 ingredients until fairly smooth, 8 to 10 seconds. Add oil and vinegar, alternately, in a fine steady stream through top opening while motor is running, about 20 seconds. Stop motor and push ingredients into blades with rubber spatula as needed. Makes about 1½ cups.

TOMATO SOUP DRESSING

1 can (10½-ounce) condensed tomato soup
⅔ cup cider vinegar
⅔ cup salad oil
⅓ cup sugar
1 thin (⅛-inch) slice onion (2-inch diameter)
1 tablespoon Worcestershire sauce
1 teaspoon salt
1 teaspoon dry mustard
¼ teaspoon pepper
½ medium clove garlic, cut into slivers

CRUMB ingredients until smooth, about 15 seconds. Makes about 2⅔ cups.

RED FRENCH DRESSING

1 cup salad oil
½ cup vinegar or lemon juice
½ cup catsup
⅓ cup sugar
1½ teaspoons paprika
1 teaspoon salt
¼ teaspoon pepper
1 thin (⅛-inch) slice onion (2-inch diameter)

CRUMB ingredients until onion is finely chopped, 10 to 15 seconds. Makes about 2¼ cups.

LOW CALORIE FRENCH DRESSING

1 can (8-ounce) tomato sauce
⅓ cup salad oil
½ teaspoon prepared mustard
2 thin (⅛-inch) slices onion, quartered
Dash of liquid hot pepper sauce
4 sprigs parsley (no stems)
½ teaspoon Worcestershire sauce
¼ cup lemon juice or vinegar

GRATE all ingredients in container until vegetables are finely chopped, about 10 seconds. Makes about 1⅓ cups.

HONEY DRESSING

½ cup honey
½ cup salad oil
⅓ cup vinegar, lemon or lime juice
⅓ cup sugar
1 teaspoon celery seed
½ teaspoon salt
2 teaspoons prepared mustard
Dash liquid hot pepper sauce
1 teaspoon paprika
1 thin (⅛-inch) slice onion (2-inch diameter)

CREAM ingredients until well mixed, about 20 seconds. Makes about 1¼ cups.

NIPPY DRESSING FOR FISH AND SEAFOOD

⅓ cup cider vinegar
2 tablespoons sugar
1 teaspoon salt
1 teaspoon paprika
¼ teaspoon pepper
½ teaspoon horseradish
2 teaspoons prepared mustard
2 (4-inch) green onions, cut in 1-inch lengths

STIR all ingredients until onions are finely chopped, about 10 seconds. Makes about ½ cup.

TARRAGON LEMON DRESSING

1 cup salad oil
2 (1-inch) pieces lemon peel
1 whole lemon, peeled
2 tablespoons tarragon vinegar
½ tablespoon sugar
1 teaspoon tarragon
½ teaspoon salt
6 peppercorns

GRIND all ingredients 40 seconds in blender container or Mini-Blend Container. Makes about 1½ cups.

CREAMY CHEESE
CUCUMBER DRESSING

¾ cup coarsely chopped unpeeled cucumber
1 thin (⅛-inch) slice unpeeled lemon, quartered
1 cup sliced (1-inch) celery
1 thin (⅛-inch) slice onion
2 packages (3-ounce) room temperature cream cheese,
   cubed
½ teaspoon salt
¼ teaspoon sugar

Add cucumber and lemon slice to container. **CHOP**
switching motor on and off until coarsely chopped,
8 to 10 seconds. Add celery and onion. **CHOP** switching motor on and off until coarsely chopped, 15 to
20 seconds. Add remaining ingredients; **CHOP** until
blended, 8 to 10 seconds. Stop motor as needed and
push ingredients into blades with rubber spatula.
Chill. Makes about 1½ cups.

SOUR CREAM
CUCUMBER DRESSING

⅓ cup dairy sour cream
¼ medium cucumber, sliced
1½ tablespoons vinegar
2 teaspoons sugar
1 slice onion
¾ teaspoon salt
⅛ teaspoon dry mustard
⅛ teaspoon pepper

GRIND all ingredients 20 seconds in blender container or Mini-Blend Container. Makes 1 cup.

SOUR CREAM DRESSING

¼ cup vinegar
¼ cup dairy sour cream
1 egg
2 tablespoons sugar
1 teaspoon salt
1 teaspoon flour
1 teaspoon dry mustard
¼ teaspoon paprika

CRUMB ingredients until smooth, 8 to 10 seconds.
Pour into heavy saucepan. Heat slowly over very low
heat, until thickened, stirring constantly. Cool. Makes
about ⅔ cup.

Sour Cream Dressing

BLENDER MAYONNAISE

Easy to make and perfect every time!

1 egg or 2 egg yolks
2 tablespoons lemon juice or vinegar
½ teaspoon sugar
½ teaspoon salt
¼ teaspoon dry mustard
1 cup salad oil

GRIND egg, lemon juice, sugar, salt and mustard 70 seconds, adding oil in a steady stream through opening in top while motor is running. Makes about 1½ cups.

NOTE: If mayonnaise curdles or liquefies, empty contents from container, blend another egg and one-fourth cup of the liquid mayonnaise until mixed, then pour remaining liquid mayonnaise instead of oil into center of container. Use rubber spatula to thoroughly blend oil into mixture.

CREAMY GARLIC DRESSING: BEAT 1 cup Blender Mayonnaise (recipe above), 1 cup dairy sour cream, ¼ teaspoon white pepper, 1 thin (⅛-inch) onion slice and 2 medium cloves garlic, sliced, 20 seconds or until onion and garlic are finely chopped. Stop motor; push ingredients into blades with rubber spatula as needed. Chill. Makes 2 cups.

THOUSAND ISLAND DRESSING: BEAT 1 cup Blender Mayonnaise (recipe above), ⅓ cup chili sauce, 1 thin (⅛-inch) onion slice (2-inch diameter), ¼ teaspoon paprika, ½ teaspoon sugar and ¼ teaspoon salt 10 seconds or until blended and onion is finely chopped. Add 2 (3-inch) sweet pickles, cut in 1-inch pieces and 2 hard-cooked eggs, quartered. **BEAT** 3 to 5 seconds or until coarsely chopped. Chill. Makes about 2 cups.

PINEAPPLE CHERRY DRESSING: Fold ½ cup well-drained canned crushed pineapple and 8 maraschino cherries, cut in eighths, into 1 cup Blender Mayonnaise (recipe above). Makes about 1½ cups.

RUSSIAN DRESSING: Stir ¼ cup Red French Dressing (recipe page 152), 2 tablespoons chili sauce or catsup, 1 tablespoon minced onion and ⅓ cup minced green pepper into ½ cup Blender Mayonnaise (recipe above). Makes about 1 cup.

CREAMY DRESSING FOR FRUITS

1 cup Blender Mayonnaise (recipe at left)
1 package (3-ounce) room temperature cream cheese, cubed
1 tablespoon thick orange marmalade
1 thin (⅛-inch) slice unpeeled orange, quartered
2 medium (1 x 1½-inch) pieces candied or preserved ginger, quartered
¼ cup pecan halves

CRUMB first 5 ingredients until smooth, 30 to 35 seconds. Stop motor and push ingredients into blades with rubber spatula as needed. Add pecan halves. Switch motor on and off 3 times or until pecans are coarsely chopped. Makes about 1½ cups.

FLUFFY CREAM CHEESE DRESSING: Fold 1 cup whipped cream or whipped dessert topping into Creamy Dressing for Fruits (recipe above). Makes about 2½ cups.

CREAM CHEESE HONEY DRESSING

See photo at right

⅓ cup pecan or walnut halves
1 cup Blender Mayonnaise (recipe at left)
2 tablespoons honey
1 slice (⅛-inch) unpeeled orange, quartered
1 package (3-ounce) room temperature cream cheese, cubed
1 or 2 pieces preserved ginger, quartered, optional
8 maraschino cherries, quartered
¼ cup well-drained canned crushed pineapple

CHOP nuts, switching motor on and off until coarsely chopped, 10 to 15 seconds. Pour into bowl; save. Combine next 4 ingredients in container in order listed. **BEAT** until mixture is smooth, 20 to 30 seconds. Stop motor as needed and push ingredients into blades with rubber spatula. Add ginger and cherries. **CHOP** switching motor on and off until cherries and ginger are finely chopped, 5 to 10 seconds. Stop motor as needed and push ingredients into blades with rubber spatula. Turn into bowl; fold in nuts and pineapple. Chill. Makes about 1¾ cups.

PINEAPPLE CREAM DRESSING

See photo at right

½ cup sugar
2 tablespoons cornstarch
½ teaspoon salt
1 cup pineapple or orange juice
2 eggs
2 thin slices unpeeled lemon or orange, quartered
½ cup drained crushed pineapple
1 cup whipped cream or whipped dessert topping

CRUMB first 6 ingredients until rind is finely chopped, about 15 seconds. Pour into heavy saucepan. Cook over very low heat until thickened, stirring constantly. Cool. Fold in pineapple and whipped cream. Makes about 2½ cups.

PEANUT-ORANGE DRESSING

See photo at right

½ cup salted peanuts
⅓ cup orange juice
1 tablespoon lemon juice
1 square (1-inch) unpeeled orange, cut in strips
2 tablespoons sugar
1 package (8-ounce) room temperature cream cheese, cubed

CHOP peanuts, switching motor on and off, until coarsely chopped, about 10 to 15 seconds. Pour into bowl; save. Add fruit juices, orange rind and sugar to container. **LIQUEFY** until orange rind is finely chopped, about 8 seconds. Add cream cheese, ½ at a time, and **BEAT** until smooth, 20 to 25 seconds. Stop motor as needed and push ingredients into blades with rubber spatula. Add remaining cream cheese and repeat process. Turn into bowl; fold in peanuts. Chill. Makes about 1⅓ cups.

COOKED SALAD DRESSING

¾ cup milk
¾ cup water
3 eggs
1 tablespoon salad oil
½ cup sugar
⅓ cup flour
2 teaspoons salt
2 teaspoons dry mustard
½ teaspoon paprika
½ cup vinegar

CHOP all ingredients except vinegar until smooth, about 10 seconds. Pour into heavy saucepan. Cook over very low heat until thickened, stirring constantly. Stir in vinegar; mix well. Cool. Makes about 2¾ cups.

COOKED SOUR CREAM SALAD DRESSING: Fold ½ cup dairy sour cream and ¼ teaspoon paprika into 1 recipe chilled Cooked Salad Dressing (recipe above). Makes about 3 cups.

Cream Cheese Honey Dressing (top), page 154
Pineapple Cream Dressing (middle),
Peanut-Orange Dressing For Fruits (bottom)

155

SANDWICHES & SPREADS

Sanwiches come in all sizes and shapes these days, plain and fancy ones for most every occasion.

With a blender it's easy to make sandwiches for a few or a bunch. The blender chops sandwich and canapé spreads and filling spreads satin smooth or crisp and crunchy, in seconds. Here are just a few suggestions that will make sandwich preparation easy.

1. Prepare small batches at a time, about 1 cup of sandwich spread. It's quicker, easier and the spread is more uniformly blended.

2. When textured spreads are being prepared **CHOP** cooked meat, sausage or poultry, hard-cooked eggs, nuts, celery, green pepper, etc., separately to the fineness desired. Blend ⅓ to ½ cup of the food at a time, switching motor on and off, until it is chopped just right, then fold it into the blended mayonnaise or cream cheese base.

3. When heavy cheese or salad mixtures are being processed stop the motor as needed and push the ingredients into the blades with rubber spatula. If the motor labors add 1 or 2 tablespoons of a suitable liquid (milk, meat stock, French dressing, etc.).

CORNED BEEF SANDWICH SPREAD

1 can (12-ounce) corned beef, chilled and cubed
⅓ cup Blender Mayonnaise (recipe page 154)
1 teaspoon prepared mustard
¼ teaspoon horseradish, optional
2 (3-inch) sweet pickles, quartered

CHOP ⅓ of corned beef cubes at a time, switching motor on and off as necessary to chop meat moderately fine, 15 to 20 seconds. Turn into mixing bowl. Add next 4 ingredients to container; **BLEND** until pickles are coarsely chopped, 20 to 25 seconds. Stop motor; push ingredients into blades with rubber spatula as needed. Add to meat; mix. Makes about 1½ cups spread.

CORNED BEEF SWISS CHEESE SANDWICH

8 slices rye or whole wheat bread, buttered
Leaf lettuce
1 recipe Corned Beef Sandwich Spread (recipe above)
8 thin tomato slices, optional
4 slices Swiss cheese

Cover ½ of bread slices with lettuce leaves; spoon ¼ of the Corned Beef Sandwich Spread onto each bread slice and top with 2 tomato slices. Cover with Swiss cheese and second bread slice. Makes 4 big sandwiches.

CORNED BEEF CHEESE SANDWICHES: Follow recipe for Corned Beef Swiss Cheese Sandwich and substitute sliced American or Cheddar for Swiss cheese. Makes 4 sandwiches.

CORNED BEEF SAUERKRAUT SANDWICH

1 recipe Corned Beef Sandwich Spread (recipe above)
4 Vienna, Kaiser or poppyseed rolls, split and buttered
Lettuce leaves
½ to ¾ cup well-drained sauerkraut

Prepare Corned Beef Sandwich Spread. Spread ¼ of the meat spread on bottom half of each roll. Cover with lettuce and top with 2 to 3 tablespoons very well-drained sauerkraut. Cover with roll top. Makes 4 big sandwiches.

WAIKIKI CHICKEN SANDWICHES

⅓ cup pecan or walnut halves or salted peanuts
½ cup Blender Mayonnaise or Cooked Salad Dressing (recipes page 154 and 155)
2 tablespoons lemon or lime juice
1 or 2 pieces preserved ginger, quartered, optional
¼ teaspoon salt
1 cup diced cooked chicken
½ cup diced celery
⅓ cup well-drained canned crushed pineapple
Leaf lettuce
10 to 12 slices raisin or nut bread, buttered.

CHOP nuts, switching motor on and off until coarsely chopped, 10 to 15 seconds. Pour into bowl; save. Combine next 4 ingredients in container. **BLEND** until ginger is finely chopped. Add to nuts. Fold in chicken, celery and pineapple. Arrange lettuce leaves on ½ of buttered bread slices. Top each with chicken mixture; cover with remaining bread slices. Makes about 1⅓ cups filling, 5 to 6 sandwiches.

WAIKIKI TURKEY SANDWICHES: Follow recipe for Waikiki Chicken Sandwiches above and substitute diced cooked turkey for chicken. Makes 5 to 6 sandwiches.

CHICKEN-ALMOND SANDWICHES: Follow recipe for Waikiki Chicken Sandwiches above and substitute toasted almonds for pecans or walnuts, reduce lemon juice to 2 teaspoons and omit pineapple. Makes about 1¼ cups filling, 5 to 6 sandwiches.

CHICKEN SALAD SPREAD

¾ cup Blender Mayonnaise (recipe page 154)
2 or 3 (3-inch) sweet pickles, in ½-inch pieces
½ thin (⅛-inch) slice onion, optional
½ teaspoon salt
1¼ cups diced cooked chicken
½ cup diced celery

Combine first 4 ingredients in container; **BLEND** until pickles are coarsely chopped, 4 to 8 seconds. Stop motor; push ingredients into blades with rubber spatula as needed. Turn into mixing bowl; fold in chicken and celery. Makes about 2⅓ cups.

TURKEY SALAD SPREAD: Follow recipe for Chicken Salad Spread above and substitute diced cooked turkey for chicken. Makes about 2⅓ cups.

HAM FILLING

Spread on tiny slices of rye bread for open-face appetizers

1 cup cooked diced ham
½ cup sliced celery
¼ cup mayonnaise

GRATE all ingredients 15 seconds, stopping motor to push ingredients to blades, if necessary. Makes 1 cup.

EGG SALAD SPREAD

⅓ cup mayonnaise
¼ cup chili sauce
½ teaspoon salt
8 hard-cooked eggs
¼ cup sliced pimiento-stuffed green olives

BLEND mayonnaise, chili sauce and salt 5 seconds. Add eggs and olives and **GRATE** 15 seconds, stopping motor to push ingredients to blades, if necessary. **GRATE** a few seconds longer for smoother spread, if desired. Makes about 2 cups.

CURRIED EGG FILLING

4 hard-cooked eggs, quartered
¼ cup mayonnaise
½ teaspoon curry powder

BLEND all ingredients 30 seconds, stopping motor to push ingredients to blades, if necessary. Makes 1 cup.

SALAMI EGG SANDWICH SPREAD

1 package (7 or 8-ounce) sliced cotto salami, cut in 6 wedges
2 hard-cooked eggs, quartered
1 package (3-ounce) room temperature cream cheese, cubed
⅓ cup Blender Mayonnaise (recipe page 154)
2 teaspoons prepared mustard
½ teaspoon horseradish
2 small (2-inch) sweet pickles, sliced

GRATE salami, a few pieces at a time, switching motor on and off until meat is desired fineness; turn into bowl. **GRATE** eggs, switching motor on and off until desired fineness. Add to salami. **GRATE** remaining ingredients until smooth; fold into salami and eggs. Makes about 2 cups.

HAM AND EGG SANDWICH SPREAD: Follow recipe for Salami Egg Sandwich Spread (recipe above); substitute 1 cup diced fully cooked ham for salami. Makes about 2 cups.

HAM SALAD SPREAD

1 cup (½-inch cubes) fully-cooked ham
⅔ cup Blender Mayonnaise (page 154)
2 (2-inch) sweet pickles, in ½-inch slices or 8 medium-size stuffed olives, cut in half
2 thin (⅛-inch) slices onion, quartered

BLEND ham, ⅓ cup at a time, switching motor on and off until ham is desired fineness, 10 to 15 seconds. Turn into mixing bowl. **BLEND** remaining ingredients until pickles are finely chopped, about 5 seconds. Add to ham; mix well. Makes about 1½ cups.

OLD VIRGINIA HAM SALAD SPREAD: Follow recipe for Ham Salad Spread above. After ham is chopped, **BLEND** ½ cup salted peanuts, switching motor on and off until chopped moderately fine. Add to ham. Proceed as directed in above recipe. Makes about 1½ cups.

BACON AND EGG SANDWICH SPREAD

4 chilled hard-cooked eggs, sliced
½ cup Blender Mayonnaise or Cooked Salad Dressing (recipes page 154 and 155)
2 (3-inch) sweet pickles, quartered
6 or 8 slices crisp broiled bacon, broken into quarters
¼ teaspoon salt

CHOP two eggs at a time, switching motor on and off until eggs are coarsely chopped. Empty into mixing bowl. Combine mayonnaise or salad dressing and pickles in container. **CHOP** pickles, switching motor on and off until chopped moderately fine, 10 to 15 seconds. Add bacon pieces and salt; **CHOP** switching motor on and off until coarsely chopped, 8 to 10 seconds. Add to eggs; mix. Makes about 1⅓ cups.

BACON 'N EGG SANDWICH ON FRENCH ROLLS

1 recipe Bacon and Egg Sandwich Spread (recipe above)
Lettuce leaves
4 or 6 individual French rolls, split and buttered
8 or 12 thin tomato slices
4 or 6 slices crisp bacon, optional

Cover bottom of rolls with lettuce and Bacon and Egg Sandwich Spread. Top each with 2 tomato slices and a crisp bacon slice. Cover with bun top. Makes 4 to 6 sandwiches depending upon size of French rolls.

A. Corned Beef Sandwich Spread page 157
B. Chicken Salad Spread page 157
C. Ham Filling page 158
D. Salami Egg Sandwich Spread page 158
E. Liver Sausage Pickle Spread page 160
F. Bacon and Egg Sandwich Spread page 158

LIVER SAUSAGE-PICKLE SPREAD

½ cup Blender Mayonnaise (recipe page 154)
¼ cup catsup or chili sauce
1 tablespoon dill pickle juice
Dash of liquid hot pepper sauce
½ small (1½-inch) onion, quartered and sliced
2 (3-inch) dill pickles, in ½-inch slices
½ pound liver sausage, cubed

Combine first 5 ingredients in container; **BLEND** until mixed and onion is coarsely chopped, 3 to 5 seconds. Add pickle slices; **BLEND** pickles, switching motor on and off until coarsely chopped, 5 to 8 seconds. Add ⅓ of the liver sausage cubes at a time and **BEAT** until mixed, 25 to 30 seconds. Stop motor and push ingredients into blades with rubber spatula as needed. Add ½ of remaining liver sausage; process as above. Add remaining liver sausage; process as above. Makes about 1½ cups spread.

LIVER SAUSAGE PEANUT SPREAD

½ cup salted peanuts
⅓ cup Blender Mayonnaise (recipe page 154)
½ pound liver sausage, cubed

CHOP peanuts, switching motor on and off until coarsely chopped, 10 to 15 seconds. Pour into mixing bowl. Add mayonnaise and ⅓ of the liver sausage cubes at a time to container; **BEAT** until mixed, 25 to 30 seconds. Stop motor and push ingredients into blades with rubber spatula as needed. Add ½ of remaining liver sausage; process as directed above. Add remaining liver sausage; process as directed above. Add to nuts; mix. Makes about 1¼ cups spread.

LIVER SAUSAGE DEVILED HAM SPREAD

½ cup Blender Mayonnaise (recipe page 154)
1 can (2¼-ounce) deviled ham
1 teaspoon horseradish
½ pound liver sausage, cubed
⅓ cup well-drained sweet pickle relish

Combine first 3 ingredients in container. **BLEND** until mixed, 4 to 5 seconds. Add ⅓ of liver sausage at a time and **BEAT** until mixed, 25 to 30 seconds. Stop motor and push ingredients into blades with rubber spatula as necessary. Add ½ of remaining liver sausage; process as directed above. Add remaining liver sausage; process as directed above. Turn into mixing bowl; mix in pickle relish. Makes about 1½ cups spread.

LIVER SAUSAGE ON POPPYSEED ROLLS

Spread bottom halves of split and buttered poppyseed rolls with 3 or 4 tablespoons liver sausage sandwich spread (use one of the spreads at left). Top with thin Bermuda onion slice, a tomato slice and a crisp lettuce leaf. Cover with bun top.

FRANKS WITH EVERYTHING SPREAD

5 frankfurters, sliced
½ cup mayonnaise
½ cup sliced pitted ripe olives
½ cup sliced sweet pickles
1 tablespoon prepared mustard

GRIND all ingredients 45 seconds, stopping motor to push ingredients to blades, if necessary. Makes 2 cups.

ZESTY BEEF SANDWICHES

1 cup Blender Mayonnaise (recipe page 154)
1½ teaspoons prepared mustard
4 small sprigs parsley (no stems)
½ teaspoon curry powder
¾ teaspoon paprika
16 slices rye or whole wheat bread
16 to 24 thin slices cold roast beef
Lettuce leaves

Combine first 5 ingredients in container; **BLEND** until parsley is minced, 5 to 8 seconds. Spread each bread slice with 1½ teaspoons of mayonnaise mixture. Top ½ of slices with 2 or 3 slices of beef. Top meat with lettuce; cover with remaining bread slices. Makes 8 sandwiches.

POLYNESIAN PORK SANDWICHES: Follow recipe for Zesty Beef Sandwich (recipe above) and change as follows: Reduce prepared mustard to ½ teaspoon. If desired, add 1 piece of preserved ginger, quartered, to mayonnaise mixture before processing. Use whole wheat bread and substitute cold roast pork for beef. For a more exotic sandwich, top lettuce leaf with a small well-drained pineapple slice and a slice of avocado before closing. Makes 8 sandwiches.

HOT HAM 'N EGG BUNWICHES

Follow recipe for Hot Tuna-Cheese Bunwiches (page 161) and substitute 1 cup finely diced fully cooked ham for tuna. Makes about 2¼ cups filling, 8 bunwiches.

SALMON SALAD SPREAD

1 cup Blender Mayonnaise (recipe page 154)
1 thin (⅛-inch) slice unpeeled lemon, quartered
1 thin (⅛-inch) slice onion, quartered
2 (3-inch) sweet pickles, quartered
½ cup (½-inch) celery slices
1 can (1-pound) salmon, drained, skinned, bonned, and flaked

Combine mayonnaise and lemon in container. **GRATE** until lemon peel is minced, about 10 seconds. Add onion; **GRATE** until onion is minced. Add pickles and celery and **CHOP** switching motor on and off until pickles and celery are chopped moderately fine 20 to 25 seconds. Stop motor as needed and push ingredients into blades with rubber spatula. Turn into mixing bowl; fold in salmon. Makes about 3 cups, filling for 6 to 8 sandwiches.

CRABMEAT SANDWICH SPREAD

½ cup Blender Mayonnaise (recipe page 154)
¼ cup catsup or chili sauce
2 teaspoons lemon juice
¼ cup sliced (½-inch) celery
2 (3-inch) sweet pickles, quartered
1 can (6½-ounce) crabmeat, drained and flaked

Combine first 5 ingredients in container. **CHOP** switching motor on and off until celery and pickles are chopped moderately fine, 10 to 15 seconds. Stop motor; push ingredients into blades with rubber spatula as needed. Turn into mixing bowl; fold in crabmeat. Makes about 1⅓ cups spread.

CRABMEAT ROLLS

6 French or Vienna rolls, split and buttered
Lettuce leaves
1 recipe Crabmeat Sandwich Spread (recipe above)

Cover bottom of rolls with lettuce. Top each with an equal amount of crabmeat mixture; cover with roll tops. Makes 6 sandwiches.

BROILED CRABMEAT SANDWICH

Prepare Crabmeat Sandwich Spread (recipe above). Spread mixture onto bottom of 6 hamburger buns; top each with a slice of process American cheese. Arrange on broiler rack along with bun tops, cut surfaces towards heat. Broil 5 to 6-inches below heating unit until sandwich warms, cheese melts and bun tops toast, 5 to 10 minutes. Makes 6 sandwiches.

SHRIMP SANDWICH SPREAD

1 cup cooked, peeled and deveined shrimp
½ cup mayonnaise
½ cup sliced celery
¼ cup coarsely chopped green pepper
1 tablespoon lemon juice
1 teaspoon prepared horseradish
¼ teaspoon onion salt

GRATE all ingredients 30 seconds, stopping motor to push ingredients to blades, if necessary. Makes 2 cups. Spread on bread slices or toast rounds.

HOT TUNA-CHEESE BUNWICHES

4 hard-cooked eggs, quartered
⅔ cup Blender Mayonnaise (recipe page 154)
8 medium stuffed olives, cut in half
2 (3-inch) sweet pickles, quartered
3 (1-inch) squares green pepper
1 thin (⅛-inch) slice onion, quartered
1 can (7-ounce) tuna, drained and flaked
8 hamburger buns, buttered
8 slices (½-pound) process American cheese

CHOP 2 eggs at a time in container, switching motor on and off until coarsely chopped, about 10 seconds; pour into bowl. Combine next 5 ingredients in blender container. **BLEND** until pickles and olives are chopped moderately fine, 20 to 25 seconds. Stop motor as needed and push ingredients into blades with rubber spatula. Add to eggs. Fold in tuna. Spoon an equal amount of mixture onto bottom of buns. Top with a cheese slice; cover with bun top. Wrap each sandwich in foil. Place on baking sheet; heat in slow oven (325°F.) about 25 minutes. Makes about 2¼ cups; 8 bunwiches.

TUNA SALAD SPREAD

Follow recipe for Salmon Salad Spread (recipe at left) and substitute 2 cans (7-ounce) tuna, drained and flaked, for salmon called for. Makes about 3 cups.

OLIVE TUNA SALAD SPREAD

Follow recipe for Salmon Salad Spread (recipe at left) and substitute 10 medium-sized stuffed olives, halved, for sweet pickles and 2 cans (7-ounce) tuna, drained and flaked, for salmon called for. Makes about 3 cups.

FRENCH TOASTED CHEESE SANDWICHES

3 eggs
¼ cup milk
½ teaspoon salt
Dash of pepper
8 slices bread, buttered on one side
4 to 8 slices American cheese
3 tablespoons butter or margarine

Combine first 4 ingredients in container, **BLEND** until mixed, 2 to 4 seconds. Pour into shallow dish or pie plate. Place 1 or 2 slices of cheese between each 2 slices of bread, buttered sides toward cheese. Dip sandwiches into egg mixture and sauté in butter or margarine in frypan over moderate heat until sandwiches brown on both sides and cheese melts; turn sandwiches once. Makes 4 sandwiches.

FRENCH TOASTED MOZZARELLA SANDWICHES: Follow recipe for French Toasted Cheese Sandwiches above and substitute processed Mozzarella for American cheese. Makes 4 sandwiches.

AVOCADO FILLING

Try this with slices of crisp-cooked bacon.

2 avocados, peeled and sliced
2 tablespoons French dressing
1 tablespoon lemon juice

BLEND all ingredients 30 seconds, stopping motor to push ingredients to blades, if necessary. Makes 1 cup.

FRUIT AND NUT CHEESE SANDWICH SPREAD

¼ cup honey
2 tablespoons cream or milk
⅓ cup creamy-style peanut butter
2 packages (3-ounce) room temperature cream cheese, cubed
⅓ cup seedless raisins

Combine honey, cream or milk and peanut butter in container. **BLEND** until smooth, 5 to 10 seconds. Stop motor; push ingredients into blades with rubber spatula as needed. Add ½ of cream cheese; **BEAT** until cheese is blended, about 15 seconds. Stop motor; push ingredients into blades with rubber spatula as needed. Add remaining cheese and raisins. **BEAT** until cheese is blended in and raisins are coarsely chopped. Stop motor; push ingredients into blades with rubber spatula as needed. If mixture is very thick and motor labors add milk, 1 tablespoon at a time. Makes about 1⅓ cups. Delicious on whole wheat, raisin, brown, nut or fruit bread or spread between graham crackers.

PEANUT BUTTER MARMALADE SPREAD: Follow recipe for Fruit and Nut Cheese Sandwich Spread and substitute orange marmalade or apricot preserves for honey called for. Makes about 1⅓ cups.

FRUITED PEANUT BUTTER SPREAD

1 cup roasted peanuts
1 medium banana, peeled
¼ cup seedless raisins
1 tablespoon salad oil
2 teaspoons lemon juice

SHRED all ingredients 2 minutes, stopping motor to push ingredients to blades, if necessary. Makes 1¼ cups.

WALNUTTY CHEESE SPREAD

1 (8-ounce) package cream cheese, cubed
½ cup walnuts
½ cup coarsely chopped green pepper
⅓ cup half and half (half milk, half cream)
⅛ teaspoon salt

GRIND all ingredients 20 seconds, stopping motor to push ingredients to blades, if necessary. Makes about 1¼ cups spread.

CHEESE 'N OLIVE SPREAD

⅓ cup walnut halves
1 cup small stuffed olives
⅓ cup dairy sour cream
1 package (3-ounce) room temperature cream cheese, cubed

CHOP walnuts, switching motor on and off until coarsely chopped, 8 to 10 seconds. Pour into bowl; save. **CHOP** olives, ⅓ cup at a time, switching motor on and off until coarsely chopped; add to nuts. Combine sour cream and ½ of cheese in container. **BLEND** until smooth, about 10 seconds. Stop motor; push ingredients into blades with rubber spatula as needed. Add remaining cheese and repeat process. Add cheese mixture to nuts and olives; mix. An excellent spread for fancy canapés or hearty sandwiches. Makes about 1⅓ cups.

Ribbon Sandwich Loaves

RIBBON SANDWICH LOAVES

A great centerpiece and main dish for a luncheon or shower

24 slices white sandwich bread
½ cup butter or margarine, softened
Curried Egg Filling, page 158
Avocado Filling, page 162
Ham Filling, page 158
1 (8-ounce) package cream cheese, cubed
½ cup dairy sour cream
2 tablespoons lemon juice
Parsley sprigs and radish slices for garnish

Trim crust from bread slices. Arrange 6 slices on cutting board or cooky sheet to form 2 loaves, each with a bottom layer of 3 slices. Spread with some of the softened butter and then with Curried Egg Filling. Top each loaf with 3 more slices each; spread with butter. Spread with Avocado Filling. Top each loaf with 3 bread slices. Spread with Ham Filling and top each loaf with 3 more bread slices. **GRIND** cream cheese, sour cream and lemon juice, stopping motor to push ingredients to blades, if necessary. Frost finished loaves with cream cheese frosting. Reserve some frosting to pipe borders with pastry tube, if desired. Garnish with parsley and radish flowers. Makes 16 servings (8 per loaf).

PRONTO PIZZA

Your teen-age chef can make a reputation with this extra-flavorful and easy recipe

1 (13¾-ounce) package hot roll mix
8 ounces Provolone or Romano cheese, cubed
8 ounces Mozzarella cheese, cubed
1 (8-ounce) can tomato sauce
1 (6-ounce) can tomato paste
½ green pepper, coarsely chopped
½ cup pimiento-stuffed green olives
½ cup pitted ripe olives
4 green onions, coarsely chopped
1 teaspoon oregano
½ teaspoon marjoram
6 parsley sprigs
1 (2-ounce) can flat anchovy fillets, drained
1 (4-ounce) can mushrooms, drained

Prepare hot roll mix for Pizza as package directs; roll or pat out and place on greased pans. **PURÉE** ½ cup Provolone cheese 10 seconds. Empty into bowl. Repeat with remaining Provolone. **PURÉE** Mozzarella, ½ cup at a time, 10 seconds and place in separate bowl. **LIQUEFY** all remaining ingredients, except anchovies and mushrooms, 15 seconds. To assemble pizzas: spread Provolone cheese over dough, then tomato mixture and then Mozzarella. Arrange anchovy fillets, spoke-like, on top. Scatter mushrooms over. Bake in moderate oven (400°F.) 15 to 20 minutes or until golden brown. Makes 2 large or 4 small pizzas.

MUSHROOM AND SAUSAGE PIZZA: Follow recipe for Short-Cut Pizza at left and substitute 1 can (2-ounce) sliced or button mushrooms, drained and ½ pound fully cooked pork sausage links, cut in 1-inch slices, for salami.

CHEESE AND BACON PIZZA: Follow recipe for Short-Cut Pizza at left and substitute ½ pound bacon, broiled until crisp and crumbled, for salami and process American for Mozzarella cheese.

DATE-NUT SANDWICH SPREAD

½ cup salted peanuts
¾ cup dairy sour cream
1 cup pitted dates (about 8-ounces), quartered
1 package (3-ounce) room temperature cream cheese, cubed

CHOP peanuts, switching motor on and off until chopped moderately fine. Pour into bowl. Add sour cream and ½ of dates to blender container; **BEAT** until dates are coarsely chopped, 20 to 25 seconds. Stop motor and push ingredients into blades with rubber spatula as needed. If mixture is very stiff and motor labors add 1 or 2 tablespoons cream. Add remaining dates and process as above. Add to chopped nuts and mix. Delicious on whole wheat, raisin or nut breads. Makes about 1¾ cups.

SHORT-CUT PIZZA

1 can (8-ounce) tomato sauce
2 tablespoons cooking oil
1 medium onion (2-inch) quartered and sliced
1½ teaspoons oregano
½ teaspoon basil
½ teaspoon garlic salt
Dash of pepper
1 can (2 or 3-ounce) sliced or button mushrooms, drained
1 can (8-ounce) refrigerated biscuits
½ cup blender-chopped Parmesan cheese (see chopping directions page 6)
2 tablespoons milk
8 slices hard or cotto salami, cut in 6 wedges
4 slices Mozzarella cheese, cut in half diagonally
8 pitted ripe olives, sliced

Combine first 7 ingredients in container; **BLEND** until onion is finely chopped, 20 to 25 seconds. Pour into saucepan; cook slowly until onion is tender and flavors blended, 10 to 15 minutes. Stir in mushrooms. Press biscuits in even layer over bottom and up sides of a 12-inch pizza pan. Bake in very hot oven (450°F.) until browned, about 5 minutes. While crust is baking combine ¼ cup Parmesan cheese and milk; mix and spread over hot crust. Remove from oven and quickly spread tomato sauce over crust; top with salami pieces. Arrange triangles of cheese in a ring 1-inch from edge of pizza. Arrange pitted ripe olive slices on sauce. Sprinkle remaining Parmesan cheese over top. Return to oven and finish baking, about 10 minutes. Cut into wedges; serve. Makes one 12-inch pizza.

TUNA PIZZA: Follow recipe for Short-Cut Pizza above and substitute 1 can (7-ounce) tuna, drained and flaked, for salami.

CHOPPED CHICKEN LIVER SPREAD

½ pound chicken livers
½ cup sliced onion
2 tablespoons rendered chicken fat
¾ teaspoon salt
⅛ teaspoon pepper
2 tablespoons half and half (half milk, half cream) or cream
1 hard-cooked egg, sliced

Wash and cut chicken livers in half; drain on paper toweling. Sauté livers and onion slices in chicken fat in frying pan over low heat until onions are limp and livers cooked. Sprinkle with salt and pepper. Add ½ of mixture and 1 tablespoon half and half or cream to container and **GRATE**, about 15 seconds or until chopped the fineness desired. Stop motor, as necessary, and push ingredients into blades with rubber spatula. Add remaining liver, onion and half and half and egg and **GRATE** until smooth, about 20 seconds or until fineness desired. Chill. Makes about 1 cup spread.

SAUCES & TOPPINGS

A perfect sauce is a culinary masterpiece that can transform prosaic foods into gourmet fare.

It's really quite simple to make perfect sauces the blender way. With the failure-proof recipes that follow and a modern multispeed blender you can whiz up a delicate Hollandaise, creamy-smooth cheese, zesty spaghetti, tempting thick chocolate and dozens of other great sauces with the skill of a French chef.

EASY-TO-FIX SAUCE FOR MAKING CREAMED DISHES GALORE!

CREAM OR WHITE SAUCE (MEDIUM)

2 cups milk or half and half (half milk, half cream)
¼ cup flour
½ teaspoon salt
Dash of pepper or cayenne
¼ cup butter or margarine

Combine first 4 ingredients in blender container; **BLEND** until smooth, 8 to 10 seconds. Pour into saucepan; add butter or margarine. Cook over low heat until thick and smooth, stirring constantly. Use for making creamed vegetable, meat, fish or poultry dishes or tasty sauces galore. Makes about 2¼ cups sauce.

THIN CREAM SAUCE: Ideal for making countless delicious cream soups. Follow recipe above for Cream or White Sauce (Medium), reduce both flour and butter or margarine to 2 tablespoons. Makes about 2¼ cups sauce.

THICK CREAM SAUCE: Wonderful for making croquettes. Follow recipe above for Cream or White Sauce (Medium) and increase flour and butter or margarine to ⅓ cup each. Makes about 2¼ cups sauce.

BECHAMEL SAUCE: Substitute 1 cup meat stock or bouillon for 1 cup of the milk or half and half called for in recipe for Cream or White Sauce (Medium) above; add a dash or two of nutmeg. Makes about 2¼ cups.

CURRY SAUCE

Add 1 chicken bouillon cube, 2 to 3 teaspoons curry powder, ⅛ teaspoon ginger, 2 thin (⅛-inch) slices onion, ¼ cup sliced celery, ¼ cup well-drained chutney to blender container with milk when making Cream or White Sauce (Medium) above. Makes 2¾ to 3 cups sauce.

CHEESE SAUCE

Add 1 teaspoon prepared mustard, ½ teaspoon Worcestershire sauce, and 2 cups blender-chopped (see chopping directions on page 6) sharp American or Cheddar cheese (about ½-pound) to hot Cream or White Sauce (Medium) above. Stir until cheese melts. Makes about 2⅔ cups.

DILL CHEESE SAUCE: Stir 2 teaspoons dried dill weed into Cheese Sauce (recipe above). Makes about 2⅔ cups.

EGG SAUCE

Cut 2 or 3 hard-cooked eggs in quarters. Add to blender container; **BLEND** switching motor on and off until coarsely chopped. Fold chopped eggs, ¼ cup diced pimiento, and 1 teaspoon mustard into Cream or White Sauce (Medium) (recipe left). Makes about 3 cups sauce.

MORNAY SAUCE

Add ¼ to ⅓ cup blender-grated Parmesan cheese (see chopping directions page 6), pinch each of nutmeg and thyme, ¼ teaspoon garlic salt, and 2 tablespoons white wine (optional) to hot Cream or White Sauce (Medium) (recipe at left); mix well. Makes about 2½ cups sauce.

VEGETABLE CREAM SAUCE

Fold 1 cup of favorite well-drained fresh cooked or cooked left-over vegetables (carrots, peas, mixed vegetables, cross cut green beans or asparagus pieces) to hot Cream or White Sauce (Medium) (recipe at left). Heat. Makes about 3 cups.

HOLLANDAISE SAUCE

½ cup butter
3 egg yolks
2 tablespoons lemon juice
¼ teaspoon salt
Dash cayenne

Melt butter and heat just until bubbling. Place remaining ingredients in blender, cover and **WHIP.** *At once* pour butter in steady stream through opening in top. Stop motor as soon as all butter has been added. Makes ¾ cup.

BÉARNAISE SAUCE

Simmer 3 tablespoons tarragon vinegar, 2 teaspoons chopped onion, 1 teaspoon dried tarragon, and ¼ teaspoon pepper until almost all liquid is gone. Add to Hollandaise Sauce (recipe above) in blender and **GRIND** 5 seconds. Serve over meats. Makes about ¾ cup.

MOUSSELINE SAUCE

WHIP ½ cup heavy cream and fold into Hollandaise Sauce (recipe above). Serve with fish. Makes about 1¼ cups.

REMOULADE SAUCE

1 cup Blender Mayonnaise (recipe page 154)
1 (4-inch) green onion, cut in 1-inch lengths
3 or 4 small sprigs parsley, no stems
2 teaspoons prepared mustard
2 teaspoons tarragon or cider vinegar
1 teaspoon horseradish
½ teaspoon leaf thyme
1 tablespoon drained sweet pickle relish or capers

Combine first 7 ingredients in blender container; **BLEND** until onion is finely chopped, 20 to 30 seconds. Add pickle relish or capers; **BLEND** just until mixed, 4 to 6 seconds. Serve cold or heat slowly and serve. Makes 1⅓ cups.

CUMBERLAND SAUCE

¾ cup currant jelly
1 can (6-ounce) frozen orange juice concentrate
1 tablespoon prepared mustard
2 (1½-inch) pieces preserved ginger or ¼ teaspoon ground ginger
2 to 3 dashes hot red pepper sauce
2 to 4 tablespoons port wine or Cointreau

GRATE first 5 ingredients until smooth, 2 to 4 seconds. Heat; stir in wine or Cointreau. Use as glaze for or sauce to serve with ham or duck. Makes about 1½ cups sauce or glaze.

CHERRY SAUCE FOR HAM

1 (1-pound) can water pack red tart cherries
¾ cup brown sugar, firmly packed
¼ cup brandy
¼ cup water
1 tablespoon dry mustard
2 teaspoons cornstarch

Drain cherries and set aside. **LIQUEFY** cherry juice, sugar, brandy, water and mustard 10 seconds. Pour over ham during last ½ hour of baking, when fat has been removed from drippings in roasting pan. Baste ham with sauce from bottom of the pan several times until it is done. Remove baked ham to a warm platter, remove rack from pan. Mix cornstarch with drained cherries. Add cherries to sauce in pan. Cook and stir over medium heat until sauce is clear and thickened. Serve with ham.

QUICK CHEESE SAUCE

½ cup cubed process Cheddar cheese
1 cup evaporated milk
2 teaspoons Worcestershire sauce
½ teaspoon salt
¼ teaspoon dry mustard

PURÉE cheese 15 seconds or until all chunks are grated. Add milk and seasonings; **GRIND** for 15 seconds. Turn into saucepan and cook over medium heat, stirring constantly, until thickened. Makes 1½ cups. Serve over vegetables, meats, cooked macaroni or spaghetti.

SWEET SOUR PINEAPPLE SAUCE

½ cup pineapple juice or water
2 tablespoons lemon juice
1 tablespoon vinegar
2 tablespoons brown or granulated sugar
1 tablespoon soy sauce
1 tablespoon cornstarch
¼ teaspoon ginger, optional
2 squares (1-inch) green pepper
1 can (9-ounce) pineapple tidbits, undrained

Combine all ingredients except pineapple tidbits in blender container. **BLEND** until ingredients are mixed and green pepper chopped moderately fine, 5 to 8 seconds. Pour into saucepan. Stir in undrained pineapple tidbits. Cook over moderate heat, stirring constantly until thick and clear. Serve on or with roast pork, ham or poultry. Makes about 1⅔ cups.

FLAMING ORANGE SAUCE

For pork, ham or poultry

1 cup orange juice
2 squares (1-inch) orange rind (no white), cut in strips
2 pieces (1-inch) preserved ginger or ¼ teaspoon ginger
2 tablespoons cornstarch
½ teaspoon salt
1 cup orange marmalade
½ cup seedless green grapes, halved
⅓ cup orange flavored liqueur, optional

Combine first 5 ingredients in blender container. **BLEND** until ingredients are mixed and ginger is finely chopped. Pour into saucepan; stir in marmalade. Cook over moderate heat, stirring constantly, until sauce is clear and thickened. Fold in grapes and heat. Stir in 2 tablespoons liqueur, if desired. Pour into small chafing dish or warmer over low heat and pour remaining liqueur over sauce. Ignite. Allow flame to die; spoon sauce over roast pork, ham or poultry servings. Makes about 2½ cups.

ORANGE SAUCE FOR HAM

1 orange, thin peel of orange and fruit only (discard white pulp)
1 cup water
½ cup sherry
1 tablespoon prepared mustard
2 teaspoons dry mustard

LIQUEFY all ingredients 15 seconds. Pour over ham during last ½ hour of baking; when fat has been removed from drippings in roasting pan. Baste ham, with sauce from bottom of the pan several times until done.

SPICY TOMATO SAUCE

1 (1-pound) can tomatoes
1 (6-ounce) can tomato paste
¼ green pepper, coarsely chopped
½ small onion, sliced
3 tablespoons butter or margarine, softened
3 tablespoons flour
¼ teaspoon oregano
⅛ teaspoon basil
2 parsley sprigs
¼ teaspoon Worcestershire sauce
Few drops hot pepper sauce

LIQUEFY all ingredients 10 seconds. Pour into a saucepan and cook and stir over medium heat until mixture comes to a boil and is thick. 3 cups.

TANGY PINEAPPLE BARBECUE SAUCE FOR RIBS

⅔ cup catsup
½ cup pineapple juice
1 tablespoon lemon juice
2 tablespoons brown sugar
1 teaspoon Worcestershire sauce
½ teaspoon liquid smoke, optional
½ teaspoon salt
⅛ teaspoon black pepper
2 to 3 drops hot red pepper sauce, optional
1 small (½-inch) onion, quartered and sliced
½ cup well-drained crushed pineapple

Combine all ingredients, except pineapple, in blender container in order listed. **CHOP** until onion is finely chopped, 10 to 15 seconds. Pour into saucepan; add crushed pineapple. Heat to simmering stage; cook slowly to blend flavors, about 10 minutes. Brush sauce over ribs several times during last 30 minutes of cooking time. Serve remaining sauce with ribs. Makes about 1½ cups sauce, enough for 2½ to 4 pounds of ribs.

SOUTHWESTERN BARBECUE SAUCE

1⅓ cups catsup or chili sauce
⅓ cup water
3 tablespoons cider or wine vinegar
2 tablespoons cooking oil
2 tablespoons brown sugar
1 tablespoon Worcestershire sauce
1 teaspoon prepared mustard
1 teaspoon celery salt
1 teaspoon liquid smoke
½ teaspoon salt
½ to 1 teaspoon chili powder
3 dashes hot red pepper sauce, optional
1 medium size (2-inch) onion, quartered and sliced
½ cup sliced (½-inch) celery

Combine all ingredients except onion and celery in blender container. **BLEND** until well mixed, about 5 seconds. Add onion and celery and **CHOP** until vegetables are coarsely chopped, 15 to 20 seconds. Stop motor and push ingredients into blades with rubber spatula as needed. Pour into saucepan. Bring to simmering stage; cook slowly to blend flavors, about 10 minutes. Makes about 2¼ cups.

STEAK SAUCE

See photo at right

¾ cup cottage cheese
2 tablespoons wine vinegar
½ teaspoon liquid sugar substitute
½ teaspoon dry mustard
1 tablespoon blue cheese

GRIND cottage cheese, vinegar, sugar substitute, and dry mustard 10 seconds. Add blue cheese. **STIR** 5 seconds or until cheese is crumbled. 1 cup. 15 calories per tablespoon. Top with chopped green onion.

STEAK OR BURGER SAUCE

¾ cup water
¾ cup chili sauce or catsup
1 teaspoon Worcestershire sauce
½ teaspoon salt
¼ teaspoon pepper
½ small (1½-inch) onion, quartered and sliced
½ cup sliced (½-inch) celery
¼ green pepper, cut in 1-inch squares
2 tablespoons butter or margarine

Combine first 5 ingredients in blender container. **STIR** to mix, about 2 seconds. Add onion, celery and green pepper and **CHOP** until vegetables are chopped moderately fine, 8 to 10 seconds. Pour into saucepan; add butter or margarine and bring to simmering stage. Cook slowly 12 to 15 minutes to blend flavors. Use as a basting sauce for steaks or hamburgers during last half of cooking time. Serve remaining sauce with cooked meat. Makes about 1⅔ cups.

COLD CHIFFON SAUCE FOR FISH

6 hard-cooked egg yolks
1 tablespoon prepared mustard
½ teaspoon salt
Dash of cayenne or pepper
1 cup Blender Mayonnaise (recipe page 154)
1 small dill pickle, cut in ½-inch slices or 2 table-spoons drained capers
2 hard-cooked egg whites
2 pitted black olives, halved

Combine first 4 ingredients in blender container. **BLEND** switching motor on and off as needed to finely chop, 15 to 20 seconds. Add mayonnaise; **BLEND** until well mixed, about 5 seconds. Add remaining ingredients; **BLEND** switching motor on and off as needed to chop egg whites moderately fine, 8 to 10 seconds. Stop motor and push ingredients into blades with rubber spatula, as needed. Chill. Serve with cold salmon, tuna or other fish. Makes about 1¼ cups.

SEAFOOD COCKTAIL SAUCE

¾ cup chili sauce
1 stalk celery, sliced
¼ cup coarsely chopped green pepper
1 tablespoon lemon juice
½ tablespoon Worcestershire sauce
½ tablespoon prepared horseradish
Dash hot pepper sauce

GRIND all ingredients 15 seconds. Chill thoroughly. Makes about 1¼ cups sauce.

SOUR CREAM SAUCE

¾ cup water
3 tablespoons flour
¼ teaspoon marjoram
¼ teaspoon dill seed
1 cup sour cream

BLEND water, flour and marjoram 10 seconds. Pour into skillet in which meat balls were browned. Stir to mix with pan drippings. Cook and stir over medium heat until thick. Add dill seed and sour cream. Heat, stirring gently, but do not boil. Serve over meat balls. Makes about 1½ cups sauce.

CUCUMBER SAUCE

Wonderful over salmon or any other fish!

1 medium cucumber, cubed
⅓ cup mayonnaise
1 teaspoon lemon juice
½ teaspoon salt
¼ teaspoon paprika
⅛ teaspoon pepper

GRATE all ingredients 30 seconds. Chill thoroughly. Makes 1 cup sauce.

Steak Sauce

TARTAR SAUCE

1 cup Blender Mayonnaise (recipe page 154)
1 (4-inch) green onion, in ½-inch lengths
3 small sprigs parsley, no stems
1 thin (⅛-inch) slice unpeeled lemon, quartered
2 or 3 (3-inch) sweet pickles, in ½-inch slices
¼ pimiento, quartered

Combine all ingredients except pimiento in blender container. **BLEND** until onion and pickles are finely chopped, 30 to 40 seconds. Add pimiento. **BLEND** switching motor on and off just until pimiento is coarsely chopped, 3 to 4 seconds. Makes about 1¼ cups sauce.

FISH AND SEAFOOD SAUCE

1 cup catsup or chili sauce
¼ cup sliced (½-inch) celery
1 thin (⅛-inch) slice onion, quartered
1 thin (⅛-inch) slice unpeeled lemon, quartered
2 teaspoons horseradish
2 teaspoons Worcestershire sauce
2 dashes hot red pepper sauce

Combine ingredients in blender container; **BLEND** until onion and celery are finely chopped. Makes about 1 cup sauce.

CORAL FISH SAUCE

1 cup Blender Mayonnaise (recipe page 154)
2 tablespoons catsup
1 thin (⅛-inch) slice unpeeled lemon, quartered
2 teaspoons horseradish
½ teaspoon Worcestershire sauce
½ pimiento, cut in quarters

Combine ingredients in blender container in order listed. **BLEND** until smooth, 20 to 30 seconds. Makes about 1 cup sauce.

FLUFFY HORSERADISH SAUCE

½ cup Cooked Salad Dressing or Blender Mayonnaise (recipes on page 154 and 155)
3 tablespoons horseradish
1 small green onion, cut in 1-inch lengths
Dash of salt
½ cup whipping cream, whipped

Combine first 4 ingredients in blender container; **BLEND** until onion is chopped moderately fine, 3 to 5 seconds. Turn into bowl. Fold in whipped cream. Makes about 1¼ cups.

VANILLA SAUCE

See photo at right

5 egg yolks
½ cup sugar
1 teaspoon cornstarch
⅛ teaspoon salt
2 cups half and half (half milk, half cream), scalded
1 teaspoon vanilla
½ cup heavy cream, optional

BLEND egg yolks, sugar, cornstarch and salt 30 seconds. **GRIND** 20 seconds adding half and half through opening in top while motor is running. Pour into a saucepan. Cook and stir over low heat until mixture is thickened and coats metal spoon. Stir in vanilla. Cool, stirring occasionally. Makes about 2¾ cups. For an extra rich sauce, **WHIP** heavy cream in blender, see page 9. Fold into vanilla sauce. Serve over fruits or cake.

APRICOT DESSERT SAUCE

See photo at right

½ cup dried apricots, cut in half
1 thin (⅛-inch) slice unpeeled lemon, quartered
⅔ cup hot water
½ cup corn syrup
½ cup sugar

Combine ingredients in saucepan; bring to boiling point over moderate heat. Reduce heat and simmer gently 5 minutes. Cool 5 minutes; pour into blender container. **BLEND** until fairly smooth, about 10 seconds. Cool. Delicious on cake or ice cream. Makes about 1½ cups.

APRICOT CHERRY DESSERT SAUCE: Fold ⅓ cup maraschino cherry quarters into Apricot Dessert Sauce (recipe above) after blending. Makes about 1¾ cups.

APRICOT ALMOND DESSERT SAUCE: Fold ½ cup blender-chopped toasted almonds into Apricot Dessert Sauce (recipe above) after blending. See directions for chopping nuts on page 7. Makes about 1¾ cups.

BUTTERSCOTCH SAUCE

1½ cups butterscotch bits
½ cup milk
2 tablespoons brown sugar or corn syrup
¼ teaspoon salt
1 teaspoon vanilla

Empty butterscotch bits into container. Pour milk, sugar or syrup and salt into saucepan; bring to simmering stage. Pour over bits. **BLEND** until smooth, about 25 seconds. Add vanilla; **STIR** until blended, 2 to 3 seconds. Serve warm or cool, stirring frequently. Delicious on cake, puddings or ice cream. Makes about 1¼ cups.

FUDGE SAUCE

4 squares (1-ounce) unsweetened chocolate, cut into
   small pieces
1 cup boiling water
1⅓ cups sugar
¼ cup cornstarch
¼ teaspoon salt
⅓ cup cold water
2 teaspoons vanilla

BLEND chocolate pieces, switching motor on and off,
until coarsely chopped. Add boiling water; **BLEND** 10
to 15 seconds or until smooth. Stop motor as needed
and push ingredients into blades with rubber spatula.
Add sugar; **BLEND** 10 seconds or until mixed. Combine cornstarch, salt and cold water in saucepan. Add
chocolate mixture; blend well. Cook over low heat,
stirring constantly until thick. Remove from heat;
stir in vanilla. Serve atop ice cream, cake, custards,
etc. Makes 2 cups.

CHOCOLATE RUM SAUCE

See photo at right

½ cup milk or half and half (half milk, half cream)
2 tablespoons sugar
½ teaspoon instant coffee powder
¼ teaspoon salt
1 package (6-ounce) semisweet chocolate bits
1 tablespoon rum or 1 teaspoon rum flavoring

Combine first 4 ingredients in heavy saucepan. Bring
to simmering stage over moderate heat. Empty
chocolate bits into container. Add hot milk mixture
and rum or rum flavoring. **MIX** until chocolate is
melted and mixture smooth, about 10 seconds. Makes
about 1 cup.

MOCHA SAUCE

1 (6-ounce) package semi-sweet chocolate pieces*
¾ cup hot coffee or ¾ cup hot water and 1 teaspoon
   instant coffee powder
⅓ cup evaporated milk

GRIND chocolate and coffee 15 seconds. Add evaporated milk and **GRIND** 10 seconds longer. Serve hot
or cold. Makes about 1¾ cups.

*You can also use mint-flavored chocolate or butter-
   scotch pieces.

A. Chocolate Rum Sauce page 171
B. Vanilla Sauce page 170
C. Apricot Dessert Sauce page 170

171

STRAWBERRY-CRANBERRY SAUCE

1 (10-ounce) package frozen strawberries or raspberries, thawed
1 cup whole cranberry sauce
1 (8-ounce) jar currant jelly

GRIND all ingredients 45 seconds. Strain, if desired,
to remove raspberry seeds. Serve over ice cream,
cakes, puddings, fresh fruits. Makes about 3 cups.
Sauce may be heated, if desired.

CARDINAL SAUCE

1 (10-ounce) package frozen raspberries, thawed
½ cup sugar
1 teaspoon cornstarch
1 tablespoon Kirsch (optional)

GRIND all ingredients 40 seconds or until smooth.
Strain and chill. Makes approximately 1 cup. Serve
over crêpes, strawberries, ice cream.

CURRANT-ORANGE SAUCE

1 cup red wine
1 (8-ounce) jar currant jelly
1 orange, peeled and quartered
1 (1-inch) piece orange peel
½ lemon, peeled and quartered
1 (1-inch) piece lemon peel

GRIND all ingredients 45 seconds. Makes about 2½
cups sauce.

ORANGE SAUCE

⅓ cup defrosted frozen orange juice concentrate,
undiluted
¼ cup sugar
¼ teaspoon salt
2 cups miniature marshmallows

Combine first 3 ingredients in saucepan; heat to simmering stage. Empty marshmallows into container.
Pour hot juice over marshmallows and **BEAT** until
marshmallows melt, about 25 to 30 seconds. Makes
about 1 cup sauce.

HARD SAUCE

*A holiday tradition over mince pie, plum, raisin or date
pudding*

⅓ cup butter or margarine, softened
2 tablespoons brandy
1 cup confectioners' sugar

GRIND all ingredients 20 seconds or until smooth.
Makes about 1 cup.

THIN HARD SAUCE

1 cup boiling water
1 cup sugar
¼ lemon (thin yellow portion of peel and fruit only)
2 tablespoons butter or margarine
1 tablespoon cornstarch
1 tablespoon brandy

STIR all ingredients except brandy 10 seconds. Pour
into saucepan and cook and stir over low heat until
thick and clear. Add brandy. Makes 1 cup.

LEMON SAUCE

1 lemon (thin yellow portion of peel and fruit only)
1 cup boiling water
1 egg
½ cup sugar
¼ cup cold water
2 tablespoons cornstarch
1 tablespoon butter or margarine
⅛ teaspoon salt
⅛ teaspoon nutmeg

GRIND all ingredients 10 seconds. Pour into saucepan and cook and stir until smooth and thick. Makes
1½ cups. Serve over Lemon Pudding, page 72.

BUTTER SAUCE

Heat ½ cup butter, 1 cup sugar and 1 cup half and
half (half milk, half cream) in saucepan until butter
melts. Add ½ teaspoon vanilla and simmer 30 minutes. Serve warm.

QUICK LEMON CUSTARD

2½ cups cold milk
1-inch square lemon rind (no white), cut in strips
1 package (3¾-ounce) instant lemon pudding and pie
filling

Combine milk and rind in container, **LIQUEFY** until
lemon is minced, about 3 seconds. Add instant lemon
pudding and pie filling. **STIR** until smooth, 3 to 5
seconds. Stop motor as needed and scrape down sides
of container with rubber spatula. Makes about 2¾
cups.

QUICK PUDDING SAUCES

For Chocolate, Vanilla and Butterscotch Puddings

2½ cups cold milk
1 package (3¾ to 4½-ounce) instant chocolate, vanilla
or butterscotch pudding and pie filling

Pour milk into blender container; add pudding and
pie filling. **STIR** until smooth, 3 to 5 seconds. Stop
motor as needed and scrape down sides of container
with rubber spatula. Makes about 2¾ cups.

SOUPS

Hundreds of teasingly different soups can be made jiffy-quick with little effort when a multispeed electric blender is used.

Nothing is more satisfying for lunch or dinner than a bowl of soup. With a few basic ingredients or leftovers and blender, chilled soups that take the sizzle out of summer meals or make warm and satisfying ones for chilly days can be whizzed up in seconds.

Try the recipes that follow. You'll like the hot and cold soups; some are old-time American favorites, others gourmet treats from far-away places.

NEW OLD-FASHIONED VEGETABLE SOUP

See photo at left

2 (10½-ounce) cans consommé
1 (8-ounce) can tomato sauce
1 cup water
1 cup diced peeled potato
½ cup sliced carrot
½ cup sliced celery stalks and leaves
2 slices onion
¼ cup diced green pepper
¾ teaspoon salt
½ teaspoon basil

GRATE all ingredients 5 to 10 seconds. Turn into saucepan, bring to boiling. Lower heat and simmer 5 minutes. Makes 1 quart.

CHICKEN VEGETABLE SOUP

2 cups chicken broth or 2 cups water and 2 chicken
   bouillon cubes
½ cup cubed cooked chicken
½ cup sliced carrot
¼ cup sliced celery
1 slice onion
1 teaspoon salt
⅛ teaspoon pepper

GRATE all ingredients 5 seconds. Turn into saucepan and heat until piping hot. Makes about 3 cups.

BLACK BEAN OR LENTIL SOUP

Old-fashioned slow-cooked flavor in half the time!

1 pound dried black beans or lentils
6 peppercorns
2½ quarts water
1½ teaspoons salt
½ teaspoon dry mustard
1 large onion, sliced
½ cup sliced celery
¼ cup butter or margarine
¼ cup sherry
2 tablespoons lemon juice

SHRED beans and peppercorns 2 minutes. Turn into large pot along with water and seasonings. **GRATE** onion and celery and add to bean mixture. Simmer, stirring occassionally, 1 to 1½ hours. Add butter, sherry and lemon juice; stir until butter melts. For extra-smooth soup, **MINCE** soup, 1 quart at a time, for 15 seconds. Reheat. Makes 12 servings. Garnish with lemon slices and pass additional sherry to be added to taste.

SPEEDY GREEN PEA SOUP

1 package (10-ounce) frozen peas
½ cup water
½ teaspoon salt
4 slices crisp bacon, broken into 1-inch lengths
2 tablespoons bacon drippings
1 cup milk

Simmer first 3 ingredients in covered saucepan about 5 minutes. Pour into container; add bacon and drippings; **GRATE** until fairly smooth, about 30 seconds. Stir in milk; heat in saucepan; serve. Makes about 2½ cups, 3 to 4 servings.

CHEDDAR CHEESE SOUP

1 cup diced (¼-inch) chilled natural Cheddar cheese
   (about 6-ounces)
4 cups milk
½ cup sliced (½-inch) fresh-cooked or canned carrots
⅓ cup sliced (½-inch) celery
2 (5-inch) green onions, in ½-inch lengths
¼ cup flour
1½ teaspoons salt
¼ teaspoon pepper
¼ cup butter or margarine

CREAM cheese, ½ cup at a time, switching motor on and off until grated, about 15 seconds. Empty container; save cheese. Repeat. **CREAM** 1½ cups milk and next 6 ingredients until vegetables are finely chopped, 15 to 20 seconds. Pour into saucepan; stir in remaining 2½ cups milk and butter or margarine. Cook, stirring constantly, until hot and slightly thickened. Lower heat; add cheese; stir until cheese melts. Makes about 5 cups, 4 to 6 servings.

AS-YOU-LIKE-IT CREAM SOUP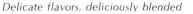

Dibs and dabs from your refrigerator are the flavoring ingredients

1½ cups milk
1 cup of any of the following: sliced raw or cooked carrots; cooked broccoli; cooked asparagus; cooked cauliflower; cooked green beans; cooked mixed vegetables; cooked lima beans; cooked corn
1 cup water
3 tablespoons flour
3 tablespoons butter or margarine
1 chicken bouillon cube or 1 teaspoon chicken bouillon granules
1 teaspoon salt
1 teaspoon Worcestershire sauce

GRIND all ingredients 30 to 45 seconds. Turn into saucepan and heat until piping hot. Makes about 1 quart soup.

CREAM OF MUSHROOM SOUP

Garnish with a spoonful of lightly salted whipped cream and tiny piece of pimiento

¼ pound fresh mushrooms, sliced
2 tablespoons butter or margarine
2 cups milk
1 slice onion
2 tablespoons flour
2 tablespoons butter or margarine
1 teaspoon salt
⅛ teaspoon pepper

Sauté mushrooms in 2 tablespoons butter until tender. **GRIND** milk, onion, flour, butter, salt and pepper 5 seconds. Turn into saucepan, add mushrooms and heat and stir until piping hot. Makes about 3 cups. Note: You may substitute 1 (4-ounce) can sliced mushrooms and liquid for fresh mushrooms and 2 tablespoons butter.

CREAM OF CORN SOUP

Garden-fresh flavor in a matter of seconds

2 cups milk
1 (1-pound) can whole kernel corn, undrained, or 1½ cups fresh cut corn
1 teaspoon salt
Dash hot pepper sauce

LIQUEFY all ingredients 1½ minutes. Turn into saucepan and heat until piping hot. Makes 1 quart soup.

CURRY CREAM SOUP

Delicate flavors, deliciously blended

1 (10½-ounce) can consommé
1 cup water
1 medium onion, quartered
1 medium apple, quartered and cored
1 teaspoon curry powder
¼ teaspoon paprika
½ cup heavy cream

LIQUEFY consommé, water, onion, apple, curry powder and paprika 30 seconds. Add cream and **BEAT** 5 seconds. Turn into saucepan and heat until piping hot. Makes 1 quart. Garnish with apple slices which have been brushed with lemon juice to keep them from darkening.

CREAM OF WATERCRESS SOUP

1 (10½-ounce) can chicken broth
1 cup half and half (half milk, half cream)
⅔ cup water
1 bunch watercress, washed
1 tablespoon flour

GRIND all ingredients 30 seconds. Turn into saucepan and heat until piping hot. Makes about 1 quart.

CELERY SOUP

Refreshing cold, delicious hot!

2 cups milk
1 cup sliced celery stalks and tops
1 slice onion
1 tablespoon flour
6 peppercorns
½ teaspoon salt

GRATE all ingredients 1 minute. Chill, or turn into saucepan and heat until piping hot. Makes about 3 cups soup.

CELERY AND CORN CREAM SOUP

1 (1-pound) can whole kernel corn, undrained
1½ cups milk
1 cup sliced celery
1 teaspoon salt
8 peppercorns

LIQUEFY all ingredients 1½ minutes. Turn into saucepan and heat until piping hot. Makes about 1 quart.

Hurry-Up Split Pea Soup

HURRY-UP SPLIT PEA SOUP

Hours of flavor in only 40 minutes

1 meaty ham bone
2½ quarts water
1 pound dried split peas
2 carrots, coarsely chopped
2 stalks celery, coarsely chopped
1 onion, coarsely chopped
½ teaspoon salt
¼ teaspoon thyme or marjoram

Place ham bone in large pan or pot with water and start simmering. **SHRED** peas 1½ minutes. Pour in with ham bone and stir. **GRATE** carrots, celery and onion and add to pot along with seasonings. Simmer 40 minutes, stirring occasionally. Remove bone, cut meat into chunks. **MINCE** soup if you wish extra-smooth texture. Return ham to soup and heat through. Makes 2½ quarts.

TEN-SECOND FRENCH ONION SOUP

4 cups hot water
3 medium onions, quartered
6 beef bouillon cubes
2 tablespoons butter or margarine

GRATE all ingredients 10 seconds. Turn into saucepan and heat to boiling. Lower heat and simmer 5 minutes. Makes 5½ cups. To serve French-style, top each serving of soup with slice of toasted French bread, sprinkle very generously with grated Parmesan cheese (page 6).

IOWA CORN CHOWDER

2 cups milk
1 (1-pound) can whole kernel corn, undrained or 1½ cups fresh cut corn
1 medium potato, cooked and cubed
4 slices bacon, cooked crisp
2 slices onion
1 teaspoon salt
6 peppercorns
Dash hot pepper sauce

GRIND all ingredients 1½ minutes. Turn into saucepan and heat until piping hot. Makes about 1 quart.

177

SURPRISE SOUP

1 (10-ounce) package frozen leaf or chopped spinach, thawed
2 cups milk
¾ cup diced cooked potato
1 slice onion
½ tablespoon soy sauce
1 teaspoon seasoned salt
½ clove garlic,
⅛ teaspoon mace or nutmeg

Cook spinach in small amount of boiling salted water for 5 minutes; drain. **GRIND** spinach with all remaining ingredients 30 seconds or until smooth. Turn into saucepan and cook and stir over medium heat until piping hot. If desired, stir in 2 tablespoons sherry just before serving. Makes 4 servings. Garnish with sprinkling of additional chopped, cooked potato and chopped parsley.

OYSTER STEW

2 cups milk or half and half (half milk, half cream)
2 tablespoons flour
1 teaspoon salt
⅛ teaspoon pepper
1 teaspoon Worcestershire sauce
3 tablespoons butter or margarine
1 can (8-ounce) defrosted frozen or ½ pint fresh undrained oysters
Paprika, optional

CREAM first 5 ingredients until smooth, about 10 seconds. Pour into saucepan. Cook slowly, stirring constantly, until mixture heats and thickens slightly. Keep warm. Melt butter or margarine in saucepan, add undrained oysters; heat slowly until edges of oysters curl; add to white sauce. Stir and heat. Serve plain or sprinkle with paprika. Makes about 3 cups, 3 to 4 servings.

CREAMY CLAM BISQUE

All the flavor of New England

2 (7-ounce) cans minced clams
1½ cups milk
⅓ cup parsley sprigs
¼ cup flour
3 tablespoons butter or margarine
1 teaspoon salt
1 teaspoon Worcestershire sauce

Drain clams and pour liquid into blender container. **GRIND** with all remaining ingredients, except clams, 30 seconds. Turn into saucepan, stir in clams and heat until piping hot. Makes about 1 quart bisque. **GRATE** additional parsley for garnish.

BEET BORSCH

See photo below

1 cup diced raw potatoes (1-medium)
1 cup hot water
2 beef bouillon cubes
¼ small onion, sliced
1 tablespoon sugar
1 teaspoon salt
½ teaspoon celery salt
1 jar (1-pound) sliced beets, undrained
2 cups water
¼ cup vinegar
½ cup dairy sour cream

Simmer first 3 ingredients in covered saucepan until potatoes are partially cooked, about 10 minutes. Pour into container; add next 4 ingredients. **GRATE** until smooth, about 30 seconds. Pour into saucepan. **GRATE** beets ½ at a time until smooth, about 3 seconds. Pour into saucepan. Add water and vinegar. Simmer to blend flavors, about 5 minutes. Serve hot topped with sour cream. Makes about 5 cups, 6 servings.

Beet Borsch

CHILLED TOMATO BUTTERMILK SOUP

1 can (10¾-ounce) condensed tomato soup
1 medium tomato, diced
2 (5-inch) green onions, in 1-inch lengths
4 sprigs parsley, no stems
¼ teaspoon salt
3 to 4 drops hot red pepper sauce
2 cups chilled buttermilk
Watercress, optional

CREAM first 6 ingredients 5 seconds or until tomato is finely chopped. Stir into buttermilk. Chill and serve. Garnish with watercress, if desired. Makes about 4 cups, 4 to 6 servings.

SWEET BASIL CARROT SOUP

2 cups half and half (half milk, half cream)
2 cups sliced carrots, cooked
½ teaspoon sweet basil
1 teaspoon sugar
1 chicken bouillon cube
2 cups Cream or White Sauce (medium) (recipe page 166)
Salt to taste

Combine ½ of half and half, carrots, basil, sugar and bouillon cube in blender container; **BLEND** until carrots are chopped very fine. Stop motor and push ingredients into blades with rubber spatula as needed. Pour into saucepan with cream sauce; stir in remaining half and half and salt to taste. Heat slowly and serve. Makes 6 to 8 servings.

COLD SWEET BASIL CARROT SOUP: Follow above recipe; chill rather than heat combined mixture. Makes 6 to 8 servings.

COLD CURRY SOUP

2 cups Cream or White Sauce (medium) (recipe page 166)
¼ cup diced celery, cooked
¼ cup thinly sliced onions, cooked
1 chicken bouillon cube
1 teaspoon curry powder
½ cup whipping cream or undiluted evaporated milk
Salt to taste
2 tablespoons flaked coconut, toasted

Combine first 5 ingredients in blender container; **STIR** until well mixed. Stir in whipping cream or evaporated milk and salt as needed. Chill thoroughly, stirring frequently until cold. Cover; continue cooling. Pour into chilled consommé cups. Top with toasted coconut. Makes 4 servings.

TOMATO BLUE-CHEESE SOUP

1½ cups cooked or canned tomatoes
¼ teaspoon fines herbes blend
⅛ teaspoon celery seed
1 thin (⅛-inch) slice onion, quartered
2 cups Cream or White Sauce (medium) (recipe page 166)
¼ cup crumbled blue cheese
Salt to taste

Combine first 4 ingredients in saucepan; heat slowly until onion is tender and flavors blended, about 10 minutes. Pour hot cream sauce in blender container; set speed at **WHIP,** turn motor on and add tomatoes slowly through top opening. Add cheese and **WHIP** until smooth. Season to taste with salt. Serve hot. Makes about 3½ to 4 cups, 4 servings.

VICHYSSOISE

Packaged instant mashed potatoes for 4 servings
1 chicken bouillon cube or 1 teaspoon chicken
   bouillon granules
1 cup hot water
½ cup cream
1 slice onion, coarsely chopped
½ teaspoon salt
Dash pepper

Heat liquid ingredients called for on instant mashed potato package and pour into blender container. Add instant mashed potatoes and **GRIND** about 10 seconds or until smooth. Add all remaining ingredients and **GRIND** about 15 seconds longer, stopping motor once to push ingredients toward blades, if necessary. Chill thoroughly. Garnish with chopped chives, if desired. Makes 6 servings.

CHILLED CUCUMBER SOUP

See photo at right

2 (5-inch) green onions, cut in ½-inch lengths
2 teaspoons butter or margarine
2 cups Thin Cream Sauce (recipe page 166)
½ teaspoon salt
1 chicken bouillon cube
1 cup (½-pint) dairy sour cream
1 medium chilled peeled cucumber, sliced

Sauté onion pieces in butter or margarine until tender. Turn into container and add next 3 ingredients. **CREAM** until smooth. Chill. **CREAM** sour cream and ½ of cucumber slices 15 seconds or until finely chopped. Add remaining cucumber slices; **STIR** 15 seconds or until finely chopped. Fold into chilled soup. Garnish, if desired, with thin unpeeled cucumber slices. Yield: About 4½ cups, 4 to 6 servings.

AVOCADO SOUP

2 chicken bouillon cubes
½ cup hot water
⅛ teaspoon black pepper
1 thin (⅛-inch) slice unpeeled lemon, quartered
½ thin (⅛-inch) slice onion
1½ cups milk
2 cups diced peeled avocado
½ cup whipping cream or dairy sour cream

GRATE first 5 ingredients in blender container until onion is finely chopped, about 20 seconds. Add milk and avocado. **GRATE** until smooth, about 20 seconds. Chill. Just before serving stir in whipping cream or sour cream. If desired, top with additional sour cream and thin slice of avocado. Serve with corn chips. Makes about 3¼ cups, 4 servings.

FROSTY LOBSTER SOUP

3 cups buttermilk
1 (5-ounce) can lobster, drained
1 small cucumber, cubed
½ bunch watercress
1 teaspoon sugar
1 teaspoon prepared mustard
½ teaspoon salt
½ teaspoon dried dill weed

GRIND all ingredients 15 seconds. Chill thoroughly. Makes about 1 quart. Garnish with chopped chives.

GAZPACHO

See photo at right

4 tomatoes, quartered
½ green pepper, seeded and cubed
½ cucumber, sliced
½ onion, sliced
2 stalks celery, sliced
3 green onions, sliced
3 parsley sprigs
2 cloves garlic, peeled
½ cup cold water
2 tablespoons tarragon wine vinegar
2 tablespoons olive or salad oil
1 teaspoon salt
½ teaspoon Worcestershire sauce
¼ teaspoon pepper

GRATE all ingredients about 12 to 15 seconds, or just until ingredients on top reach blades. Chill thoroughly. Makes 6-7 servings.

JELLIED MUSHROOM SOUP

2 (10½-ounce) cans consommé
½ pound fresh mushrooms, coarsely chopped
1 envelope unflavored gelatin
½ cup water
1 (2-inch) piece lemon peel
¼ lemon, peeled
¼ cup white wine
Salt and pepper to taste
½ cup yogurt
Chopped dill or chives for garnish

Simmer consommé and mushrooms about 20 minutes. **LIQUEFY** gelatin, water, lemon peel and fruit 20 seconds. Add mushrooms and consommé and **PURÉE** 20 seconds. Add wine, salt and pepper to taste. **STIR** 10 seconds. Chill until served. Makes 8 servings, approximately 44 calories per serving. Garnish with yogurt and chopped dill or chives.

SENEGALESE SOUP

See photo at right.

2 cups Curry Sauce (recipe page 166)
1 cup whipping cream or undiluted evaporated milk
Curry powder, to garnish
3 tablespoons shredded coconut, toasted

Prepare Curry Sauce as directed. Cool slightly; stir in cream and chill. Pour into 6 chilled consommé cups; sprinkle with curry powder and top each serving with coconut. Makes 6 servings.

A. Chilled Cucumber Soup; B. Gazpacho; C. Senegalese Soup

BLENDER PREPARATION OF BABY AND JUNIOR FOODS

Foods for babies and juniors can be prepared economically and quickly right along with the family dinner with the help of a blender. This allows for a greater variety of flavors, textures and consistencies. The choice of baby's food and the introduction of new foods should be determined by the doctor.

To test for smoothness of food rub a small portion of mixture between your fingers. **GRATE** ingredients a few seconds longer if mixture is not smooth enough. If food with more texture is desired, process at **BLEND** rather than **GRATE.**

BABY VEGETABLES, MEATS OR POULTRY

¼ cup milk or bouillon
1 cup well-drained cooked fresh, frozen or canned vegetables, meats or poultry, cut in ½-inch cubes
Dash of salt

Combine ingredients in blender container. **GRATE** until satin smooth, about 30 seconds. Stop motor and push ingredients into blades with rubber spatula as needed. Test for smoothness by rubbing a small amount of food between fingers. If too coarse, continue processing. Makes about 1 cup, 2 servings.

JUNIOR OR TODDLER VEGETABLES MEATS OR POULTRY

Follow above recipe for Baby Vegetables, Meats or Poultry; **BEAT** 15 to 20 seconds or to desired fineness.

BABY FRUITS

¼ cup fruit juice or fruit syrup
1 cup well-drained cooked or canned fruits
Sugar or honey, as desired.

Prepare as directed for Baby Vegetables (recipe above). Makes about 1 cup, 2 servings.

JUNIOR OR TODDLER FRUITS

Follow recipe for Baby Fruits at left and **BEAT** 15 to 20 seconds or to desired fineness. Test for particle size by rubbing a bit of food between fingers.

BEEF DINNER

GRATE ½ cup milk, ½ cup cubed cooked lean beef, 2 tablespoons drained cooked or canned vegetables, 1 piece crisp-cooked bacon, ½ tomato and ¼ cup cooked rice or mashed potatoes 60 seconds or until smooth. Season as required for child or convalescent. Heat to serving temperature. Makes about 1½ cups.

CHICKEN DINNER

GRATE ½ cup milk, ½ cup diced cooked chicken, ⅓ cup drained cooked or canned vegetables and ¼ cup cooked rice or mashed potatoes 60 seconds or until smooth. Season as required for child or convalescent. Heat to serving temperature. Makes about 1½ cups.

APRICOT APPLESAUCE

Cover 30 dried apricot halves with water; simmer 15 minutes in covered pan. Add 1 apple, peeled, cored and sliced; simmer 15 minutes longer. **GRATE** 30 seconds or until smooth. Freeze individual portions in small paper cups or plastic ice cube containers. Defrost and serve cold or heat, as desired. Makes about 1¼ cups.

APPLEY COTTAGE CHEESE

Peel, core and slice ½ apple. Add ¼ cup water and cook slowly until apple is tender. **GRATE** with ½ cup cottage cheese 20 seconds or until smooth. Season to taste with salt, and sugar. Well-drained canned or cooked fruit may be substituted for apple if desired. Makes about 1 cup.

BANANA CEREAL

GRATE 1 ripe banana, peeled and sliced, with 3 tablespoons dry baby cereal and 3 tablespoons fruit juice or formula, milk or other liquid, 15 seconds or until smooth. Makes ½ cup.

FRUIT DESSERT

Drain 1 can (8 or 9-ounce) fruit or mixed fruit; **GRATE** 30 seconds or until smooth. Makes ⅔ cup.

CONVALESCENT, LIQUID OR SEMISOFT DIET FOODS

Foods for invalids on liquid or semisoft diets, or for senior citizens, can be tasty and tempting. Follow the recipes for Baby or Junior Foods (page 183) and process to fineness desired. Dinner foods served to the family take just seconds to process to the desired fineness for family invalids. Season the foods to taste or as a specific diet directs, using salt or sugar substitutes when necessary.

ORANGE-CARROT NOG

1 cup chilled milk or half and half (half milk, half cream) as diet requires
⅔ cup drained sliced cooked or canned carrots
1 tablespoon orange juice
2 teaspoons sugar or honey
Dash of salt
Dash of nutmeg
1 scoop vanilla ice cream

Combine milk or half and half, carrots, orange juice, sugar or honey, salt and nutmeg in blender container; **LIQUEFY** until carrots are smooth. Add ice cream and **WHIP** until blended. Pour into serving glass. Makes 1 serving.

ORANGE FLUFF

6 graham crackers
½ cup cold water
1 envelope (1 tablespoon) unflavored gelatin
¾ cup hot water
1-inch square orange peel (no white), cut in strips
⅔ cup orange juice
1 teaspoon liquid artificial sweetener
2 egg whites, stiffly beaten

Blender-chop graham crackers (see chopping directions page 8); save. Combine cold water and gelatin in container; **WHIP** until mixed, 2 or 3 seconds. Add hot water and orange peel. **GRATE** until gelatin is dissolved and orange rind is very finely chopped, 5 to 8 seconds. Add orange juice and artificial sweetener; **WHIP** to mix, 1 or 2 seconds. Pour into bowl. Chill until mixture has set ¾ of the way from edge to center of bowl. Beat until frothy with hand or electric beater. Fold in egg whites; spoon into chilled sherbet glasses or custard cups. Sprinkle blender-chopped graham crackers over top; chill. Makes 4 servings.

FROSTED CAFF-AU-LAIT

½ cup crushed ice
1 cup cold water
½ cup nonfat dry milk solids
¾ teaspoon instant coffee
½ teaspoon vanilla
6 drops liquid artificial sweetener
Pinch of salt

Combine ingredients in container; **CRUSH** until milk solids and coffee are dissolved, 40 to 50 seconds. Pour into chilled glass. Serve plain or topped with whipped dietary topping. Makes one tall or 2 medium sized drinks.

TWO-CALORIE WHIPPED TOPPING

1 teaspoon unflavored gelatin
1 tablespoon cold water
½ cup instant nonfat dry milk
1 (2-inch) piece lemon peel
¼ lemon, peeled
1 teaspoon vanilla
1 teaspoon liquid sugar substitute
½ cup ice water

Sprinkle gelatin over cold water. Dissolve over hot water or low heat. **LIQUEFY** milk, gelatin, lemon peel and fruit, vanilla and sugar substitute 60 seconds. Chill until cool to the touch. Add ice water and **WHIP** 3 minutes or until consistency of whipped cream. Stop motor at 30 second intervals and push ingredients to center of container with rubber spatula. Makes about 2 cups, approximately 2 calories per tablespoon.

EGGNOG

1 egg
1 tablespoon sugar*
1 cup chilled milk or half and half (half milk, half cream)
½ teaspoon vanilla
Pinch of salt, optional
Pinch of nutmeg, optional

Combine ingredients in container. Set speed at **CREAM,** switch motor on and off 2 or 3 times or until mixed. Pour into chilled glass. Makes 1 serving.

*Or substitute an equivalent amount of artificial sweetener.

DIET LEMONADE OR LIMEADE

¼-inch square lemon or lime rind (no white), cut into
   thin strips
⅓ cup lemon or lime juice
6 large ice cubes
1½ cups cold water
Liquid, powdered or granulated artificial sweetener to
   taste*

Combine rind and lemon or lime juice in container.
GRATE until rind is very finely chopped, 10 to 15
seconds. Add ice cubes, water and **GRATE** until ice
cubes are crushed, 8 to 10 seconds. Pour into glasses;
stir in artificial sweetener to taste. Makes about 2
cups, 2 servings.

*If sugar is preferred to artificial sweetener add ⅓
   cup granulated sugar to container with ice cubes
   and process as directed in above recipe.

WHEAT GERM NUT LOAF

1½ cup pecan halves
1½ cups ½-inch celery slices
1 cup ½-inch carrot slices
1½ cups milk
½ medium-size onion, cut in ¼-inch slices
3 eggs
⅓ cup flour
1½ teaspoons salt
⅛ teaspoon pepper
1 cup shredded American process or Cheddar cheese
¾ cup wheat germ

Line a 9 x 5 x 3-inch loaf pan with aluminum foil;
grease foil. Add ½ cup pecans to container. Set speed
at **BLEND**; switch motor on and off until nuts are
coarsely chopped. Repeat process 2 times; save nuts.
Add ½ cup celery to container. Set speed at **PURÉE**
switch motor on and off until celery is coarsely
chopped. Turn into saucepan. Repeat process 2 times.
Add ½ cup carrot slices to container. Set speed at
BEAT; switch motor on and off until coarsely
chopped. Add to saucepan. Repeat. Add milk, onion,
eggs, flour, salt and pepper to container. Set speed
at **BEAT**; process until well mixed, 2 to 3 seconds.
Pour into saucepan. Cook slowly, stirring constantly,
until mixture thickens. Add cheese, pecans and wheat
germ; mix well. Turn into loaf pan. Bake in moderate
oven (350°F.) until done, about 50 minutes. Cool 10
minutes before removing from pan. Serve plain or
topped with favorite cheese or cream sauce. Makes
6 servings.

MOCK SOUR CREAM FOR DIETERS

½ cup skim milk
1½ cups cottage cheese
½ thin slice onion
2 tablespoons lemon juice
¼ teaspoon salt
Dash of white pepper

Combine ingredients in container. **CHOP** until
smooth, 25 to 30 seconds. Stop motor as needed and
push ingredients into blades with rubber spatula.
Serve as salad dressing, a base for dips, on vegetables
or meats. Makes about 1½ cups.

PEANUTTY CHOCOLATE BREAKFAST-IN-A-GLASS

1 package (1.2 ounce) chocolate instant breakfast
   drink
1 cup chilled milk
3 tablespoons creamy-style peanut butter
¼ pint chocolate ice cream, cut in chunks

Combine first 3 ingredients in container. Set speed at
STIR and switch motor on and off 4 to 6 times or
until well mixed. Add ice cream and repeat processing
just until smooth. Pour into chilled glasses. Makes
2 servings.

DIETER'S BREAKFAST-IN-A-GLASS

2 eggs
2 cups chilled orange juice
⅔ cup nonfat dry milk solids
Liquid or powdered artificial sweetener to taste

Combine first 3 ingredients in container. Set speed
at **WHIP**; 2 or 3 seconds or until milk solids are recon-
stituted. Pour into 2 glasses; let each person stir in
sweetener to taste. Makes 2 servings.

LOW CALORIE ICE CREAM GINGER FIZZ

⅔ cup drained canned dietetic fruit cocktail
1 egg
1 or 2 scoops dietetic vanilla, New York or cherry ice
   cream
¼ cup chilled low calorie ginger ale

Combine fruit, egg and 1 scoop ice cream in container. **BLEND** until smooth, 10 to 15 seconds. Stop
motor; push ingredients into blades with rubber spatula as needed. Pour into a tall glass; stir in ginger
ale. Serve as is or top with a scoop of ice cream.
Makes 1 serving.

MORE FOODS DIETERS WILL LIKE

Beverages
    Carrot Cocktail   22
    Cherry Whiz   22
    Four Fruit Whiz   22
    Gelatin Pick-Me-Up   21
    Lime Lift   20
    Low Calorie Ice Cream Ginger Fizz   185
Desserts
    Orange Fluff   184
    Slim-Jim Cherry Pie   120
Meat, Fish, Seafood, and Poultry
    Barbecued Chicken   100
    Barbecued Chuck Steak   112
    Barbecued Fish Steaks   116
    Broiled Lobster Tails   116
    Charcoal Broiled Sirloin Steak   112
    Herbed Lamb Chops   116
    Lamb Kabobs   92
    Meat Balls   85
    Meat Loaves   81
    Sauerbraten   82
    Seven Tempting Hamburgers   111
Salads
    Ambrosia   146
    Cabbage Patch Slaw   145
    Caesar Salad   144
    Cool-As-A-Cucumber Mold   142
    Creamy Tomato, Vegetable, and Salmon Molds   142
    Cucumber Slices In Sour Cream Or Yogurt   144
    Low Calorie French Dressing   152
    Mock Sour Cream for Dieters   185
    Molded Tomato Salad   140
    Tuna-Tomato Aspic   142

A FEW HEALTH FOODS THAT PLEASE

Beverages
    Apricot Shake   23
    Carrot Cocktail   23
    Gelatin Pick-Me-Up   21
    Orange Carrot Nog   184
    Orange Glow   23
    Sunny Sipper   20
Breads
    Banana Bran Muffins   34
    Banana Wheat Germ Bread   29
    Bran Nut Muffins   34
    Whole Grain Wheat Bread   31
Cookies
    Mincemeat Oat Drops   62
    Pecan-Raisin Bran Drops   61
Desserts
    Applesauce   78
    Apricot or Baked Caramel Custard   78
    Apricot or Prune Whip   74
    Orange Fluff   184
Meats, Poultry and Fish
    Baked Stuffed Trout   96
    Barbecued Chuck Steak   112
    Barbecued Fish Steaks   116

    Barbecued Herb Chicken   116
    Broiled Lobster Tails   116
    Herbed Lamb Chops   116
    Lamb Kabobs   92
    Meat Balls   85
    Meat Loaves   81
    Seven Tempting Hamburgers   111
Salads
    Ambrosia   146
    Avocado Mold   139
    Cabbage Patch Slaw   145
    Crabmeat Salad in Avocado Shells   148
    Cucumber Slices in Sour Cream or Yogurt   144
    Green Goddess Salad   144
    Tuna-Tomato Aspic   142

MORE TEMPTING EASY-TO-EAT AND SEMISOLID FOODS FOR SENIOR CITIZENS AND INVALIDS

Beverages
    Hot Cocoa   25
    Hot Peanut Chocolate Toddy   25
    Peach Splash   19
Breads
    Banana Bran Muffins   34
    Banana Wheat Germ Bread   29
    Buttermilk Corn Bread   33
    Gingerbread, Old Fashioned   29
Cheese and Eggs
    Baked Macaroni and Cheese   99
    Cheese Rarebit   100
    Golden Soufflé   99
    Omelets and Scrambled Eggs   100
Desserts
    Applesauce   78
    Apricot or Prune Whip   74
    Chocolate Chiffon Pie   127
    Lemon, Caramel Rice and Chocolate Puddings   72
    Pots de Crème, Chocolate and Maple   73
    Pumpkin Pie   125
    Red Devil's Food Cake   45
    Spicy Applesauce Cake   46
    Strawberry Bavarian Cream   70
Fish, Meat and Poultry
    Baked Stuffed Trout   96
    Cheese Topped Cube Steaks   112
    Chicken Fricassee, Croquettes and Noodle Casserole   93
    Meat Balls   85
    Meat Loaves   81
    Seven Tempting Hamburgers   111
Salads
    Ambrosia   146
    Frosty Pineapple Mold   139
    Molded Tomato Salad   140
    Stuffed Peach or Pear Salad   147
Vegetables
    Cauliflower Polonaise   188
    Florentine Spinach   191
    Southern Yam Pudding   190
    Zucchini Custard   193

VEGETABLES

Vegetables are so important in the diet they should always be made into attractive dishes with an unusually fine flavor.

The blender can help make vegetable dishes easy to concoct and pretty as a picture. Count on the blender to mince or chop onion, garlic or other vegetables just the size desired. Use it to blend the velvety smooth sauces to serve with vegetables, grate the cheese needed for au gratin dishes, make the crumbs for sprinkling over vegetables or topping casseroles, etc.

Try the recipes that follow; they will encourage you to use the blender to prepare or garnish other tempting vegetable dishes.

CAULIFLOWER POLONAISE

Try polonaise crumbs over Brussels sprouts, broccoli, cabbage slices, green beans or boiled potatoes

1 medium head cauliflower
2 slices bread
2 tablespoons butter or margarine
1 hard-cooked egg yolk
3 parsley sprigs (optional)

Cook cauliflower in boiling salted water to cover for 12 to 15 minutes; drain. Toast bread and spread with butter; cut into 1-inch squares and **CRUMB** along with egg yolk. Scatter crumbs over cauliflower to serve. Makes 6 servings.

TWICE-BAKED POTATOES

Substitute triple-purpose process cheese spread for half of the sour cream for extra richness

6 baking potatoes
1½ cups sour cream
⅓ to ½ cup milk
4 green onions, sliced
3 slices bacon, crisp-cooked
1½ teaspoons salt

Bake potatoes in hot oven (425°F.) 40 to 60 minutes. Make crosswise cut in top, turn peel back and scoop out. **GRIND** sour cream and all remaining ingredients with scooped-out potato 1 minute, stopping motor to push ingredients to blades. Pile potato mixture into potato shells, sprinkle with paprika; return to oven for 5 to 10 minutes. Makes 6 servings.

FRUIT-STUFFED SWEET POTATOES

You can use raisins, pitted prunes or dried peaches instead of dates and apricots, if you wish

6 medium sweet potatoes or yams
¾ cup milk
¼ cup butter or margarine
½ cup pitted dates
¼ cup dried apricots
½ teaspoon salt
¼ teaspoon cloves

Bake potatoes in hot oven (425°F.) for 40 minutes or until done. Cut slice from top and scoop out inside, leaving shell intact. **GRIND** milk and all remaining ingredients with scooped-out potato 1 minute, stopping·motor to push ingredients to blades. Pile in potato shells; bake in moderate oven (350°F.) 15 to 20 minutes. Makes 6 servings.

GREEN BEANS VINAIGRETTE

Garnish with additional chopped pimiento and green pepper for a pretty confetti look

1 pound fresh green or wax beans
⅓ cup salad oil
¼ cup vinegar
1 slice onion
¼ small green pepper
½ canned pimiento
2 tablespoons parsley sprigs
¾ teaspoon salt
¼ teaspoon dry mustard

Clean beans, cook in boiling salted water until tender; drain. **GRIND** all remaining ingredients 15 seconds. Pour over beans. Cook over medium heat until hot. 4 to 6 servings. Note: Chill beans in vinaigrette sauce and serve cold as vegetable or salad.

GREEN BEANS ROMANO

Remember this rapid tomato topping for asparagus, peas, corn or wax beans

1 (10-ounce) package frozen green beans
1 medium tomato, quartered
½ cup cubed ham (optional)
1 tablespoon olive oil
1 clove garlic, peeled
½ teaspoon salt
½ teaspoon sugar

Cook green beans; drain. **GRIND** all remaining ingredients 30 seconds. Pour over beans and cook and stir over medium heat until piping hot. Makes 4 servings.

ORANGE-GLAZED SWEET POTATOES

⅔ cup honey
⅓ cup orange juice
⅔ cup sugar
1 teaspoon salt
½ medium (2½-inch) washed orange, cut into sixths
¼ cup butter or margarine
6 large sweet potatoes, cooked, peeled and halved*

Combine first 5 ingredients in container. **GRATE** until orange rind is finely chopped, about 20 seconds. Melt butter or margarine in large skillet. Add orange mixture. Bring to a boil; simmer gently until sugar is melted and syrup thickens slightly. Turn heat to low. Add potato halves and baste with sauce until potatoes are well glazed. Transfer potatoes to heated serving dish; pour thickened syrup over potatoes. Makes about 6 to 8 servings.

*2 cans (1-pound 10-ounce) vacuum packed sweet potato halves, without syrup, may be substituted for fresh cooked ones.

Twice-Baked Potatoes, Cauliflower Polonaise, Fruit-Stuffed Sweet Potatoes, Green Beans Romano

SOUTHERN YAM PUDDING

So rich and chewy it could become a holiday tradition!

3 cups diced peeled raw sweet potatoes or yams
1½ cups milk
1 cup sugar
1 egg
1½ tablespoons butter or margarine
1 teaspoon salt
½ teaspoon vanilla
½ teaspoon cinnamon
¼ teaspoon allspice

GRATE all ingredients 20 seconds. Pour into greased 1½-quart casserole. Bake in moderate oven (350°F.) 1 hour to 1 hour and 10 minutes, stirring once or twice during baking. Makes 6 servings.

APPLE-SAUCED BEETS

2 small apples, cored and diced
1 slice onion, coarsely chopped
2 tablespoons butter or margarine
1 (1-pound) can sliced beets, drained
½ teaspoon salt
Dash pepper
Dash mace

GRATE apples and onion 5 seconds or until coarse. Melt butter in saucepan; add apples, onion, beets and seasonings. Stir to mix. Cover and cook over medium heat until piping hot. Makes 6 servings.

GREEN BEAN BAKE

1 cup sour cream
2 slices onion
1 (1-inch) piece lemon peel
1 tablespoon parsley sprigs
1 teaspoon salt
¼ teaspoon pepper
5 cups drained cooked or canned green beans
2 slices bread
2 tablespoons butter or margarine

BLEND first six ingredients 20 seconds. Arrange beans in 1½-quart casserole; pour sour cream over. Spread bread with butter, tear each slice into 5 or 6 pieces and **CRUMB** 15 seconds. Sprinkle over beans. Bake in hot oven (400°F.) 10 minutes. 6 servings.

SCANDINAVIAN LIMA BEANS

⅓ cup sour cream
¼ cup milk
3 ounces blue cheese
1 tablespoon parsley sprigs
1 (10-ounce) package frozen lima beans, cooked and drained

GRIND sour cream, milk, cheese and parsley 15 seconds. Pour over lima beans. Cook over medium heat until hot. **GRATE** additional parsley for garnish. Makes 4 servings.

YAMS IN ORANGE SHELLS

3 oranges
1 (1-pound 2-ounce) can sweet potatoes, drained
½ cup walnuts or pecans
¼ cup cranberry juice
¼ cup butter or margarine, softened
½ teaspoon salt

Halve oranges. Scoop out fruit and **GRIND** fruit along with all remaining ingredients 45 to 50 seconds. Spoon into orange shells, arrange shells on baking sheet and bake in moderate oven (350°F.) for 15 to 20 minutes. Makes 6 servings.

CRISPY CARROT SAUTÉ

2 cups diced carrots
3 tablespoons butter or margarine
¼ teaspoon salt
¼ teaspoon ginger
¼ cup parsley sprigs

GRATE carrots, ½ cup at a time, about 15 seconds or until all pieces have been chopped. Melt butter in saucepan, add carrots and sprinkle with salt and ginger. Cover and cook over medium heat about 5 minutes or until crisp-tender. **GRATE** parsley for 2 to 5 seconds; use for garnish. Makes 3-4 servings.

SEVEN-MINUTE CABBAGE

Fresh, tender and delicious! Just remember not to over-chop or over-cook!

1 medium head cabbage, sliced (about 5 cups)
¼ cup water
2 tablespoons butter or margarine
½ teaspoon salt
Dash pepper

Fill blender container with cabbage; add cold water to cover and **GRATE** 2 to 3 seconds, *no longer!* Drain in strainer or colander. Turn into saucepan; repeat to chop remaining cabbage. Add all remaining ingredients. Heat to boiling, lower heat, cover and simmer 7 minutes. Makes 6 servings.

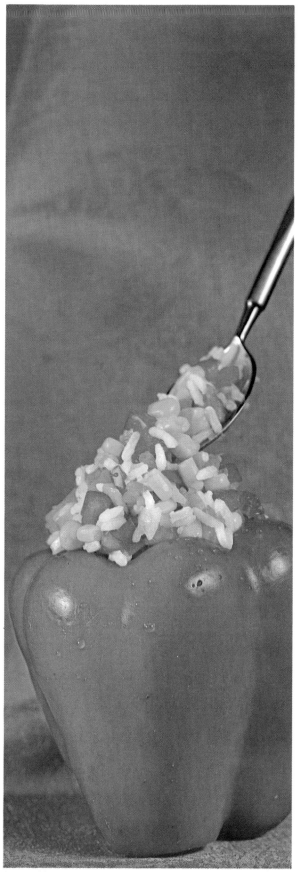

Vegetable — Stuffed Peppers

SWEET-SOUR CABBAGE

Seven-Minute Cabbage (page 190)
3 slices bacon, diced
2 tablespoons brown sugar
2 tablespoons flour
⅓ cup water
⅓ cup vinegar
1 slice onion
¼ teaspoon salt

Prepare Seven-Minute Cabbage as recipe directs. Meanwhile, cook bacon until crisp. Drain, reserving 2 tablespoons drippings. **GRIND** reserved drippings with all remaining ingredients 15 seconds. Pour in pan with bacon; cook and stir until thick. Pour over Seven-Minute Cabbage, mix and serve. Makes 6 to 8 servings.

VEGETABLE-STUFFED PEPPERS

See photo at left

3 green peppers
1 large tomato, quartered
1 stalk celery, sliced
1 slice onion
1 (1-pound) can whole kernel corn, drained
2 cups cooked rice
2 slices bread
¼ cup cubed American cheese

Remove tops and seeds from pepper; trim tops from stems and place in blender container. Parboil peppers in boiling salted water for 5 minutes; drain. **GRATE** pepper tops, tomatoes, celery and onion 10 seconds, stopping motor to push ingredients to blades, if necessary. Turn into bowl with corn and rice; mix. Place peppers in baking dish; spoon vegetable filling in. Tear each slice bread into 5 or 6 pieces. **CRUMB** 1 slice of bread 10 seconds. **CRUMB** remaining bread and cheese 10 seconds. Sprinkle crumbs over peppers. Bake in moderate oven (350°F.) 30 minutes. Makes 3 main dish or 6 vegetable servings. If desired, halve peppers lengthwise, fill and bake.

FLORENTINE SPINACH

1 (10-ounce) package frozen leaf spinach
½ cup sour cream
2 eggs
1 slice onion
1 teaspoon Worcestershire sauce
½ teaspoon salt
Dash pepper

Cook spinach in small amount boiling salted water until tender. Drain. **GRATE** with all ingredients 15 seconds. Pour into custard cups or individual bakers. Set in pan filled to 1-inch depth with hot water. Bake in moderate oven (350°F.) 15 to 20 minutes. Makes 4 servings.

TOMATOES PROVENCALE

A wonderful go-along for broiled steaks or chops

3 large ripe tomatoes
3 slices bread, toasted
½ clove garlic
2 green onions, sliced
3 tablespoons olive oil
½ teaspoon salt
⅛ teaspoon pepper

Halve tomatoes; place on baking sheet. Tear each slice toast into 5 or 6 pieces and **CRUMB**, 1 slice at a time, 10 seconds, or until fine. **GRIND** garlic and remaining ingredients 10 seconds. Pour over crumbs; toss to mix. Pile crumbs on tomatoes. Broil 4 inches from heat for 8 to 10 minutes. Makes 6 servings.

SCALLOPED TOMATOES

4 stalks celery, sliced
2 slices onion, coarsely chopped
2 tablespoons mustard pickles
2 tablespoons flour
1 tablespoon sugar
1 teaspoon salt
1 (1-pound 12-ounce) can tomatoes
3 slices bread, toasted and cubed

GRATE celery, onion and pickles 10 seconds. Turn into 1½-quart casserole. Stir in flour, sugar and salt, then tomatoes. **CRUMB** toast and stir half the crumbs into tomato mixture. Bake in moderate oven (350°F.) 30 minutes. Scatter remaining crumbs over top and bake 20 minutes longer. Makes 8 servings.

SWEDISH BAKED BEANS

¾ cup catsup or chili sauce
½ medium onion, quartered and sliced
¼ cup seedless raisins
1 medium apple, peeled, cored, and cut into 1-inch chunks
⅓ cup well-drained sweet pickle relish
1 tablespoon brown sugar
1 teaspoon prepared mustard
2 cans (1-pound 4-ounce) pork and beans

Combine catsup or chili sauce, onion and raisins in blender container. **BLEND** until onion is coarsely chopped, about 30 seconds. Stop motor as needed and push ingredients into blades with rubber spatula. Add apple chunks, ½ at a time; **BLEND** until coarsely chopped, 20 to 25 seconds. Pour into covered frypan. Add remaining ingredients; mix. Bring to simmering stage; cover and cook slowly until heated and flavors are well blended, 25 to 30 minutes, stirring frequently. Makes about 6 servings.

HAM-STUFFED ACORN SQUASH

See photo at right

2 medium Acorn squash
1 cup cubed cooked ham
½ cup coarsely chopped green pepper
1 stalk celery, sliced
2 hard-cooked eggs, quartered
3 slices bread
2 tablespoons melted butter or margarine

Halve squash, remove seeds. Place, cut side down, in shallow pan. Bake in moderate oven (350°F.) 40 minutes. **GRATE** ham, green pepper and celery; turn into bowl. **GRATE** hard-cooked eggs; add to ham. Tear each slice of bread into 5 or 6 pieces. **CRUMB** bread, 1 slice at a time, and add to ham. Toss to mix. Pile in squash. Drizzle with butter. Bake at 350° 15 minutes. Makes 4 servings.

HASH-BROWN POTATOES

3 cups diced peeled potatoes
¼ green pepper, coarsely chopped
¼ cup parsley sprigs
¼ cup butter or margarine
1½ teaspoons salt
¼ teaspoon pepper

GRATE potatoes, ½ cup at a time, 5 seconds. **GRATE** green pepper and parsley 5 to 10 seconds. Melt butter in 10-inch skillet; spread potatoes, green pepper and parsley evenly in skillet. Cover and cook over low heat 10 to 15 minutes. Remove cover and cook over medium heat another 10 to 15 minutes, or until bottom is brown and crisp. Makes 4 to 6 servings.

MEXICANA GREEN BEANS

2 medium tomatoes, peeled and cut into 8 wedges
½ small (1½ to 2-inch) onion, quartered and sliced
¼ small green pepper, cleaned and cut into 1-inch squares
2 tablespoons cooking oil, or melted butter or margarine
1½ teaspoons salt
¼ teaspoon sugar
¼ teaspoon chili powder
Dash of pepper
2 packages (10-ounce) cross cut green beans, partially defrosted and separated

Combine first 8 ingredients in container; **BEAT** until tomato and green pepper are finely chopped, 40 to 60 seconds. Stop motor; push ingredients into blades with rubber spatula as needed. Pour into covered saucepan or frypan. Heat to simmering stage. Empty beans into sauce; mix. Cover tightly; cook slowly until beans are tender. Makes 6 servings.

INSTANT MASHED POTATOES

To Blender-Cook packaged instant mashed potatoes, simply heat the liquid ingredients called for on the package and pour into blender container. Add dry potatoes and **GRIND** until smooth and thick. Serve at once.

CORN TOMATO CUSTARDS

1½ cups milk
2 eggs
⅓ medium-size green pepper, cleaned and cut into 1-inch squares
2 teaspoons sugar
1½ teaspoons salt
Dash of pepper
3 tablespoons melted butter or margarine
1 can (12-ounce) whole kernel corn, drained
6 fresh tomato slices
6 (1½-inch) crisp bacon slices, optional

Combine first 6 ingredients in container; **BLEND** just until green pepper is chopped moderately fine, 10 to 15 seconds. Pour into bowl; add 1 tablespoon melted butter or margarine and corn; mix. Spoon into six 6-ounce custard cups or baking dishes. Place dishes in shallow pan; fill pan ½ full of hot water. Bake in slow oven (300°F.) until set, 30 to 35 minutes. When custards are done a blade of knife will come out clean when inserted into center. Sauté tomato slices quickly in remaining butter or margarine. Arrange tomato slices on corn custards; top each with a bacon slice, if desired. Makes 6 servings.

BROILED TOMATO SLICES

½ cup blender-grated Parmesan cheese (see grating directions page 6)
½ cup finely blender-chopped buttered bread crumbs (see crumbing directions on page 8)
1 teaspoon salt
Dash of pepper
3 large (3-inch) firm tomatoes, cut in 4 slices
¼ cup melted butter or margarine

Combine cheese, crumbs, salt and pepper; mix. Brush each tomato slice with butter or margarine; dip in cheese-crumb mixture, coating slices on both sides. Place slices on buttered shallow baking pan. Broil 5 to 6 inches from heat source until lightly browned; turn slices carefully with pancake turner. Brown second side and allow tomato to warm through. Makes 6 servings.

ZUCCHINI CUSTARD

6 medium zucchini, halved
2 tablespoons butter or margarine
3 eggs
1 cup evaporated milk
1 slice onion
1 whole canned pimiento
½ garlic clove
1 teaspoon salt

Place zucchini halves, cut side down, in 11½ x 7½-inch baking pan with butter. Bake in hot oven (400°F.) 15 minutes. **BLEND** all remaining ingredients 30 seconds. Pour over zucchini. Place baking pan in larger pan, fill larger pan with hot water to 1-inch deep and bake at 350° 40 minutes. Makes 6 servings.

Ham-Stuffed Acorn Squash page 192

INDEX

A

Alexander 27
Almond Crust 119
Almond Paste, Blender-Made 56
Almond Stuffed Apples 78
Anchovy Dip, Creamy 15
Appetizers
  Apple-Stuffed Edam 16
  Bacon Dip 15
  Bagna Cauda 13
  Black Bean Dip, Hot 13
  Caviar Dip 14
  Cheese Duo Dip 15
  Cheese Nut Ball 11
  Chicken Filled Puffs 11
  Chili Con Queso 15
  Chopped Chicken Liver
    Spread 164
  Chutney-Cheese Spread 13
  Corned Beef Dip 16
  Crabmeat Dip Or Spread 11
  Crabmeat Filled Puffs 11
  Creamy Anchovy Dip 15
  Danish Herring Dip 14
  Deviled Ham Dunk 15
  Down East Clam Dip 14
  Easy Swiss Fondue 17
  Franks Fondue 17
  Gaucamole 15
  Ham And Egg Sandwich
    Filling 14
  Ham And Mushroom Dunk 14
  Ham Fondue 17
  Ham Sandwich Spread 15
  He-Man Garlic Dip 16
  Hot Black Bean Dip 13
  Hot Orange Marmalade Dip
    Hot Franks Or Meat Balls 16
  Midget Meat Balls 85
  Pineapple-Blue Cheese Dip 16
  Pizza Fondue 17
  Pronto Chicken Spread 15
  Rousing Roquefort Dip 13
  Salami Pizza Fondue 17
  Saucy Sardine Dip 14
  Shrimp 'N Dill Dip 14
  Shrimp Fondue 15
  Shrimp In Beer 16
  Shrimp Newburgh Dip 14
  Stuffed Kumquats 11
  Sunshine Dip 16
  Tangy Ham Dip 11
  Tasty Tuna Dip 13
  Wisconsin Dunk 13
Apples
  Almond Stuffed 78
  Applesauce 78
  Apple-Sauced Beets 190
  Appley Cottage Cheese 183
  Butter, Old Fashioned 131
  Delight Pudding 72
  Doughnuts 104
  Fritters 103
  Pancakes 35
  Raisin Stuffing 91
  Stuffed Edam 16
Apricots
  Almond Dessert Sauce 170
  Applesauce 183
  Squares, Rich 65

B

Baby And Junior Foods
  Applesauce 78
  Appley Cottage Cheese 183
  Apricot Applesauce 183
  Baby Fruits 183
  Baby Vegetables, Meats Or
    Poultry 183
  Banana Cereal 183
  Beef Dinner 183
  Chicken Dinner 183
  Custard 73
  Fruit Dessert 183
  Junior Or Toddler Fruits 183
  Junior Or Toddler Vegetables,
    Meats Or Poultry 183
Bacardi 26
Bacon
  'N Egg Sandwich On
    French Rolls 158
  And Egg Sandwich Spread 158
  Dip 15
  Muffins 33
  Or Ham Hot Cakes 36
  Cheese And Bacon Pizza 164
Bagna Cauda 13
Bagna Cauda Vegetables 13
Baked Beans, Swedish 192
Baked Ham 87
Baked Macaroni And Cheese 99
Baked Stuffed Spareribs 87
Bananas
  Bran Muffins 34
  Bread 183
  Chiffon Cake 48
  Fritters 103
  Ice Cream 76
  Muffins 33
  Nut Cake 41
  Nut Doughnuts 104
  Pancakes 35
Banbury Tarts 129
Barbecue
  Sauce, Southwestern 168
  Sauce For Ribs, Tangy
    Pineapple 168
  Chicken 94
  Chuck Steak 112
  Fish Steaks 116
  Herb Chicken 116
  Pork Loin 114
  Pork Loin, Orange Glazed 114
Basic Meat Loaf 81
Batter, Fritter For Fruits 103
Batter, Fritter For Seafood And
  Vegetables 103
Bavarian Cream, Mocha 70
Bavarian Cream, Strawberry 70
Beans
  Bake, Green 190
  Romano, Green 188
  Scandinavian Lima 190
  Vinaigrette, Green 188
Bearnaise Sauce 166
Bechamel Sauce 166
Beef
  Basic Meat Loaf 81
  Blender Hash 86
  Burgers Italiano 111
  Burgers Mexicana 111
  Burgundy 82

Cake, Broiled 46
Cherry Dessert Sauce 170
Chiffon Pie 126
Coconut Balls 58
Crème 69
Custard 78
Muffins 33
Or Prune Whip 74
Pecan Balls 58
Shake 23
Soufflé Pie 128
As-You-Like-It Cream Soup 176
Avocado
  Dressing 151
  Filling 162
  Guacamole 15
  Mold 139
  Soup 180

Cheese Topped Cube Steaks 112
Cheesy Bacon Burgers 111
Chuck Steak, Barbecued 112
Corned Beef Cheese
  Sandwiches 157
Corned Beef Dip 16
Corned Beef Sandwich
  Spread 157
Corned Beef Sauerkraut
  Sandwich 157
Corned Beef Swiss Cheese
  Sandwich 157
Dinner 183
Flank Steak Tarragon,
  Grilled 112
Frenchy Burgers 111
German Meat Balls 84
Honolulu Burgers 111
Meat And 'Tater Loaf 81
Patio Burgers 111
Peanut Burgers 111
Sauerbraten 82
Sirloin Steak, Charcoal
  Broiled 112
Steak, Small Chuck 112
Zesty Beef Sandwiches 160
Beet Borsch 178
Beet Relish, Horseradish 136
Beets, Apple-Sauced 190
Berry Cream 70
Berry Cream Filling 55
Beverages, Alcoholic
  Alexander 27
  Bacardi 26
  Bloody Mary 26
  Commodore Cocktail 26
  Daiquiri, Frozen 26
  Emerald Fizz 26
  Frozen Daiquiri 26
  Grasshopper 26
  Holiday Eggnog 19
  Orange Blossom 27
  Orange Frappé 23
  Pink Lady 27
  Sherry Flip 27
  Silver Fizz 26
  Sloe Gin Fizz 26
  Stinger 26
  Tom Or Rum Collins 26
  Whiskey Sour 27
Beverages, Non-Alcoholic
  After-Dinner Mocha 25
  Apricot Shake 23
  Best Banana Milk Shake 21
  Brazilian Chocolate 24
  Calypso Chocolate 25
  Carrot Cocktail 23
  Cherry-Vanilla Float 21
  Cherry Whiz 23
  Chocolate, Peppermint Or
    Coffee Floats 20
  Choco-Mint Float 21
  Diet Lemonade Or Limeade 185
  Dieters Breakfast-
    In-A-Glass 185
  Double Chocolate Floats 20
  Double Ginger Punch 19
  Double Raspberry Soda 21
  Eggnog 184
  Four Fruit Whiz 23
  Fresh Rhubarb Cocktail 23
  Frosted Cafe-Au-Lait 184
  Fruit-Nut Milk Shake 24
  Gelatin Pick-Me-Up 21
  Hot Butterscotch Toddy 25
  Hot Chocolate 24
  Hot Cocoa 25
  Hot Peanut Chocolate
    Toddy 25
  Lime Freeze 20
  Lime Lift 20
  Low-Calorie Ice Cream
    Ginger Fizz 185
  Malts, Shakes and 20
  Mint Punch 19
  Minted Ice Tea 25
  Mocha Float 21
  Moscow Hot Chocolate 25
  Orange-Carrot Nog 184
  Orange Glow 23
  Party Punch For Many 18

Peach Splash 19
Peanut Butterscotch Toddy 25
Peanutty Chocolate Breakfast-
  In-A-Glass 185
Pineapple-Mint Whip 20
Pineapple-Orange Frost 21
Pink Peppermint Velvet 24
Quick Cocoa 25
Quick-Fix Fruit Juices 19
Raspberry Fizz 20
Shakes and Malts 20
Sparkling Fruit Punch 19
Strawberry-Banana Milk
  Shake 21
Strawberry Frost 23
Sunny Sipper 20
Taffy Peppermint Smoothie 21
Thick Mocha Shake 20
Tropical Floats 19
Black Bean Or Lentil Soup 175
Black Bottom Pies 124
Black Satin Chocolate Frosting 52
Blackberry, Blueberry and
  Boysenberry Jam, Frozen 131
Blender Beef Hash 86
Blender-Make Almond Paste 56
Blender Mayonnaise 154
Blender Basics 4
Blintzes, Pancakes For Crêpes
  And Blintzes 37
Blitz Torte, Modern-Made 50
Bloody Mary 26
Blueberries
  Funny Cake 48
  Jam, Spiced 133
  Muffins 33
  Pancakes 36
Blue Cheese Dressing 151
Bombay Chicken Curry 95
Bran
  Muffins, Banana 34
  Nut Muffins 34
  Pecan-Raisin Bran Drops 61
  Pumpkin Spice Bran Drops 62
Brazilian Chocolate 24
Breads, Miscellaneous
  Garlic Bread, Hot 117
  Italian Cheese Bread 117
Breads, Quick
  Apple Pancakes 35
  Apricot Muffins 33
  Bacon Muffins 33
  Bacon Or Ham Hot Cakes 36
  Banana Bran Muffins 34
  Banana Muffins 33
  Banana Pancakes 35
  Banana Wheat Germ Bread 29
  Berry Crêpes 37
  Blueberry Muffins 33
  Blueberry Pancakes 36
  Bran Nut Muffins 34
  Buttermilk Corn Bread 33
  Buttermilk Pancakes 35
  Cheese Buttermilk Corn
    Bread 33
  Cheese Waffles 35
  Chocolate Chip Waffles 35
  Corn Muffins 33
  Corn Sticks 33
  Country Kitchen Muffins 33
  Cranberry Nut Bread 29
  Crispy Waffles 35
  Date Corn Bread 33
  Fix-Ahead Popovers 35
  Herb Popovers 35
  Nut Waffles 35
  Oatmeal Muffins 33
  Old Fashioned Gingerbread 29
  Orange Nut Bread 29
  Orange Pecan Pancakes 36
  Pancakes 35, 36
  Pancakes For Crêpes And
    Blintzes 37
  Parmesan Popovers 35
  Pineapple Waffles 35
  Popover Mixes 195
  Popovers 34, 35
  Potato Pancakes 36
  Prune Or Date Muffins 33
  Speedy-Made Muffins From
    A Mix 34

Spice Popovers 35
Spicy Apple Waffles 35
Wheat Germ Banana Muffins 34
Whole Grain Wheat
Pancakes 36
Whole Wheat Muffins 33
Yorkshire Pudding 35
Breads, Yeast
Cinnamon Pecan Rolls 31
Cinnamon Swirl 31
Golden Cheese 31
Luscious Yeast Rolls 31
Orange Nut 117
Stollen 32
Tutti-Fruitti Rolls 32
Whole Grain Wheat 31
Breakfast-In-A-Glass, Dieters 185
Broiled Apricot Cake 46
Broiled Coconut Frosting 55
Broiled Crabmeat Sandwich 161
Broiled Lobster Tails 116
Broiled Nutty Chocolate
Frosting 55
Brown Edge Or Vanilla Wafer
Crust 121
Brownies 64
Brownies, Best-Ever Blender 64
Burger Sauce, Steak Or 168
Burgers
Cheesy-Bacon 111
Frenchy 111
Honolulu 111
Italiano 111
Mexicana 11
Patio 111
Peanut 111
Burnt Sugar Praline Squares 58
Butter Chews 66
Butter Pecan Crust 119
Butter Sauce 72
Butters and Butter Spreads
Churned Butter 39
Cinnamon Butter 38
Cinnamon Honey Butter 38
Curry Butter 39
Garlic Butter 39
Herb Butter 39
Homemade Nut Butter 39
Honey Butter 38
Lemon Parsley Butter 39
Maple Butter 38
Mustard Butter 39
Nut Butter, Homemade 39
Onion Butter 39
Orange Marmalade Butter 38
Peanut Butter 39
Strawberry Butter 39
Sweet Butters 38
Sweet Fruity Butter 38
Toffee Butter 39
Buttermilk Corn Bread 33
Buttermilk Pancakes 35
Butterscotch
Frosting 52
Pecan Ice Cream Pie 122
Sauce 170
Hot Toddy 25
Peanut Toddy 25

C

Cabbage
Cabbage Patch Slaw 145
Seven-Minute 190
Sweet-Sour 191
Ceasar Salad 144
Cakes
Banana, Spiced 41
Banana Chiffon 48
Banana Nut 41
Blueberry Funny 48
Broiled Apricot 46
Mixes 41
Carrot 46
Cherry Nut 44
Chocolate Angel Torte 50
Chocolate Caramel 44
Chocolate Cream 48
Chocolate Nut Torte 50
Cup 44
Devil's Food, Red 45

Double Rich Devil's Food 44
Feathery Fudge 44
Fluffy Prune With Lemon
Frosting 41
Fruit, Last Minute Holiday 46
Graham Cracker Torte 49
Hot Milk Sponge 48
Last Minute Holiday Fruit 46
Lemony-Light Cheese 43
Mocha Spice 44
Modern-Made Blitz Torte 50
Orange Cheese 43
Orange Ice Box 77
Orange Spice 41
Patriotic 107
Peach Chiffon Party 48
Pecan Or Walnut 44
Pretty Party 107
Quick And Easy Dobos Torte 48
Red Devil's Food 45
Regal Cheese 43
Spiced Banana 41
Spicy Applesauce 46
Sponge, Hot Milk 48
Torte Elegante 49
Yellow 44
Wheat And Apple Nut 45
Zoo Parade Birthday 107
Cake Frostings And Fillings
Berry Cream Filling 55
Black Satin Chocolate
Frosting 52
Black Satin Frosting, Quick 50
Broiled Coconut Frosting 55
Broiled Nutty Chocolate
Frosting 55
Butterscotch Frosting 52
Cherry Frosting 53
Chocolate Butter Cream
Frosting 52
Chocolate Icing 52
Chocolate Mint Frosting 52
Coconut Pecan Frosting 55
Coffee Frosting 53
Confectioners' Sugar Frosting 53
Creamy Frosting Mixes 50
Cream Lemon Frosting 55
French Butter Cream 52
Lady Baltimore Frosting 53
Lemon Frosting 53
Marshmallow Frosting 55
Milk Chocolate Frosting 52
Mocha Frosting 52
Orange Frosting 53
Peanut Butter Frosting 53
Peppermint Frosting 55
Quick Black Satin Frosting 52
Snowy Cake Icing 53
Whipped Cream Frosting 53
Calypso Chocolate 25
Candies and Confections
Apricot Coconut Balls 58
Apricot Pecan Balls 58
Burnt Sugar Praline Squares 58
Caramel Apples, Peanutty 106
Chocolate Angel Confection 57
Chocolate Marshmallow
Bites 106
Date Pecan Rolls 58
Peanut Butter Panoche 57
Praline Clusters 58
Praline Squares, Burnt Sugar 58
Quick Chocolate Pecan
Fudge 57
Quick Pralines 58
Rum Balls 57
Candy Coated Ice Cream
Paddle Dips 108
Caper Dressing 151
Caramel Apples, Peanutty 106
Caramel Custard, Baked 78
Caramel Rice Pudding 72
Cardinal Sauce 172
Carrot Cake 46
Carrot Salad, Sunny 146
Carrot Sauté, Crispy 190
Carrot Soup, Cold Sweet Basil 179
Carrot Soup, Sweet Basil 179
Catsup 137
Catsup, Tomato Apple 137
Cauliflower Polonaise 188

Caviar Dip 14
Celery And Corn Cream Soup 176
Celery Soup 176
Celery Stuffing 94
Cereal Flake Crumb Crust 121
Ceylon Chicken Salad 148
Charcoal Broiled Sirloin Steak 112
Cheddar Cheese Soup 175
Cheese
'N Olive Spread 162
And Bacon Pizza 164
And Egg Puffs 99
Apple-Stuffed Edam 16
Bacon Burgers 111
Baked Macaroni And Cheese 99
Blue Cheese Dressing 151
Buttermilk Corn Bread 33
Cake, Regal 43
Cheddar Cheese Soup 175
Chutney Spread 13
Corned Beef Sandwiches 157
Creamy Cucumber Dressing 153
Dill Sauce 166
Duo Dip 15
Easy Swiss Fondue 17
Franks Fondue 17
French Toasted Sandwiches 162
French Toasted Mozzarella
Sandwiches 162
Frozen Roquefort Dressing 151
Fruit And Nut Sandwich
Spread 162
Fruit Tarts 129
Golden Bread 31
Ham Fondue 17
He-Man Garlic Dip 16
Hot Tuna Bunwiches 161
Italian Bread 117
Italian Dressing 151
Lemony-Light Cake 43
Mexicana Rarebit 100
Nut Ball 11
Orange Cake 43
Parmesan Popovers 35
Pastry 119
Pineapple-Blue Dip 16
Pizza Fondue 17
Pronto Pizza 163
Rarebit 100
Roquefort Cream Dressing 151
Roquefort Dressing 152
Rousing Roquefort Dip 13
Sauce 166
Sauce, Quick 167
Scrambled Eggs 100
Sunshine Dip 16
Tomato-Blue Cheese Soup 179
Topped Cube Steaks 112
Waffles 35
Walnutty Cheese Spread 162
Wisconsin Dunk 13
Cherry
Coconut Macaroons 64
Frosting 53
Jubilee Pie 120
Nut Cake 44
Pecan Ice Cream Pie 122
Sauce For Ham 167
Vanilla Float 21
Whiz 23
Chicken
Almond Sandwiches 157
Barbecued 94
Barbecued Herb 116
Bombay Curry 95
Cacciatore 94
Ceylon Salad 148
Country 94
Croquettes 93
Dinner 183
Filled Puffs 11
Fricassee 93
Liver Spread, Chopped 164
Noodle Casserole 93
Pronto Spread 15
Salad Spread 157
Turkey Or Ham Salad 148
Vegetable Soup 175
Waikiki Sandwiches 157
Chiffon Sauce For Fish, Cold 169
Chiffonade Dressing 151

Children's Delights
Candy Ice Cream
Paddle Dips 108
Chocolate Marshmallow
Bites 106
Cool Cat Cones 107
Crazy Cutouts 108
Firecrackers 108
Fruit Ice Sticks 108
Ice Cream Flower Pots 108
Ice Cream Tepees 106
Icy Paddle Sticks 108
Jewel Paddle Dips 108
Minty Paddle Dips 108
Nutty Candy Paddle Dips 108
Orange Paddle Dips 108
Patriotic Cakes 107
Peanut Balls 108
Peanutty Caramel Apples 106
Pretty Party Cakes 107
Rocky Road Balls 108
Snow Cones and Slush Cups 106
Spooky Paddle Dips 108
Tricky Doughnut Treats 107
Zoo Parade Birthday Cakes 107
Chili Con Carne 84
Chili Con Queso 15
Chili Sauce 137
Chilled Tomato Buttermilk
Soup 179
Chinese Chews 66
Chocolate and Cocoa
Best-Ever Blender Brownies 64
Black Satin Chocolate
Frosting 52
Brazilian Chocolate 24
Broiled Nutty Chocolate
Frosting 55
Brownies 64
Calypso Chocolate 25
Chocolate Almond Crisps 62
Chocolate Angel Confection 57
Chocolate Angel Pie 128
Chocolate Angel Torte 50
Chocolate Butter Cream
Frosting 52
Chocolate Caramel Cake 44
Chocolate Chiffon Pie 127
Chocolate Chip Drops 61
Chocolate Chip Waffles 35
Chocolate Nut Macaroons 64
Chocolate Cream Cake 48
Chocolate Freeze 74
Chocolate Frosting, Broiled
Nutty 55
Chocolate, Hot 24
Chocolate Icing 52
Chocolate Marshmallow
Bites 106
Chocolate Mint Frosting 52
Chocolate Nut Fondue
With Orange Sauce 69
Chocolate Nut Torte 50
Chocolate Pecan Frosting 55
Chocolate Pecan Fudge,
Quick 57
Chocolate Peppermint Pie 122
Chocolate Pots De Crème,
Quick 73
Chocolate Pudding 72
Chocolate Rum Sauce 171
Chocolate Sundae Pie 122
Chocolate Wafer Crust 121
Choco-Mint Foat 21
Cocoa, Hot 25
Cocoa, Quick 25
Double Chocolate Banana
Pie 125
Double Chocolate Floats 20
Double Rich Devil's Food
Cake 44
Feathery Fudge Cake 44
Frosted Chocolate Drops 61
Frozen Chocolate
Peppermint Torte 77
Fudge Sauce 171
Heavenly Chocolate Pie 128
Milk Chocolate Frosting 52
Mocha Sauce 171
Moscow Hot Chocolate 25
Quick Black Satin Frosting 52

195

Quick Chocolate Pots
De Crème 73
Peanut Chocolate Toddy,
Hot 25
Red Devil's Food Cake 45
Chopped Chicken Liver
Spread 164
Chopping
Brittles, Peanut, Coconut, etc. 6
Candy Canes 6
Candy Sticks 6
Cheeses 6
Chocolate 6
Coconut, Fresh
Eggs, Hard-Cooked
Fruits, Dry Chop Method 6
Meat And Poultry, Cooked 6
Nuts
Rind, Lemon, Orange Or Lime
Vegetables (Raw Or Cooked),
Dry Chop Method 7
Vegetables For Salads And
Relishes, Water Chop Method 7
Chuck Steak,
Small 112
Chutney Grilled Lamb Chops 116
Cinnamon Butter 38
Cinnamon Honey Butter 38
Cinnamon Pecan Rolls 31
Cinnamon Swirl Bread 31
Clam Bisque, Creamy 178
Clam Dip, Down East 14
Cocoa, Hot 25
Coconut Frosting, Broiled 55
Coconut Pastry 119
Coconut Pecan Frosting 55
Coffee
After-Dinner Mocha 25
Coffee Frosting 53
Frosted Cafe-Au-Lait 184
Cold Chiffon Sauce For Fish 169
Cold Sweet Basil Carrot Soup 179
Coleslaw, Fruited 146
Coleslaw, Salmon 146
Coleslaw With Sour Cream
Dressing 145
Commodore Cocktail 26
Confectioners' Sugar 53
Confectioners' Sugar Frosting 53
Convalescent, Liquid, Semi-Soft
Diet Or Health Foods
Applesauce 78
Appley Cottage Cheese 183
Apricot Applesauce 183
Apricot Custard And Baked
Caramel Custard 78
Apricot Or Prune Whip 74
Baked Prune Whip 73
Banana Cereal 183
Custard 73
Diet Lemonade Or Limeade 185
Dieter's Breakfast-
In-A-Glass 185
Eggnog 184
Frosted Cafe-Au-Lait 184
Health Foods That Please 186
Low Calorie Ice Cream Ginger
Fizz 185
Mock Sour Cream For Dieters 185
More Foods Dieters
Will Like 186
More Semisolid Foods For
Invalids And Senior
Citizens 186
Orange-Carrot Nog 184
Orange Fluff 184
Peanutty Chocolate Breakfast-
In-A-Glass 185
Wheat Germ Nut Loaf 185
Cooked Salad Dressing 155
Cooked Sour Cream Salad
Dressing 155
Cookies
Best-Ever Blender Brownies 64
Brownies 64
Butter Chews 66
Cherry Coconut Macaroons 64
Chinese Chews 66
Chocolate Almond Crisps 62
Chocolate Chip Drops 61
Chocolate Nut Macaroons 64

Frosted Chocolate Drops 61
Fruit Squares 66
Fruit Treasures 65
Linzer Bars 66
Mexican Wedding Cakes 67
Mincemeat Bars 64
Mincemeat Oat Drops 62
Molasses Drops 61
Pecan-Raisin Bran Drops 61
Pineapple Nut Drops 62
Pumpkin Spice
Bran Drops 62
Rich Apricot Squares 65
Rum Balls 57
Shortbread Crumb Cookies 67
Yummy Frosted Bars 67
Cool-As-A-Cucumber Mold 142
Cool Cat Cones 107
Coral Fish Sauce 170
Corn
And Bacon Fritters 103
Celery And Corn Cream
Soup 176
Chowder, Iowa 177
Fritters 103
Muffins 33
On The Cob 117
Relish, Speedy 136
Tomato Custards 193
Cream Of Corn Soup 176
Corn Bread
Buttermilk 33
Cheese Buttermilk 33
Corn Muffins 33
Date Corn Bread 33
Sticks 33
Corned Beef
Cheese Sandwiches 157
Dip 16
Sandwich Spread 157
Sauerkraut Sandwich 157
Swiss Cheese Sandwich 157
Cottage Cheese Apricot Pie 124
Country Kitchen Muffins 33
Crab
Broiled Crabmeat Sandwich 161
Crabmeat Dip Or Spread 11
Crabmeat Rolls 161
Crabmeat Salad In Avocado
Shells 148
Crabmeat Sandwich Spread 161
Deviled Crab 98
Cranberries
Cranberry Marshmallow
Salad 146
Cranberry Nut Bread 29
Cranberry-Orange
Marmalade 131
Cranberry Pecan Relish 134
Cranberry Relish, Spiced
Orange 134
Cranberry Relish Pie 129
Cranberry Sauce,
Strawberry 172
Cranberry-Waldorf Salad 139
Crazy Cutouts 108
Cream Cheese Dressing, Fluffy 154
Cream Cheese Honey Dressing 154
Cream Of Corn Soup 176
Cream Of Mushroom Soup 176
Cream Of Watercress Soup 176
Cream Or White Sauce
(Medium) 166
Cream Sauce, Thick 166
Cream Sauce, Thin 166
Creamy Cheese Cucumber
Dressing 153
Creamy Cherry Banana Pie 125
Creamy Clam Bisque 178
Creamy Dressing For Fruits 154
Creamy Frosting Mixes 52
Creamy Garlic Dressing 154
Creamy Lemon Frosting 55
Creamy Salmon Ring Mold 142
Creamy Tomato Mold 142
Creamy Vegetable Mold 142
Crêpes
Berry Crêpes 37
Pancakes For Crêpes And
Blintzes 37
Crispy Carrot Sauté 190

Crispy Waffles 35
Crown Roast Of Lamb With
Apple Raisin Stuffing 91
Crumb Crust, Spicy 121
Crumbs—Crumbing
Bread Crumbs 8
Bread Crumbs, Buttered 8
Bread Crumbs, Cheese 8
Cereal Crumbs 8
Cookie Crumbs 8
Cracker Crumbs 8
Crunchy Peanut Pie 125
Crusts
Almond Crust 119
Blender Pastry 119
Butter Pecan Crust 119
Cereal Flake Crumb Crust 121
Cheese Pastry 119
Chocolate Wafer Crust 121
Coconut Pastry 119
Gingersnap Crust 121
Graham Cracker Crumb
Crust 119
Nut Pastry 119
Nutty Crumb Crust 121
Seed Pastry 119
Spicy Crumb Crust 121
Vanilla Or Brown Edge Wafer
Crust 121
Wheat Germ Crumb Crust 121
Whole Wheat Pastry 119
Cucumber
Cool-As-A-Cucumber Mold 142
Relish, Fresh 136
Sauce 169
Scandinavian 144
Slices In Sour Cream 144
Soup, Chilled 180
Sour Cream Dressing 153
Cumberland Sauce 167
Cup Cakes 44
Currant-Orange Sauce 172
Curry
Bombay Chicken 95
Butter 39
Cold Soup 179
Cream Soup 176
Dressing 151
Egg Filling 158
Lamb 93
Sauce 166
Scrambled Eggs 100
Senegalese Soup 180
Shrimp 98
Soup, Cold 179
Custard
Apricot 78
Baked Caramel 78
Custard 73
Zucchini 193

D

Daiquiri, Frozen 26
Danish Herring Dip 14
Dates
Corn Bread 33
Cream Pie 124
Nut Roll 70
Or Prune Muffins 33
Pecan Rolls 58
Pudding, Steamed 72
Desserts
Almond Dessert Cream 69
Almond Stuffed Apples 78
Apple Delight Pudding 72
Apple Fritters 103
Applesauce 78
Apricot Applesauce 183
Apricot Crème 69
Apricot Custard 78
Apricot Or Prune Whip 74
Baked Caramel Custard 78
Baked Prune Whip 73
Banana Fritters 103
Banana Glace 78
Banana Ice Cream 76
Berry Cream 70
Blitz Torte, Modern-Made 50
Caramel Rice Pudding 72

Chocolate Angel Torte 50
Chocolate Freeze 74
Chocolate Nut Fondue With
Orange Sauce 69
Chocolate Pudding 72
Cool Cat Cones 107
Custard 73
Date Nut Roll 70
Firecrackers 108
Frozen Chocolate Peppermint
Torte 77
Fruit Dessert 183
Ginger Cream 70
Ice Cream Flower Pots 108
Ice Cream Tepees 106
Instant Pudding Mixes 195
Jewel Paddle Dips 108
Lemon Ice 74
Lemon Pudding 72
Lemony-Light Cheese Cake 43
Lime Divine 70
Maple Nut Ice Cream 76
Minty Paddle Dips 108
Mocha Bavarian Cream 70
Mock Devonshire Cream 77
Nutty Candy Paddle Dips 108
Orange Cheese Cake 43
Orange Divine 70
Orange Fluff 184
Orange Ice Box Cake 77
Orange Paddle Dips 108
Orange Pistachio Parfait 74
Party Parfait 74
Peach Ice Cream 76
Peach Pecan Crisp 69
Peanut Balls 108
Pineapple Cream 70
Quick Chocolate
Pots De Crème 73
Quick Maple Pots De Crème 73
Regal Cheese Cake 43
Rocky Road Balls 108
Snow Cones And Slush Cups 106
Spooky Paddle Dips 108
Steamed Date Pudding 72
Strawberry Bavarian Cream 70
Strawberry Ice Cream 74, 76
Strawberry Ice Cream Dessert 73
Strawberry Trifle 78
Tortoni Squares 77
Vanilla Custard Ice Cream 76
Dessert Topping Mixes,
Whipped 72
Devil's Food Cake, Double
Rich 44
Deviled Crab 98
Deviled Eggs, Spicy Sauced 100
Deviled Ham Dunk 15
Devonshire Cream, Mock 77
Diet Lemonade Or Limeade 185
Dieter's Breakfast-In-A-Glass 185
Dill Cheese Sauce 166
Dips
Bacon 15
Caviar 14
Cheese Duo 15
Chili Con Queso 15
Corned Beef 16
Crabmeat Dip Or Spread 11
Creamy Anchovy 15
Danish Herring 14
Deviled Ham Dunk 15
Down East Clam 14
Easy Swiss Fondue 17
Guacamole 15
Ham And Mushroom Dunk 14
He-Man Garlic 16
Hot Black Bean 13
Orange Marmalade For
Franks Or Meat Balls, Hot 16
Pineapple-Blue Cheese 16
Rousing Roquefort 13
Saucy Sardine 14
Shrimp 'N Dill 14
Shrimp Newburgh 14
Sunshine 16
Tangy Ham 11
Tasty Tuna 13
Wisconsin Dunk 13
Double Apple Salad 139
Double Chocolate Banana Pie 125

Double Rich Devil's Food Cake 44
Doughnuts
    Apple 104
    Banana Nut 104
    Orange Potato 104
    Spicy 104
Down East Clam Dip 14
Dutch Apple Pie 120

E

Easy Swiss Fondue 17
Eggs
    Bacon 'N Egg Sandwich
      On French Rolls 158
    Bacon And Egg Sandwich
      Spread 158
    Cheese And Egg Puffs 99
    Cheese Scrambled 100
    Curried Filling 158
    Curry Scrambled 100
    Foo Yung 99
    Eggnog 184
    Eggnog, Holiday 19
    Salad Spread 158
    Sauce 166
    Ham And Egg Sandwich
      Filling 14
    Ham And Egg Sandwich
      Spread 158
    Ham Scrambled Eggs 100
    Hot Ham 'N Egg Bunwiches 160
    Onion Scrambled 11
    Quiche Lorraine 101
    Ranch Style Omelet 100
    Salami Egg Sandwich
      Spread 158
    Scrambled 100
    Spicy Sauced, Deviled 100
Emerald Fizz 26
Entrées
    Bagna Cauda 13
    Baked Ham 87
    Baked Macaroni And Cheese 99
    Baked Stuffed Spareribs 87
    Baked Stuffed Trout 96
    Barbecued Chicken 94
    Basic Meat Loaf 81
    Beef Burgundy 82
    Blender Beef Hash 86
    Bombay Chicken Curry 95
    Cheese And Egg Puffs 99
    Cheese Rarebit 100
    Cheese Scrambled Eggs 100
    Chicken Cacciatore 94
    Chicken Crocquettes 93
    Chicken Fricassee 93
    Chicken Noodle Casserole 93
    Chili Con Carne 94
    Country Chicken 94
    Crown Roast Of Lamb With
      Apple Raisin Stuffing 91
    Curry Scrambled Eggs 100
    Deviled Crab 98
    Egg Foo Yung 99
    German Meat Balls 84
    Golden Soufflé 99
    Halibut Creole 96
    Ham Scrambled Eggs 100
    Ham Timbales 88
    Indian Lamb Skewers 92
    Individual Pork Pies 87
    Italian Spaghetti Sauce 88
    Jambalaya 88
    Java Pork Kabobs 87
    Lamb Curry 93
    Lamb Kabobs 92
    Lasagne 88
    Marinated Leg Of Lamb 92
    Meat And 'Tater Loaf 81
    Mexican Enchiladas 90
    Mexican Rarebit 100
    Midget Meat Balls 85
    Minute Meat Loaf 81
    Onion Scrambled Eggs 100
    Quiche Lorraine 101
    Pork 'N Sweets Casserole 86
    Ranch-Style Omelet 100
    Rock Cornish Hens 94
    Roast Turkey With Giblet
      Stuffing 96

Sauerbraten 82
Scrambled Eggs 100
Shrimp Curry 98
Spanish Pork Tenderloin 87
Spicy Sauced, Deviled Eggs 100
Stuffed Lamb Shoulder Roast 92
Stuffed Veal Breast 81
Swedish Meat Balls 85
Sweet-Sour Ham Balls 84
Sweet-Sour Spareribs 114
Swiss Style Goulash
    On Buttered Noodles 82
Tasty Tuna Turnovers 98
Veal Scallopine 84
Wheat Germ Nut Loaf 185

F

Feathery Fudge Cake 44
Fish
    Baked Stuffed Trout 96
    Barbecued Fish Steaks 116
    Creamy Anchovy Dip 15
    Creamy Salmon Ring Mold 142
    Danish Herring Dip 14
    Halibut Creole 96
    Hot Tuna-Cheese
      Bunwiches 161
    Olive Tuna Salad Spread 161
    Salmon Coleslaw 146
    Salmon Salad Spread 161
    Salmon Salad With Louis
      Dressing 148
    Saucy Sardine Dip 14
    Tasty Tuna Dip 13
    Tasty Tuna Turnovers 98
    Tuna-Mac Salad 148
    Tuna Pizza 164
    Tuna Salad Spread 161
    Tuna-Tomato Aspic 142
Fix-Ahead Popovers 35
Flaming Orange Sauce 167
Flank Steak Tarragon, Grilled 112
Floats
    Cherry Vanilla Float 21
    Chocolate, Peppermint Or
      Coffee Floats 20
    Choco-Mint Float 21
    Coffee, Chocolate Or
      Peppermint Floats 20
    Double Chocolate Floats 20
    Mocha Float 21
    Tropical Floats 19
Florentine Spinach 191
Fluffy Cream Cheese Dressing 154
Fluffy Horseradish Sauce 170
Fluffy Prune Cake With Lemon
    Frosting 41
Fondue
    Bagna Cauda 13
    Easy Swiss Fondue 17
    Franks Fondue 17
    Ham Fondue 17
    Pizza Fondue 17
    Salami Pizza Fondue 17
    Shrimp Fondue 17
Foreign
    Bagna Cauda 13
    Beef Burgundy 82
    Brazilian Chocolate 24
    Burgers Italiano 111
    Burgers Mexicana 111
    Chicken Cacciatore 94
    Chili Con Queso 15
    Danish Herring Dip 14
    Egg Foo Yung 99
    Frenchy Burgers 111
    Gazpacho 180
    German Meat Balls 84
    Guacamole 15
    Italian Spaghetti Sauce 88
    Java Pork Kabobs 87
    Lasagne 88
    Mexican Enchiladas 90
    Mexican Rarebit 100
    Mexicana Greeen Beans 192
    Moscow Hot Chocolate 25
    Polynesian Pork
      Sandwiches 160

Sauerbraten 82
Scandinavian Cucumbers 144
Scandinavian Lima Beans 190
Senegalese Soup 180
Spanish Pork Tenderloin 87
Swedish Baked Beans 192
Swedish Meat Balls 85
Swiss Style Goulash
    On Buttered Noodles 82
Ten-Second French Onion
    Soup 177
Veal Scallopine 84
Vichyssoise 179
Yorkshire Pudding 35
Franks With Everything Spread 160
French Butter Cream 52
French Dressing 151
French Onion Soup,
    Ten-Second 177
French Toasted Cheese
    Sandwiches 162
French Toasted Mozzarella
    Sandwiches 162
Fritters And Doughnuts
    Apple Doughnuts 104
    Apple Fritters 103
    Banana Fritters 103
    Banana Nut Doughnuts 104
    Corn And Bacon Fritters 103
    Corn Fritters 103
    Fried Shrimp 103
    Fritter Batter For Fruits 103
    Fritter Batter For Seafood
      And Vegetables 103
    Orange Potato Doughnuts 104
    Pineapple Fritters 103
    Spicy Doughnuts 104
    Tricky Doughnut Treats 107
Frosted Cafe-Au-Lait 184
Frosted Chocolate Drops 61
Frosty Lobster Soup 180
Frozen Fruit Cream 140
Frozen Neopolitan Pie 122
Frozen Roquefort Dressing 151
Fudge, Quick Chocolate Pecan 57
Fudge Cake, Feathery 44
Fudge Sauce 171

G

Garden Relish 136
Garlic Bread, Hot 117
Garlic Butter 39
Garlic Dip, He-Man 16
Garlic Dressing 151
Garlic Dressing, Creamy 154
Gazpacho 180

Gelatin Pick-Me-Up 21
German Meat Balls 84
Giblets For Gravy 194
Ginger Cream 70
Ginger Dressing 151
Gingerbread, Old-Fashioned 29
Gingersnap Crust 121
Glaze, Strawberry 43
Golden Cheese Bread 31
Golden Orange Marmalade 133
Golden Salad Freeze 139
Golden Soufflé 99
Goulash, Swiss Style On Buttered
    Noodles 82
Graham Cracker Crumb Crust 119
Graham Cracker Torte 49
Grasshopper 26
Gravy, Giblets For 194
Gravy, Lump-Free
Green Bean Bake 190
Green Beans, Mexicana 192
Green Beans Romano 188
Green Beans Vinaigrette 188
Green Goddess Salad 144
Guacamole 15

H

Halibut Creole 96
Ham
    Bacon Or Ham Hot Cakes 36
    Baked Ham 87

Chicken, Turkey Or Ham
    Salad 148
Deviled Ham Dunk 15
Ham And Egg Sandwich
    Filling 14
Ham And Egg Sandwich
    Spread 158
Ham And Mushroom Dunk 14
Ham Balls, Sweet-Sour 84
Ham Filling 158
Ham Fondue 17
Ham Mousse 144
Ham Salad Spread 158
Ham Sandwich Spread 15
Ham Scrambled Eggs 100
Ham-Stuffed Acorn Squash 192
Ham Timbales 88
Hot Ham 'N Egg Bunwiches 160
Liver Sausage Deviled Ham
    Spread 160
Old Virginia Ham Salad
    Spread 158
Tangy Ham Dip 11
Hard Sauce 172
Hard Sauce, Thin 172
Hash Blender Beef 86
Hash-Brown Potatoes 192
Health Foods That Please 186
Heavenly Chocolate Pie 128
Herb Butter 39
Herbed Lamb Chops 116
Holiday Eggnog 19
Hollandaise Sauce 166
Honey
    Cinnamon Honey Butter 38
    Honey Butter 38
    Honey Cream Cheese
      Dressing 154
    Honey Dressing 152
Horseradish Beet Relish 136
Horseradish Sauce, Fluffy 170
Hurry-Up Split Pea Soup 177

I

Ice Cream And Freezes
    Banana Ice Cream 76
    Butterscotch Pecan
      Ice Cream Pie 122
    Candy Ice Cream
      Paddle Dips 108
    Cherry Pecan Ice Cream Pie 122
    Chocolate Freeze 74
    Chocolate Sundae Pie 122
    Cool Cat Cones 107
    Crazy Cutouts 108
    Firecrackers 108
    Frozen Chocolate Peppermint
      Torte 77
    Frozen Neopolitan Pie 122
    Fruit Ice Sticks 109
    Ice Cream Flower Pots 108
    Ice Cream Tepees 106
    Icy Paddle Sticks 108
    Jewel Paddle Dips 108
    Maple Nut Ice Cream 76
    Minty Paddle Dips 108
    Nutty Candy Paddle Dips 108
    Orange Paddle Dips 108
    Peach Ice Cream 76
    Peanut Balls 108
    Rocky Road Balls 108
    Snow Cones And Slush Cups 106
    Spooky Paddle Dips 108
    Strawberry Ice Cream 74, 76
    Tortoni Squares 77
    Vanilla Custard Ice Cream 76
Ice, Blender Crushed
Individual Pork Pies 87
Instant Mashed Potatoes 193
Instant Pudding Mixes 73
Iowa Corn Chowder 177
Italian Cheese Bread 117
Italian Cheese Dressing 151
Italian Spaghetti Sauce 88

J

Java Pork Kabobs 87
Jellied Mushroom Soup 180

Jewel Paddle Dips 108
Juices, Quick-Fix Fruit 19

K

Kumquats, Stuffed 11

L

Lady Baltimore Frosting 53
Lamb
    Chutney Grilled Lamb
      Chops 116
    Crown Roast Of Lamb With
      Apple Raisin Stuffing 91
    Herbed Lamb Chops 116
    Indian Lamb Skewers 92
    Lamb Curry 93
    Lamb Kabobs 92
    Leg Of Lamb, Marinated 92
    Stuffed Lamb Shoulder Roast 92
Lasagne 88
Lemon
    Angel Pie 128
    Custard Sauce, Quick 172
    Frosting 53
    Ice 74
    Light Cheese Cake 43
    Parsley Butter 39
    Pudding 72
    Sauce 172
Lime
    Divine 70
    Freeze 20
    Lift 20
Linzer Bars 66
Liver Sausage
    Liver Sausage Deviled Ham
      Spread 160
    Liver Sausage
      On Poppyseed Rolls 160
    Liver Sausage Peanut Spread 160
    Liver Sausage-Pickle Spread 160
Lobster
    Broiled Lobster Tails 116
    Lobster Soup, Frosty 180
Lorenzo Dressing 151
Low Calorie Foods
    Ambrosia 146
    Barbecued Chuck Steak 112
    Barbecued Fish Steaks 116
    Broiled Lobster Tails 116
    Broiled Tomato Slices 193
    Cabbage Patch Slaw 145
    Caesar Salad 194
    Carrot Cocktail 23
    Charcoal Broiled
      Sirloin Steak 112
    Cherry Whiz 23
    Cool-As-A-Cucumber Mold 142
    Creamy Vegetable Mold 142
    Cucumber Slices In Sour Cream
      Or Yogurt 144
    Dieters Breakfast-
      In-A-Glass 185
    Dieters Lemonade
      Or Limeade 185
    Frosted Cafe-Au-Lait 184
    Gelatin Pick-Me-Up 21
    Hamburgers 111
    Herbed Lamb Chops 116
    Hot Grilled Tomatoes 117
    Lamb Kabobs 92
    Low Calorie French
      Dressing 152
    Low Calorie Ice Cream
      Ginger Fizz 185
    Marinated Leg Of Lamb 92
    Meat Balls, 84, 85
    Meat Loaves 81
    Mock Devonshire Cream 77
    Mock Sour Cream
      For Dieters 185
    Molded Tomato Salad 140
    Orange-Carrot Nog 184
    Orange Fluff 184
    Sauerbraten 82
    Scrambled Eggs 100
    Seven-Minute Cabbage 190
    Stuffed Pear Or Peach Salad 145

Two-Calorie Whipped
    Topping 184
Tuna-Tomato Aspic 142
Luscious Yeast Rolls 31

M

Macaroons, Cherry Coconut 64
Macaroons, Chocolate Nut 64
Malts, Shakes And 20
Maple Butter 38
Maple Nut Ice Cream 76
Maple Pots De Crème, Quick 73
Marshmallow Frosting 55
Mayonnaise, Blender 154
Meat
    Bacon Dip 15
    Baked Ham 87
    Baked Stuffed Spareribs 87
    Barbecued Chuck Steak 112
    Barbecued Pork Loin 114
    Basic Meat Loaf 81
    Beef Burgundy 82
    Broiled Pork Chops, Caribbean
      Style 114
    Burgers Italiano 111
    Burgers Mexicana 111
    Charcoal Broiled
      Sirloin Steaks 112
    Cheese Topped Cube Steaks 112
    Cheesy-Bacon Burgers 111
    Chutney Grilled
      Lamb Chops 116
    Corned Beef Cheese
      Sandwiches 157
    Corned Beef Dip 16
    Corned Beef Sandwich
      Spread 157
    Corned Beef Sauerkraut
      Sandwich 157
    Corned Beef Swiss Cheese
      Sandwich 157
    Crown Roast Of Lamb With
      Apple Raisin Stuffing 91
    Flank Steak Tarragon,
      Grilled 112
    Franks Fondue 17
    Frenchy Burgers 111
    German Meat Balls 84
    Ham And Egg Sandwich
      Spread 158
    Ham Fondue 17
    Ham Mousse 144
    Ham Timbales 88
    Herbed Lamb Chops 116
    Honolulu Burgers 111
    Indian Lamb Skewers 92
    Individual Pork Pies 87
    Java Pork Kabobs 87
    Lamb Curry 93
    Lamb Kabobs 92
    Leg Of Lamb, Marinated 92
    Liver Sausage On
      Poppyseed Rolls 160
    Liver Sausage
      Peanut Spread 160
    Liver Sausage-Pickle Spread 160
    Meat And 'Tater Loaf 81
    Midget Meat Balls 85
    Orange Glazed Barbecued
      Pork Loin 114
    Patio Burgers 111
    Peanut Burgers 111
    Polynesian Pork
      Sandwiches 160
    Pork 'N Sweets Casserole 86
    Salami Egg Sandwich
      Spread 158
    Sauerbraten 82
    Sausage Vegetable Salad 147
    Small Chuck Steak 112
    Southwestern Spareribs 114
    Spanish Pork Tenderloins 87
    Stuffed Lamb Shoulder Roast 92
    Stuffed Veal Breast 81
    Swedish Meat Balls 85
    Sweet-Sour Ham Balls 84
    Sweet-Sour Spareribs 114
    Swiss Style Goulash
      On Buttered Noodles 82

Veal Scallopine 84
Zesty Beef Sandwiches 160
Mexican Enchiladas 90
Mexican Rarebit 100
Mexican Wedding Cakes 66
Midget Meat Balls 85
Milk Chocolate Frosting 52
Milk-Shakes And Malts 20
Mincemeat
    Mincemeat Bars 64
    Mincemeat Oat Drops 62
    Mincemeat Pie 129
    Old-Fashioned Mincemeat 137
Mint Punch 19
Minty Paddle Dips 108
Mocha
    After-Dinner Mocha 25
    Mocha Bavarian Cream 70
    Mocha Float 21
    Mocha Frosting 52
    Mocha Sauce 171
    Mocha Spice Cake 44
Mock Sour Cream For Dieters 185
Molasses Drops 61
Molded Tomato Salad 140
More Foods Dieters Will Like 186
More Semi-Solid Foods For
    Invalids And Senior Citizens 186
Mornay Sauce 166
Mousseline Sauce 166
Muffins
    Apricot 33
    Bacon 33
    Banana Bran 34
    Banana 33
    Bran Nut 34
    Corn 33
    Country Kitchen 33
    Oatmeal 33
    Prune Or Date 33
    Speedy-Made 34
    Wheat Germ Banana 34
    Whole Wheat 33
Mushroom And Sausage Pizza 164
Mushroom Soup, Cream Of 176
Mushroom Soup, Jellied 180
Mustard Butter 39

N

Nesselrode Chiffon Pie 127
New Old-Fashioned
    Vegetable Soup 175
Nippy Dressing For Fish
    And Seafood 152
Non-Fat Dry Milk Solids 195
Nut Butter, Homemade 39
Nut Pastry 119
Nut Waffles 35
Nutty Candy Paddle Dips 108
Nutty Crumb Crust 121

O

Oatmeal Muffins 33
Old Virginia Ham Spread 158
Olive Tuna Salad Spread 161
Omelet, Ranch Style 100
Onion Butter 39
Onion Scrambled Eggs 100
Onion Soup, French 177
Orange
    Blossom 27
    Carrot Nog 184
    Cheese Cake 43
    Cranberry Relish 134
    Divine 70
    Fluff 184
    Frappé 23
    Frosting 53
    Glazed Sweet Potatoes 188
    Glow 23
    Ice Box Cake 77
    Marmalade, Golden 133
    Marmalade Butter 38
    Marmalade Dip, For
      Franks Or Meat Balls, Hot 16
    Nut Bread 29, 117
    Paddle Dips 108
    Pecan Pancakes 36

Pistachio Parfait 74
Potato Doughnuts 104
Sauce 172
Sauce, Currant 172
Sauce For Ham 168
Sauce, Flaming 167
Spice Cake 41
Oyster Stew 178

P

Pancakes
    Apple Pancakes 35
    Bacon Or Ham Hot Cakes 36
    Banana Pancakes 35
    Berry Crêpes 37
    Blueberry Pancakes 36
    Buttermilk Pancakes 35
    Orange Pecan Pancakes 36
    Pancakes 35, 36
    Pancakes For Crêpes
      And Blintzes 37
    Potato Pancakes 35
    Whole Grain Wheat
Panoche, Peanut Butter 57
Parfait
    Orange Pistachio 74
    Party 74
Parsley French Dressing 151
Party Cakes, Pretty 107
Party Punch For Many 18
Pasta
    Baked Macaroni And Cheese 99
    Italian Spaghetti Sauce 88
    Lasagne 88
    Tuna-Mac Salad 148
    Patio Burgers 111
    Patriotic Cakes 107
Patio Burgers 111
Patriotic Cakes 107
Peach
    And Pear Jam 133
    Chiffon Party Cake 48
    Fresh Jam 133
    Ice Cream 76
    Pecan Crisp 69
    Pecan Pie 122
    Short-Cut Preserves 133
    Splash 19
Peanuts And Peanut Butter
    Crunchy Peanut Pie 125
    Fruited Peanut Butter
      Spread 162
    Peanut Balls 108
    Peanut Burgers 111
    Peanut Butter 39
    Peanut Butter Frosting 53
    Peanut Butter Marmalade
      Spread 162
    Peanut Butter Panoche 57
    Peanut Butterscotch Toddy 25
    Peanut-Orange
      Dressing 155
    Peanutty Chocolate Breakfast-
      In-A-Glass 185
Pear Or Peach Salad, Stuffed 147
Pecan
    Butterscotch Pie 125
    Cinnamon Rolls 31
    Or Walnut Cake 44
    Pumpkin Pie 125
    Raisin Bran Drops 61
    Southern Pie 125
Pepper Relish 137
Peppers, Vegetable-Stuffed 191
Peppermint
    Chiffon Pie 125
    Frosting 55
    Velvet, Pink 24
    Taffy Smoothie 21
Perfection Salad 140
Peter Rabbit Ring 140
Pickle Relish, Sweet 134
Pie Crusts
    Almond Crust 119
    Blender Pastry 119
    Butter Pecan Crust 119
    Cereal Flake Crumb Crust 121
    Cheese Pastry 119
    Chocolate Wafer Crust 121
    Coconut Pastry 119

Gingersnap Crust 121
Graham Cracker Crumb
  Crust 119
Nut Pastry 119
Nutty Crumb Crust 121
Seed Pastry 119
Spicy Crumb Crust 121
Vanilla Or Brown Edge Wafer
  Crust 121
Wheat Germ Crumb Crust 121
Whole Wheat Pastry 119
Pies And Pastries
Apricot Chiffon Pie 126
Apricot Soufflé Pie 128
Banbury Tarts 129
Black Bottom Pies 124
Butterscotch Pecan
  Ice Cream Pie 122
Butterscotch Pecan Pie 125
Cheese Fruit Tarts 129
Cherry Jubilee Pie 120
Cherry Pecan Ice Cream Pie 122
Chocolate Angel Pie 128
Chocolate Chiffon Pie 127
Chocolate Peppermint Pie 122
Chocolate Sundae Pie 122
Cottage Cheese Apricot Pie 124
Cranberry Relish Pie 129
Creamy Cherry Banana Pie 125
Crunchy Peanut Pie 125
Date Cream Pie 124
Double Chocolate
  Banana Pie 125
Dutch Apple Pie 120
Frozen Neopolitan Pie 122
Heavenly Chocolate Pie 128
Lemon Angel Pie 128
Lemon Chiffon Pie 128
Mincemeat Pie 129
Nesselrode Chiffon Pie 127
Peachy Pecan Pie 122
Pecan Pumpkin Pie 125
Mincemeat Pie 129
Peppermint Chiffon Pie 126
Preserve Tarts 129
Pumpkin Pie 125
Quiche Lorraine 101
Rhubarb Cream Pie 124
Slim-Jim Cherry Pie 120
Southern Pecan Pie 125
Strawberry, Raspberry
  Or Peach Pie 125
Valentine Party Pies 122
Pineapple
Barbecue Sauce 168
Blue Cheese Dip 16
Cherry Dressing 154
Cream 70
Cream Dressing 155
Mint Whip 22
Mold, Frosty 139
Nut Drops 62
Orange Frost 21
Sauce, Sweet Sour 167
Waffles 35
Pink Lady 27
Pink Peppermint Velvet 24
Pizza
Cheese And Bacon 164
Fondue 17
Mushroom And Sausage 164
Pronto 163
Short-Cut 164
Tuna 164
Plum Relish, Spicy Fresh 134
Popovers
Fix-Ahead 35
Herb 35
Parmesan 35
Popovers 34
Spice 35
Pork
Baked Stuffed Spareribs 87
Barbecued Loin 114
Barbecued Loin,
  Orange Glazed 114
Broiled Chops,
  Caribbean Style 114
Individual Pies 87
Java Kabobs 87
Polynesian Sandwiches 160

Pork 'N Sweets Casserole 86
Southwestern Spareribs 114
Spanish Pork Tenderloin 87
Sweet-Sour Spareribs 114
Potatoes
Hash-Brown 192
Instant Mashed 193
Potato Pancakes 36
Potato Salad, Hot 148
Potato Salad, Sour Cream 147
Twice-Baked 188
Potatoes, Sweet
Fruit-Stuffed 188
Orange-Glazed 188
Pork 'N Sweets Casserole 86
Southern Yam Pudding 190
Yams In Orange Shells 190
Pots De Crème,
  Quick Chocolate 73
Pots De Crème, Quick Maple 73
Poultry
Barbecued Chicken 94
Bombay Chicken Curry 95
Ceylon Chicken Salad 148
Chicken, Barbecued Herb 116
Chicken, Cacciatore 94
Chicken Croquettes 93
Chicken Dinner 183
Chicken Fricasse 93
Chicken Noodle Casserole 93
Chicken Vegetable Soup 175
Country Chicken 94
Pronto Chicken Spread 15
Rock Cornish Hens 94
Roast Turkey With Giblet
  Stuffing 96
Turkey Salad Spread 157
Praline Clusters 58
Pralines, Quick 58
Praline Squares, Burnt Sugar 58
Preserves And Relishes
Catsup 137
Cherry Raisin Conserve 134
Chili Sauce 137
Cranberry-Orange
  Marmalade 131
Cranberry Pecan Relish 134
Fresh Cucumber Relish 136
Frozen Blackberry, Blueberry
  And Boysenberry Jam 131
Frozen Fresh Red
  Raspberry Jam 131
Frozen Fresh Strawberry
  Jam 131
Frozen Strawberry Jam 131
Garden Relish 136
Golden Orange Marmalade 133
Horseradish Beet Relish 136
Old Fashioned Apple Butter 131
Old-Fashioned Mincemeat 137
Orange Cranberry Relish 134
Peach And Pear Jam 133
Peach Jam, Fresh 133
Pepper Relish 137
Short-Cut Peach Preserves 133
Short-Cut Raspberry 133
Short-Cut Strawberry 133
Speedy Corn Relish 136
Spiced Blueberry Jam 133
Spiced Orange Cranberry
  Relish 134
Spicy Fresh Plum Relish 134
Sweet Pickle Relish 134
Tomato Apple Catsup 137
Preserve Tarts 129
Pronto Pizza 163
Prune Cake With Lemon
  Frosting 41
Prune Or Apricot Whip 74
Prune Or Date Muffins 33
Prune Whip, Baked 73
Pudding
Apple Delight Pudding 72
Caramel Rice Pudding 72
Chocolate Pudding 72
Instant Pudding Mixes 71
Lemon Pudding 72
Steamed Date Pudding 72
Pumpkin
Pecan Pumpkin Pie 125
Pumpkin Pie 125

Pumpkin Spice Bran Drops 62

Q
Quiche Lorraine 101
Quick Cheese Sauce 167
Quick Lemon Custard Sauce 172
Quick Pudding Sauces
  (Chocolate, Vanilla And
  Butterscotch) 172

R
Ranch Style Omelet 100
Rarebit, Cheese 100
Raspberry Fizz 20
Raspberry Preserves,
  Short-Cut 133
Raspberry Soda, Double 21
Red And Green Slaw 146
Red Devil's Food Cake 45
Red French Dressing 152
Red Raspberry Jam 131
Regal Cheese Cake 43
Remoulade Sauce 167
Rhubarb Cocktail, Fresh 23
Rhubarb Cream Pie 124
Ribbon Sandwich Loaves 163
Rice
  Caramel Rice Pudding 72
  Jambalaya 88
Roast Turkey With Giblet
  Stuffing 96
Rock Cornish Hens 94
Rocky Road Balls 108
Roquefort Cream Dressing 151
Roquefort Dressing 152
Rum Balls 57
Rum Or Tom Collins 26
Russian Dressing 154

S
Salads, Fish And Seafood
Crabmeat In Avocado
  Shells 148
Creamy Salmon Ring Mold 142
Salmon Coleslaw 146
Salmon With Louis Dressing 148
Tuna-Mac 148
Tuna-Tomato Aspic 142
Salads, Fruit
Ambrosia 146
Avocado Mold 139
Cranberry Marshmallow 146
Cranberry-Waldorf 139
Double Apple 139
Frosty Pineapple Mold 139
Frozen Fruit Cream 140
Golden Salad Freeze 139
Perfection 140
Seabreeze 139
Stuffed Pear Or Peach 147
Sunny Carrot 146
Two-Grape Fruit 140
Salads, Meats And Sausage
Ham Mousse 144
Salmagundi 147
Sausage Vegetable 147
Salads, Poultry
Ceylon Chicken 148
Chicken, Turkey Or Ham 148
Salads, Vegetable
Cabbage Patch Slaw 145
Caesar 144
Coleslaw With Sour Cream
  Dressing 145
Cool-As-A-Cucumber Mold 132
Creamy Tomato Molds 142
Creamy Vegetable Mold 142
Cucumber Slices In Sour Cream
  Or Yogurt 144
Fruited Coleslaw 146
Green Goddess 144
Molded Tomato 140
Peter Rabbit Ring 140
Potato Salad, Hot 148
Potato Salad, Sour Cream 147
Red And Green Slaw 146

Scandinavian Cucumbers 143
Vegetable Basket 144
Salad Dressings
Avocado 151
Blue Cheese 151
Caper 151
Chiffonade 151
Cream Cheese Honey 154
Creamy Cheese Cucumber 153
Creamy Dressing For Fruits 154
Creamy Garlic 154
Curry 151
Fluffy Cream Cheese 154
French 151
Frozen Roquefort 151
Garlic 151
Ginger 151
Honey 142
Italian Cheese 151
Lorenzo 151
Low Calorie French 152
Mayonnaise, Blender 154
Mock Sour Cream 185
Nippy Dressing For Fish
  And Seafood 152
Parsley French 151
Peanut-Orange 155
Pineapple Cherry 154
Pineapple Cream 155
Red French 152
Roquefort Cream 151
Roquefort 152
Russian 154
Salad Dressing, Cooked 155
Salad Dressing, Cooked Sour
  Cream 155
Sour Cream Cucumber 153
Tarragon Lemon 152
Tarragon Cream 153
Thousand Island 154
Tomato Soup 152
Sandwiches
Bacon 'N Egg Sandwich
  On French Roll 158
Broiled Barbecue Cheese
  Bunwiches 162
Broiled Crabmeat 161
Chicken-Almond 157
Chicken Waikiki 157
Corned Beef Cheese 157
Corned Beef Sauerkraut 157
Corned Beef Swiss Cheese 157
Crabmeat Rolls 161
French Toasted Cheese 162
French Toasted Mozzarella 162
Ham 'N Egg Bunwiches 160
Liver Sausage On Poppyseed
  Rolls 160
Polynesian Pork 160
Ribbon Sandwich Loaves 163
Tuna-Cheese Bunwiches,
  Hot 161
Turkey Waikiki 157
Waikiki Chicken 157
Waikiki Turkey 157
Zesty Beef 160
Sandwich Spreads
Avocado Filling 162
Bacon And Egg Sandwich 158
Cheese 'N Olive 162
Chicken Salad 157
Chopped Chicken Liver 164
Chutney-Cheese 13
Corned Beef Sandwich 157
Crabmeat Sandwich 161
Curried Egg Filling 158
Date-Nut Sandwich 164
Egg Salad 158
Franks With Everything 160
Fruit And Nut Cheese
  Sandwich 162
Fruited Peanut Butter 162
Ham And Egg Filling 14
Ham And Egg Spread 158
Ham Filling 158
Ham Salad 158
Ham Sandwich 15
Liver Sausage Deviled Ham 160
Liver Sausage Peanut 160
Liver Sausage-Pickle 160
Old Virginia Ham Salad 158

Olive Tuna Salad 161
Peanut Butter Marmalade 162
Pronto Chicken 15
Salami Egg Sandwich 158
Salmon Salad 161
Shrimp Sandwich 161
Tuna Salad 161
Turkey Salad 157
Walnutty Cheese 162
Sauces, Dessert
Apricot Almond Dessert 170
Apricot Cherry Dessert 170
Apricot Dessert 170
Butter 72
Butterscotch 170
Cardinal 172
Chocolate Rum 171
Currant-Orange 172
Fudge 171
Hard 172
Lemon 172
Mocha 171
Orange 172
Quick Lemon Custard 172
Quick Pudding (Chocolate,
Vanilla And Butterscotch) 172
Strawberry-Cranberry 172
Thin Hard 172
Vanilla 170
Sauces, General
Bearnaise 166
Bechamel 166
Cheese 166
Cherry For Ham 167
Cold Chiffon For Fish 169
Coral Fish 170
Cream Or White (Medium) 166
Cream, Thick 166
Cream, Thin 166
Cucumber 169
Cumberland 167
Curry 166
Dill Cheese 166
Egg 166
Fish And Seafood 170
Flaming Orange 167
Hollandaise 166
Horseradish, Fluffy 170
Mornay 166
Mousseline 166
Orange, For Ham 168
Quick Cheese 167
Remoulade 167
Seafood Cocktail 169
Sour Cream 169
Southwestern Barbecue 168
Spicy Tomato 168
Steak Or Burger 168
Steak 168
Sweet Sour Pineapple 167
Tangy Pineapple Barbecue,
For Ribs 168
Taratar 170
Vegetable Cream 166
Sauerbraten 82
Sausage
Franks With Everything
Spread 160
Liver Sausage Deviled Ham
Spread 160
Liver Sausage On Poppyseed
Rolls 160
Liver Sausage Peanut
Spread 160
Liver Sausage-Pickle Spread 160
Mushroom And Sausage
Pizza 164
Salami Pizza Fondue 17
Sausage Vegetable Salad 147
Scalloped Tomatoes 192
Scandinavian Lima Beans 190
Scrambled Eggs 100
Seafood
Broiled Crabmeat Sandwich 161
Broiled Lobster Tails 116
Crabmeat Dip Or Spread 11
Crabmeat Filled Puffs 11
Crabmeat Rolls 161
Crabmeat Salad In Avocado
Shells 148
Crabmeat Sandwich Spread 161

Creamy Clam Bisque 178
Deviled Crab 98
Down East Clam Dip 14
Frosty Lobster Soup 180
Oyster Stew 178
Seafood Cocktail Sauce 169
Shrimp, Fried 103
Shrimp 'N Dill Dip 14
Shrimp Curry 98
Shrimp Fondue 17
Shrimp In Beer 16
Shrimp Newburgh Dip 14
Shrimp Sandwich Spread 161
Semi-Solid Diet Foods 186
Seven-Minute Cabbage 190
Shakes
Apricot 23
Best Banana Milk 21
Fruit-Nut Milk 24
Mocha, Thick 20
Shakes and Malts 20, 21
Sherry Flip 27
Strawberry-Banana Milk 21
Shortbread Crumb Cookies 67
Short-Cut Pizza 164
Shrimp
'N Dill Dip 14
Curry 98
Fondue 17
Fried 103
In Beer 16
Newburgh Dip 14
Sandwich Spread 161
Silver Fizz 26
Sirloin Steak, Charcoal
Broiled 112
Sloe Gin Fizz 26
Snow Cones And Slush Cups 106
Snowy Cake Icing 53
Soups
As-You-Like-It Cream 176
Avocado 180
Beet Borsch 178
Black Bean Or Lentil 175
Celery And Corn Cream 176
Celery 176
Cheddar Cheese 175
Chicken Vegetables 175
Chilled Cucumber 180
Chilled Tomato Buttermilk 179
Cold Curry 179
Cold Sweet Basil Carrot 179
Corn Chowder, Iowa 177
Cream Of Corn 176
Cream Of Mushroom 176
Cream Of Watercress 176
Creamy Clam Bisque 178
Curry Cream 176
Frosty Lobster 180
Gazpacho 180
Jellied Mushroom 180
New Old-Fashioned
Vegetable 175
Onion, Ten-Second French 177
Oyster Stew 178
Senegalese 180
Speedy Green Pea 175
Split Pea, Hurry-Up 177
Surprise 178
Sweet Basil Carrot 179
Tomato-Blue Cheese 179
Vichysoise 179
Sour Cream Sauce 169
Southern Pecan Pie 125
Southern Yam Pudding 190
Spanish Pork Tenderloin 87
Spareribs, Baked Stuffed 87
Spareribs, Southwestern 114
Spareribs, Sweet-Sour 114
Spice Popovers 35
Spiced Banana Cake 41
Spicy Apple Waffles 35
Spicy Applesauce Cake 46
Spicy Crumb Crust 121
Spicy Doughnuts 104
Spicy-Sauced Deviled Eggs 100
Spinach, Florentine 191
Spooky Paddle Dips 108
Squash, Ham-Stuffed Acorn 192
Stinger 26
Stollen 32

Strawberry
Banana Milk Shake 21
Bavarian Cream 70
Butter 39
Cranberry Sauce 172
Frost 23
Ice Cream 74, 76
Ice Cream Dessert 73
Jam, Frozen 131
Jam, Frozen Fresh 131
Preserves, Short-Cut 133
Strawberry, Raspberry
Or Peach Pie 125
Trifle 78
Stuffed Lamb Shoulder Roast 92
Stuffed Veal Breast 81
Sunshine Dip 16
Swedish Baked Beans 192
Swedish Meat Balls 85
Sweet Butters 38
Sweet Fruity Butter 38
Sweet Potatoes, Fruit-Stuffed 188
Sweet Potatoes,
Orange-Glazed 188
Sweet-Sour Cabbage 191
Sweet-Sour Ham Balls 84
Sweet-Sour Spareribs 114
Swiss Style Goulash on Buttered
Noodles 82

Taffy Peppermint Smoothie 21
Tangy Pineapple Barbecue Sauce 168
Tarragon Lemon Dressing 152
Tartar Sauce 170
Tarts
Banbury 129
Cheese Fruit 129
Preserve 129
Tea, Minted Ice 25
Ten-Second French Onion
Soup 177
Thin Hard Sauce 172
Thousand Island Dressing 154
Toffee Butter 39
Tom Or Rum Collins 26
Tomatoes
Apple Catsup 137
Blue Cheese Soup 179
Buttermilk Soup, Chilled 179
Hot Grilled 117
Molds, Creamy 142
Provencale 192
Salad, Molded 140
Sauce, Spicy 168
Scalloped 192
Slices, Broiled 193
Soup Dressing 152
Tortes
Chocolate Angel 50
Chocolate Nut 50
Frozen Chocolate Peppermint 77
Graham Cracker 49
Modern-Made Blitz 50
Quick And Easy Dobos 50
Torte Elegante 49
Tortoni Squares 77
Tropical Floats 19
Trout, Baked Stuffed 96
Tuna
Hot Tuna-Cheese
Bunwiches 161
Olive Salad Spread 161
Pizza 164
Salad Spread 161
Tasty Dip 13
Tasty Turnovers 98
Tomato Aspic 142
Tuna-Mac Salad 148
Turkey
Chicken, Or Ham Salad 148
Roast, With Giblet
Stuffing 96
Salad Spread 157
Waikiki Sandwiches 157
Tutti-Fruitti Rolls 32
Twice-Baked Potatoes 188
Two-Calorie Whipped
Topping 184
Two-Grape Fruit Salad 140

V
Valentine Party Pies 122
Vanilla Custard Ice Cream 76
Vanilla Or Brown Edge Wafer
Crust 121
Vanilla Sauce 170
Veal
Stuffed Breast 81
Scallopine 84
Vegetable Cream Sauce 166
Vegetable Soup, New
Old Fashioned 175
Vegetables
Bagna Cauda 13
Beans, Swedish Baked 192
Beet Borsch 178
Beets, Apple-Sauced 190
Cabbage, Seven-Minute 190
Cabbage, Sweet-Sour 191
Carrot Sauté, Crispy 190
Cauliflower Polonaise 188
Corn And Bacon Fritters 103
Corn Fritters 103
Corn-On-The-Cob 117
Corn Tomato Custards 193
Cucumber Slices
In Sour Cream 144
Cucumbers, Scandinavian 143
Green Bean Bake 190
Green Beans, Mexicana 192
Green Beans Romano 188
Green Beans Vinaigrette 188
Lima Beans, Scandinavian 190
Peppers, Vegetable-Stuffed 191
Potato Pancakes 36
Potatoes, Hash-Brown 192
Potatoes, Instant Mashed 193
Potatoes, Twice-Baked 188
Spinach, Florentine 191
Squash, Ham-Stuffed Acorn 192
Sweet Potatoes,
Fruit-Stuffed 188
Sweet Potatoes,
Orange-Glazed 188
Tomato Slices, Broiled 193
Tomatoes, Hot Grilled 117
Tomatoes Provencale 192
Tomatoes, Scalloped 192
Yams In Orange Shells 190
Yam Pudding, Southern 190
Zucchini Custard 193
Vichyssoise 179

W
Waffles
Cheese 35
Chocolate Chip 35
Crispy 35
Nut 35
Pineapple 35
Spicy Apple 35
Waikiki Chicken Sandwiches 157
Waikiki Turkey Sandwiches 157
Walnut Or Pecan Cake 44
Walnutty Cheese Spread 162
Watercress Soup, Cream Of 176
Whipped Cream
Whipped Cream Frosting 53
Whipped Dessert Topping
Mixes 72
Whipped Topping,
Two-Calorie 184
Whiskey Sour 27
White Or Cream Sauce
(medium) 166

Y
Yams In Orange Shells 190
Yam Pudding, Southern 190
Yellow Cake 44
Yorkshire Pudding 35
Yummy Frosted Bars 67

Z
Zesty Beef Sandwiches 160
Zoo Parade Birthday Cakes 107
Zucchini Custard 193